Abandoning historical conflict?

Former political prisoners and
reconciliation in Northern Ireland

Peter Shirlow, Jonathan Tonge, James McAuley
and Catherine McGlynn

Manchester University Press
Manchester and New York
distributed exclusively in the USA by Palgrave Macmillan

Published by Manchester University Press
Oxford Road, Manchester M13 9NR, UK
and Room 400, 175 Fifth Avenue, New York, NY 10010, USA
www.manchesteruniversitypress.co.uk

Distributed exclusively in the USA by
Palgrave Macmillan, 175 Fifth Avenue, New York,
NY 10010, USA

Distributed exclusively in Canada by
UBC Press, University of British Columbia, 2029 West Mall,
Vancouver, BC, Canada V6T 1Z2

British Library Cataloguing-in-Publication Data
A catalogue record for this book is available from the British Library

Library of Congress Cataloging-in-Publication Data applied for

ISBN 978 0 7190 8011 1 hardback

First published 2010

The publisher has no responsibility for the persistence or accuracy of URLs for external or any third-party internet websites referred to in this book, and does not gurantee that any content on such websites is, or will remain, accurate or appropriate.

Typeset
by Helen Skelton, Brighton, UK
Printed in Great Britain
by the MPG Books Group

Abandoning historical conflict?

MANCHESTER
1824

Manchester University Press

Contents

Acknowledgements

The authors acknowledge with grateful thanks the generous financial assistance for this research project provided by the Leverhulme Trust. We are also very grateful for the hard work and diligence of the project's research assistants, Michael Culbert and Dawn Purvis MLA, in organising and conducting interviews with republican and loyalist former prisoners respectively. The facilitation of the research by various former prisoners' organisations, Coiste, EPIC, Charter and Teach na Failte, is also acknowledged with thanks. We pay tribute to the late Noel Gilzean, whose posthumous PhD, awarded in 2008, was richly earned. We thank all our families for tolerating our long absences during the research for this project. Finally, we offer our thanks to all the former prisoners who participated, for their time and frankness in the articulation of their ideas.

List of abbreviations

AMODEG	Mozambican Association of the War Demobilised
ANC	African National Congress
AVT	Association of Victims of Terrorism
CIRA	Continuity IRA
CRJ	Community Restorative Justice
CTI	Conflict Transformation Initiative
DDR	Demilitarisation, Demobilisation and Re-integration
DUP	Democratic Unionist Party
EACTP	East Antrim Conflict Transformation Process
EPIC	Ex-Prisoners' Interpretive Centre
ETA	Euskadi Ta Askatasuna
EXPAC	Ex-Prisoners Action Committee
GAL	Grupos Antiterroristas de Liberacion
IICD	Independent International Commission on Decommissioning
INLA	Irish National Liberation Army
IPLO	Irish People's Liberation Organisation
IRA	Irish Republican Army
IRSP	Irish Republican Socialist Party
LVF	Loyalist Volunteer Force
MLA	Northern Ireland Assembly member
NGO	non-governmental organisation
NIACRO	Northern Ireland Association for the Care and Resettlement of Offenders
NIO	Northern Ireland Office
NUPRG	New Ulster Political Research Group
ODC	'Ordinary Decent Criminal'
OIRA	Official IRA
PIRA	Provisional Irish Republican Army
PNV	Partido Nacionalista Vasco

POW	Prisoner-of-War
PP	Partido Popular
PSNI	Police Service of Northern Ireland
PSOE	Partido Socialista Obrero Espanol
PUP	Progressive Unionist Party
RHC	Red Hand Commando
RIRA	Real IRA
RUC	Royal Ulster Constabulary
SDLP	Social Democratic and Labour Party
SF	Sinn Fein
UCAG	Ulster Community Action Group
UDA	Ulster Defence Association
UDP	Ulster Democratic Party
UFF	Ulster Freedom Fighters
ULDP	Ulster Loyalist Democratic Party
UPRG	Ulster Political Research Group
UUP	Ulster Unionist Party
UVF	Ulster Volunteer Force

Introduction

This book arose from a Leverhulme Trust research project of the same title, conducted from 2006 to 2008, involving individual and group interviews with 147 republican and loyalist former prisoners and examination of the roles played by combatants in effecting political change. The aim of the book is to assess the extent to which the peace process in Northern Ireland developed as a result of the repudiation or maintenance of previously held views by those who had 'fought the war' and spent time in prison as a consequence of their actions. The level of analysis was crucial; most contemporary accounts of the peace and political processes were concentrated at elite level, examining the ability of political representatives to construct and maintain an inclusive set of compromises. In our view, none of these compromises were sustainable without backing from 'combatants' in the conflict. As such, any account of the peace process which failed to take account of why so many former prisoners supported the 1998 Good Friday Agreement was incomplete. Moreover, it was necessary to ascertain whether this backing for the peace process involved renunciation of previous articles of faith amongst former combatants, or instead represented ideological continuity amid new circumstances.

In undertaking these tasks, we begin, in Chapter 1, with a more detailed outline of the objectives of the project and discuss the main research questions. Our intellectual interest in the project was heightened by suspicion of the neat symmetry associated with explanations of the end of the Northern Ireland conflict grounded in theories of mutually hurting stalemate. Claims of symmetry and stalemate were juxtaposed with contrasting explanations from those involved in the 'war' as to why they had stopped fighting; one side (loyalists) believing they had won; the other (republicans) they would eventually win, with new tactics; in other words, not a perceived stalemate, let alone a mutually hurting one, at all. Chapter 1 raises the possibilities of alternative explanations of why conflict ended amid ideological *continuity* not change, and these are examined in the respective studies of loyalism and republicanism in later chapters.

Chapter 2 highlights the importance of prisoner releases in peace processes beyond Northern Ireland. Where the terms of such releases are ambiguous, or freedom is used overtly as a bargaining chip, the beneficial effects are often only brief. The chapter offers a set of 'ideal-type' conditions for prisoner releases, to maximise the chances of such measures making a positive contribution to sustainable peace. This section of the book also highlights how the literature on demilitarisation, demobilisation and reintegration has tended to overlook the centrality of prisoner releases to a successful peace process. Moreover, the focus has often been upon the mechanics of demobilisation of 'armies' at the expense of a serious consideration of whether those former combatants have adapted their political views.

Following this, the book traces the ideological development of those incarcerated during the conflict. Chapter 3 deploys the qualitative material to analyse the motivations underpinning participation in the conflict. Experiential and situational factors were more important than historical belief and family tradition. Motivations for joining were often reactive and ideological development followed, rather than preceded, violent actions and imprisonment.

Chapter 4 reviews the literature on the struggle for legitimacy conducted by republican and loyalist prisoners during the 1970s and 1980s. Although similar tactics were used by both sides in refusing to comply with prison authorities, the larger and more enduring campaigns conducted by republican prisoners were to reshape the Northern Irish conflict. The determination to be recognised as prisoners-of-war was replicated by republicans by their desire to prove that they enjoyed a sizeable electoral mandate. Due to their willingness to endure deprivation and hunger and view prison as another site of struggle, republican prisoners helped shape the direction of their movement, although the precise extent of influence remains disputed. Loyalist prisoners were disoriented by the experience of imprisonment by the state they purported to defend and loyalism struggled, within and beyond prison, to develop a political role.

The interplay of ideological, political, military, structural and personal factors which shaped prisoner arguments in favour of a peace process are examined in Chapter 5. These factors were not equally weighted and differed between republicanism and loyalism, but the political and the military aspects were inextricably linked in what both sides saw as an ostensibly political struggle, notwithstanding its military outworking. A combination of tactical flexibility, societal change, perceptions of victory or continuing change and outworking of the longstanding recognition of the limited utility of violence contributed to ceasefires and concentration upon politics.

Having analysed the motivations behind conflict transformation, Chapter 6 assesses the extent to which republicans and loyalist former prisoners have changed their views of each other. The chapter suggests a need to disaggregate pragmatic and cordial working relations between former inmates from ideological convergence. The working relationships established between former prisoners across the communal divide have been important in defusing tensions, particularly at sectarian interfaces, but should not be conflated with an acceptance of the legitimacy of a rival ideology.

Chapter 7 explores the positive roles played by former prisoners within their communities. Community restorative justice schemes, in particular, brought former prisoners into ever-closer contact with state agencies and moved armed groups away from the arbitrary dispensing of local 'justice'. The chapter again indicates the greater level of social capital within republican communities, affording a greater level of opportunities for developmental work for republican prisoners. There remain issues for former prisoners; although the Good Friday Agreement promised the promotion of their reintegration into society, their continued identification as previous combatants may act as a barrier to entry to some jobs, whilst their plight and their constructive offerings have diminished in importance to government as peace has consolidated.

The book concludes by summarising the roles played by former prisoners in conflict transformation and assesses the extent to which they can assist in the desectarianisation of Northern Ireland. Former prisoners have made significant political contributions to the development and maintenance of peace. Without forfeiting all of the views that contributed to their incarceration, republicans have been obliged to work with the state; loyalists have been required to accept republicans within state structures and explore means of working with the historic 'enemy' across the communal divide. Memories of conflict will fade; the local 'stature' of republican and loyalist former prisoners may reduce and funding for conflict transformation may diminish, potentially reducing the possibilities for positive societal change that could be engendered by those who learned lessons from their period as combatants. Nonetheless, we argue that former prisoners made a significant impact in the formulation and consolidation of peace.

1 Politically motivated prisoners in Northern Ireland

Long after the signing of the 1998 Good Friday Agreement – hereafter the Agreement – in Northern Ireland, the far-reaching consequences envisaged in the consociation of the competing political groupings of Ulster unionism and Irish nationalism became manifest. A long and tortuous path led to the formation of an inclusive coalition government headed by the supposed political extremes of the Democratic Unionist Party (DUP), representing the Unionist-British position, and Sinn Fein (SF), part of the wider Irish republican movement.

The formation of a DUP-Sinn Fein dominated coalition followed a long-term decline in politically motivated violence, with cessations and virtual disbandment from the main combatant groups. The Provisional Irish Republican Army (IRA) destroyed its arsenal and formally ended its armed campaign in 2005; the Ulster Volunteer Force (UVF) formally renounced violence and dissolved its military structures. Even the most reticent of the major groupings, the Ulster Defence Association (UDA), has engaged in processes of conflict transformation and disbanded the Ulster Freedom Fighters (UFF), its overtly military wing. The Irish National Liberation Army (INLA), although opposed to the Agreement, has also disengaged from politically motivated violence.

In the light of such dramatic change there has been a general focus upon formal party political leaderships as the agents of transformation. Analysis at the elite level obscures an appreciation of the efforts, structures and approaches taken at grassroots level to uphold and sustain conflict transformation and a reduction in violence (Shirlow and McEvoy 2008). Yet, as we argue in Chapter 2, via an analysis of other conflictual arenas, the delivery, impact and prospects of transformation are best aided when the issue of political prisoners and the evaluation of them as peace-builders are prominent within peace negotiations. Moreover, a failure to fully comprehend and explain the political and peace processes in Northern Ireland without adequate evaluation of the role played by former prisoners, amounts to an incomplete analysis.

In assessing the role played by former non-state combatants in conflict transformation we have obtained significant access to those former prisoners, many of whom are engaged in processes of societal transition. These former combatants have provided evidence regarding their own political and combatant biographies, the reasons for their involvement in conflict and their roles in transforming war into peace. In both personal and structural terms there is evidence of former combatants working to diminish the political tensions that remain as a result of the long-term inter-communal hostility developed across decades of violence. However, the evidence produced indicates that former combatants involved in personal and group transformation do so without discarding key ideological goals and interpretations. Moreover, we suggest that ideological antipathy remains intact and in this respect the past has 'not' been abandoned. Nonetheless a more pragmatic approach to the articulation and advancement of ideological goals has been adopted.

Analysis of post-conflict violence generally examines renewed conflict between enemies, the rise of dissidents opposed to peace-making initiatives and those who morph into criminal gangs (Keen 2001; Moran 2004). In South Africa and Serbia some paramilitaries sought the maintenance of status through 'punishment' violence, revenge or extensive criminality. Dowdney (2005) argues that such violence maintained lost status, while Stedman (1997) and Boyce (2002) assert that dissenters aim to 'spoil' what they view as unjust peace accords. In the condemnation of former prisoners in Northern Ireland, via media sources and the legal structures of criminalisation, there is insufficient space dedicated to how these former combatants have smoothed and guided the transition to conflict transformation and not acted in the deleterious manner found in other conflicts. No one doubts that there are elements within the former prisoner community who dissent from peace and practice criminal activity but the constant reference to the 'ruthlessness' of former prisoners and the presentation of them as 'psychotic' or 'deluded' depoliticises the meaning of conflict and its transformation in Northern Ireland (Arena and Arrigo 2006).

In making such an assertion, we do not naively eulogise non-state combatant actions, nor are we 'ivory tower' academics removed from the harsh realities of conflict. Instead, we argue that it is important to study conflict transition in an inclusive manner that includes those who were involved in violence. There is also a responsibility among academics to lift the cover off uncomfortable realities and in so doing challenge the fiction of blamelessness that is part of the general body politic.

In the fascination with violence and victims much of what is understood about conflict and former political prisoners is purposely intangible. Loyalism, for example, has been presented as an 'idiocy that comes with a fragmented culture that has lost both memory and meaning' (Howe 2005: 2). In other readings, republicanism is capable and loyalism is deemed as 'lacking'. As noted by Alison (2004: 447) 'liberatory' forms (Irish republicanism) also usually incorporate fairly wide-ranging goals of social transformation as part of their political programmes, while state and pro-state nationalisms (loyalism) do not.

Those who reject loyalism and republicanism see both as having failed to promote the positive in terms of their identity and actions. The realities of former prisoner groups challenging interface violence, building social capital, defying criminality and racism and removing those opposed to peaceful accord are hidden behind a plethora of negativity. In challenging such negative portrayals it is important to locate the arenas within which former prisoner groups have led conflict-transformation initiatives, have done much to quell elements intent upon a return to conflict, have created networks that encourage dialogue with former adversaries, have undermined the efficacy of violence as a rational practice and have developed links with statutory agencies in order to encourage social justice and accountability (Shirlow and McEvoy 2008). Such a transitional role, as discussed in Chapter 7, is under-explored despite these transitions being crucial with regard to ending victimi-sation, encouraging citizenship and removing threat.

As argued in Chapters 3 and 6, the capacity to shift loyalism and republi-canism into the realm of transition has generally come from among adherents to those ideologies and has not been based upon an imposition of state or wider political authority. Transitional attitudes and models are being advanced by former political prisoner groups, effecting a shift from a destabilising past. However, the internal and organic nature of conflict transformation and the models being advanced by former prisoners, which have an international appeal and resonance, remain obscured by the unconstructive representation of former prisoners, who are often deemed as 'all that is wrong' with Northern Ireland.

The outplaying of conflict transformation also, as shown within this book, is not based upon simplistic ideas that concern a 'mutually hurting stalemate', in which combatants fought each other to a standstill before 'coming to their senses', but instead is led by those formerly engaged in conflict, who are taking responsibility in the design and rolling out of post-conflict solutions. This is achieved without acceding to an alternative ideology or accepting the past as 'illegitimate', but instead is fused around maintaining core values of social inclusion, human rights and inter- and intra-community challenge. Former prisoner groups are dealing with the issues that caused and reproduced conflict through identifying the healing of society via inclusion. Attitudes towards the peace process do not relate directly to academic determinations of conflict and peace-building, as they remain grounded in much closer experiences of conflict. The interpretation of moving out of violence is not understood as a process of ideological 'ditching' or the emergence of a 'mutually hurting stalemate' (Zartman 2003a) but of the development of tactics and the impact of conflict upon opening up means to promote republican and loyalist discourse.

For IRA respondents, violence engendered the peace process in two ways. First, it had forced the British state into adopting anti-discrimination legislation and second, the IRA had elicited an acceptance by the British state that they were a political organisation rather than common criminals, a perception epitomised by early releases under the provisions of the Agreement. Loyalist respondents argued that their violence had stalled republicans and upheld the constitutional link. Ironically these differing perspectives, rather than an acceptance of a mutually hurting stalemate, achieved the capacity to move beyond violence. In sum, the use of violence was not rejected via a primarily moral concern, although that was for many respondents important, but instead conditioned by a sense that it had bolstered negotiating entry 'rights', as evidenced by the Manchester bombing in 1996, the largest bomb ever used by the IRA. This legitimacy had been 'proven' as opposed to 'defeated'.

Conflict transformation and the maintenance of ideology

This study considers the extent to which former political prisoners 'abandoned' the ideological compass, which 'legitimised' violence. Much has been written concerning the 'ditching' of ideological beliefs in the pursuit of peace. For example, in *Gunsmoke and Mirrors* (2008) the journalist Henry McDonald writes of the IRA as those engaged in a 360 degree turn in mainstream republican ideology, one which has been associated elsewhere with cunning and deception exercised by the Sinn Fein leadership, against hapless members of the IRA and the Sinn Fein grassroots, to a level which would make Machiavelli look like an amateur (McIntyre 2008; Moloney 2002: see also Alonso 2006; McIntyre 1995, 2001; Patterson 1997; White 2006).

Among the extensive range of interviews conducted there is was a near complete rejection that the peace process and demilitarisation was either a rejection of violence as being terrorist-inspired and that previous military activity lacked ideological reason (Alonso 2006) or that the discursive value of loyalism or republicanism had been abandoned (McInytre 1995, 2001, 2008). Among republicans there was an acceptance of Bean's argument that the nature of demilitarisation was paralleled by the socio-economic shaping of contemporary Northern Ireland and the 'complexities of this relationship between movement and community' (Bean, 2007: 13). For loyalists the sense that republicanism was defeated militarily is presented as having endorsed both violent enactment and a cessation of that violence. It is worth noting that those who have claimed that the IRA has ditched their ideological beliefs usually produce evidence to support this argument from those dissatisfied with, or dismissive of, 'transitional' tactics (McIntyre 2008; Moloney 2002; Rolston

1989; Ryan 1994; Shirlow and McGovern 1998). The account presented within this book pertains to a wider array of voices and includes ideas and opinions that are not necessarily scripted by the leadership of respective movements (see also English 2003, 2006). This volume produces a more heterogeneous account that highlights the broad range of ideas and perspectives located among former loyalist and republican prisoners.

In examining the nature and intent of loyalism and republicanism, the differing electoral fortunes of each movement provides a dichotomy of achievement in wider political terms. Republican consciousness, as it pertained to demilitarisation and demobilisation of the IRA, has been closely allied to the fortunes of Sinn Fein, although not all former IRA prisoners are supportive of that particular political party. For loyalism, the comparably low level of political representation, confined to Progressive Unionist Party (PUP) and independent councillors, plus a solitary Assembly member (Dawn Purvis) means that the role played by former loyalist prisoners is located mostly in conflict transformation work.

Among former IRA prisoners the rejection of ideological ditching is accompanied by a presentation of tactical shifts as key to a wider explanation of transition and transformation. Thus tactical awareness, whether that has involved the use of violence, serving in the Northern Ireland Assembly (in a still-partitioned Ireland) or campaigning for the promotion of equality, is mutually inclusive and seen as part of a long-term strategy that will gain Irish unification. These attitudes form part of a broader teleology associated with republicanism in which the end of history – a united Ireland – remains achievable even if military impulses disappear for periods (Smith, 1995). Republican belief in ultimate success does not deny the complexities of post-conflict political, cultural and social practice, nor does in dismiss the unevenness of the struggle at times, but there were constant reminders during interviews with former IRA prisoners, that present strategies are tied to an unambiguous, verifiable and long-term ideological intent. In sum, former IRA prisoners contend that it is not the constitution of republican ideology that has shifted, but the practice of ideology and alternative methods that have been allied to what is a potentially more 'successful' political and community strategy (Adams 1995; Maillot 2004).

Conflict transformation is interpreted within loyalism as a process of contestation within and beyond loyalism. Conflict is understood as not only removing violence but also challenging the wider social arenas of ethnosectarian disputation linked to suspicion, mistrust and the need to develop human rights agendas for working-class communities. Transformation is generally about establishing relationships that challenge inequitable social, cultural and political definitions and categories and in so doing promoting Protestant working-class identities that stretch beyond sectarian renditions and practices. As with republicans the goal of contemporary activism has not been based upon ideological ditching, but instead the enveloping of loyalist ideas into changing conditions and solutions. This is an important point in that it undermines the idea of former prisoners as merely 'criminals' and helps construct a more accurate understanding of how tactics and ideas are shaped by conflict, wider social changes and through the reasoning that the deliverance of democratic accountability requires the consent and approval of adversaries both within and beyond each respective community. As noted by Shirlow and Monaghan (2006: 3):

> The desire to prevent future occurrences of violent disunity has been divided into two general perspectives. Firstly, a conflict transformation perspective encourages an analysis of the antecedents of conflict as a way out of disagreement. Secondly, seeking out better ways to represent loyalism within a process of capacity building has also emerged. Additional features include lifting loyalism out of insularity and into a host of civic and inter-community based relationships; developing better relationships with government and statutory agencies; promoting restorative justice schemes; creating alternative community narratives which link loyalism into a post-ceasefire process; and challenging the mythic status of violence and in so doing diverting youth attention away from paramilitaries and sectarian violence.

An important factor in the promotion of non-violence is the extent to which post-conflict approaches are found to be credible among the rank and file. Credibility has been important with regard to dissuading a return to violence, as it provides legitimacy to anti-violence discourse, but operates as a further example of the internally generated transition. Given the internalised nature of transition and the dominance of narratives that have examined peace-building in Northern Ireland, at the elite level, this book is based upon developing and accounting for personal experiences of former prisoners in order to determine more about the nature of non-state combatant violence and the endorsement of peaceful former prisoner activity. The interview work undertaken aimed to determine; the reasons for joining a paramilitary organisation; the influence of imprisonment in terms of abandoning, developing or acquiring ideological beliefs; examining if support for past actions has been diminished, reinvented or remains constructed around contested interpretations of 'truth' and legitimacy; determining the post-imprisonment support base for - or rejection of - former political prisoners and how this has shaped the capacity and meaning of post-conflict transformation and appreciating and explaining the development of political and community leadership strategies by former political prisoners.

Two further objectives are developed. First, as discussed in Chapters 2, 6 and 7, the development of former prisoner groups was tied to promoting ideological beliefs via community activism and the role of former political prisoners as 'organic intellectuals' (Cassidy 2005, 2008). Second, as shown in Chapter 3, the presentation of loyalist and republican discourses relates to wider interpretations of conflict and peace-building, in terms of countering 'traditional' models of conflict cessation, the relationship with political elites and the balance between endogenous and exogenous factors in achieving conflict transformation.

Studying former politically motivated prisoners

This is the largest study of republican and loyalist former prisoners undertaken via qualitative analysis. Former prisoner groups who provided a gatekeeping role to access groups and individuals greatly aided the study. Using gatekeeper organisations ensured that all respondents were former prisoners. Moreover, the views expressed by respondents did not merely mimic group interpretations as a range of different experiences, criticisms and viewpoints emerged. We did not seek approving or disapproving voices regarding the development of the peace process, but instead aimed to cover a range of perspectives and viewpoints from within these groups. The approach undertaken sought to determine if ideas regarding legitimacy and the past amounted to ideological change, adaptation or political pragmatism. Evidently, there has been insufficient work on this regarding former combatants and we reached 147 respondents to maximise the number of prisoner voices on which to construct academic analysis.

The first phase of contact was based upon developing and explaining the research themes to the following prisoner groups: Coiste na Ichimi (Provisional IRA); EPIC (UVF/Red Hand Commando); Charter (UDA/UFF) and Teach na Failte (INLA). The second phase of analysis involved a range of semi-structured interviews and focus group work. In sum, eighty-seven republicans and sixty loyalists were involved in interviews and of these around three-quarters of all interviews and meetings were recorded. Interviews and focus groups also included women and had a geographical spread, including fourteen focus groups in South Derry, Derry City, South Armagh, Belfast and Armagh City. Other focus groups and interviews were conducted with serving IRA prisoners in Roscrea, members of Sinn Fein and that organisation's *ard chomairle* (executive) and the PUP and its executive.

The study centred on an inductive approach, which examined the nature of narrative and ideology among former prisoners. We aimed to test the experiences and narratives of being former combatants with regard to the complexities of the shifting out of violence and whether such a shift was tied to ideological 'ditching', or the use of ideology to confirm the movement away from armed violence. Research themes were initially agreed and debated with former prisoners groups so that the emergent narratives would guide the research objectives beyond those already set.

A semi-structured schedule of questions was utilised in order to permit each respondent's voice to emerge. This study contributes to an awareness of the meaning of belief and experiences from the perspective of combatants who are considered as individuals. The primary means of research involved interviews with individuals in order to ensure that they express freely given attitudes. These interviews were centred upon the respondent's responses to a known situation (conflict/imprisonment/post-conflict) and how they perceived concepts of narrative and ownership so vital in interpreting violence and the post-conflict situation. The research undertaken was exploratory in nature and not an attempt to provide definite truths, but instead to explore the motivations, significance and consequences of a transition from armed conflict to non-violence and the maintenance or rejection of key political goals.

In terms of acquiring specific information on the geographical spread of former prisoners and information on gender and age there was, perhaps surprisingly, a dearth of information from official sources and the precise number of prisoners jailed for 'political' offences during the conflict is unknown. The prisoner groups themselves do not have exact records. The use of a qualitative approach aimed to not only fill a void in academic discussion of former prisoners from within both loyalism and republicanism but to also evaluate how language constructs social relations and the constituting of ideas and their interpretation. Both loyalist and republican ideals are presented as the outcome of discursively fabricated classifications of belonging (Burton and Carlen 1979) and both groups understand their present situation as being part of a tradition of inter- and intra-group engagement and analysis.

In locating such voices we are reminded that representation is fused around the notion of loyalty and both precise and different interpretations and imaginings of variant notions of community, harm, suffering and ontological togetherness. For former IRA prisoners the reiteration of a republican discourse is generally seen as unproblematic, whereas for loyalists and INLA respondents there is a more evident questioning of intent and practice, although the legitimacy of motivation remains. Thus language and the verbal reasoning behind support of the peace process is at times exclusivist in terms of a loyalist and republican reading of transition, but also inclusive given the realisation that the inclusion and or consent of the 'other' is necessary in formulating conflict transformation. Resistance, as shown in Chapter 5, to an identified 'other' remains and the peace process, for former prisoners and local political elites, is based upon removing extensive animosity between groups, but at the same time continuing to promote activities and concerns that are practised and conditioned upon the needs of the 'self' that are represented as respective electorates. Thus the disputed understanding of Northern Ireland's constitutional future remains as a guide to the limitations of post-conflict meaning, practice and intention.

The language of loyalist and republican identity is seen as having been secured through the various stages of revolt, political development and more recently commemoration and conflict transformation. In essence the journey

of political vocabulary has been guided by the shift in tactics and more importantly from an IRA perspective transition has been an ongoing method that
was linked to the shift from 'powerlessness' due to asymmetrical state relations,
through to political 'achievement' within an ever-changing cultural,
economic, social and political landscape. In recoding the language and
meaning of that transition we are reminded that the issue is not one of ideological disjuncture, but of what is understood as evolving situations and the
manner in which violence produces a range of options and sometimes even
unintended outcomes. The material recorded herein highlights how ideology
is an umbrella under which the expression of values and material practice is
outplayed.

What is understood as ideology and belief has been reproduced via realities
and the idea that the expression of ideas was fluid, but remained conditioned
by oppositional constitutional perspectives. There is no sense among the
respondents that ideological practice would have remained static or
unwavering. A sense that ideological ditching had occurred would have undermined the peace process in a much more influential way than has been the case
among those represented as republican and loyalist dissidents. It is in the sense
that violence succeeded and that loyalism prevented Irish unification or that
republicanism will usher in a united Ireland now that Northern Ireland has
changed irrevocably, that the conditions and interpretation of discourse is
located. Ultimately in examining attitudes via a qualitative approach we learn
more about the system and dimensions of conflict, but in so doing also experience more about how imprisonment and conflict fashions understanding and
interests. Paradoxically, in the Northern Ireland case conflict, imprisonment,
debate and tactics ushered in the cessation of a conflict that was not resolved,
but managed and transformed.

The ideas and beliefs of former prisoners are largely self-referential and self-
sustained by notions of republican and loyalist legitimacy. This does not mean,
with regard to victims, that there is not regret about human loss, nor lack of
cognisance of the unacceptability of some actions, but it also highlights how
many combatants wondered how conflict could be ceased. In the 1970s this
was generally understood as military victory, but such a perspective was never
independent of other ideological ideas and concerns, being conditioned by
notions of the practical or aspirational. Once the practical limitations were
exposed as limited the fusing of alternative but existing approaches was
ushered forth.

Key arguments and observations

Two key interpretations argue that militant behaviour is a result of individual
psyche; one perspective suggests that there exists a 'terrorist' personality
(Crenshaw 2000) while others (Arena and Arrigo 2006) argue that non-state

combatants engage in political violence as a result of high levels of commit-ment and well-developed ideological positions. However, we argue that partic-ipation in conflict is neither attached to a 'terrorist' psyche nor simply rooted in ideological belief. In so doing we offer alternative frames of explanation – the definition and fusion of experiential factors (driven by the onset of violence, brutality and perceived community violation), 'ideological' frame-works strengthened by a strong sense of collective identity and structural factors (political leadership, social injustice, discrimination and socio-economic position).

This book provides a more coherent understanding of involvement in conflict, the delivery of a peace process and the influence over that process as understood by former political prisoners and the social worlds within which they are situated. It grounds experience, legitimacy and the mobilisation of long-serving interpretations of history and conflict and the merger of these around ideas of developing and sustaining conflict transformation.

There has evidently been no abandoning of a historical past and in many ways the beliefs regarding the 'other' are sustained despite the development of inter-group activity. Legitimacy and interpretations of the past have not shifted in order to sustain the peace process, but instead conflict transformation has been assembled around locating shared concerns and promoting the efficacy of ideologies of community activism as opposed to violence. Political resistance is now articulated around non-violent means and the capacity to shift out of violence has been based upon discourses of loyalty to the group and the communities that uphold support for that organisation. Imprisonment built up trust within groups and their respective leaderships due to the latter having themselves been imprisoned. Experience of imprisonment, as shown in Chapters 3 and 4, provides a legitimacy in itself that is now invoked to provide community-led strategies of transformation. Transformation is not about ideological decline or a separation from past motivations, but is instead based upon the promotion of republican and loyalist ideas within an environment they believe was altered by 'successful' military interventions.

Membership motivations

The joining of paramilitary groups was generally based upon 'events more than anything else' and violence that emanated from an identifiable 'other'. Some respondents were cultivated into organisations, others came from families steeped in republican and loyalist-defender traditions and others succumbed to peer pressure. The importance of 1966 to a few republicans later to join the IRA (a connection virtually invisible in academic analyses of the Provisionals) as the fiftieth anniversary of the 1916 Rising was attached to senses of consciousness-raising and a need for republican remobilisation. Such ideolog-ical discovery and rebirth was attached to structural and experiential contexts.

This was paralleled within loyalism as a need to recast and reform the original UVF as a defender of unionist territory. Those imprisoned after the mid 1970s located or had been supplied with a more defined ideological position.

With regard to overall senses of legitimacy, it was found that former republican and loyalist prisoners view the conflict as a reaction to state or republican oppression and or aggression. Like previous and contemporary forms of identity-based violence the most significant condition for mobilisation is to be found in the agency of activists (Bean 2007). Within both groupings, the base has been attached to creative cultural mediums and organisational structures that sought to define collective identity (Shirlow and McGovern 1998). The IRA deployed the language of community to not only instill nationalist 'unity', but to also establish hegemony within the nationalist community. The building of such hegemony has been partly achieved through recent electoral politics, with Sinn Féin emerging as the dominant voice of Northern nationalism (McAllister 2004; Murray and Tonge 2005; Shirlow and Murtagh 2006). For loyalists and the INLA the sense of community is caste more tightly as corroboration for their activities was more bounded in terms of scale and much less significant than that achieved by the IRA. For loyalists in particular, there is a sense of community being fused around the notion of 'the people' and having acted in the interests of 'the people', with 'the people' constituted as Protestant unionists, whose defence by armed loyalists was seen as the main articulation of the 'defender' role (McAuley 1991: 45–55; McAuley 1998).

The reality of societal and political deterioration in the early stage of the conflict was a paramount cause of mobilisation. Many of those imprisoned in the early 1970s saw themselves as reacting to violence, unionist hegemony and state indifference. The sense of 'hitting back' as a mode of becoming involved and then adopting a more defined discourse, especially among IRA members, was commonplace. For all respondents the sense of being part of a violated community was important.

For some the capacity to locate republican family histories was important in that it established a sense of ideological lineage that was brought to the fore by the collapse of social relationships in the 1960s and 1970s. Several factors influenced the discursive journey of republicanism; ideological mobilisation through the use of commemoration, socialisation and the goal of Irish unity; situational violence and the response to state and loyalist activity; structural factors conditioned by 'second-class' citizenship and the demands for equality of recognition and anti-discrimination legislation. The fusion of these was constantly understood by the respondents as being the basis on which to utilise violence. For loyalists, the sense that republican violence was not being sufficiently challenged by pro-state actions was combined with the knowledge and experience of assault and inter-community violence. Yet a sense of 'second-class' citizenship was not confined to republicans. It was also evident among those loyalists who felt duped by 'Middle Unionism', comprising those who represent the unionist electorate and the middle classes. The disconnection between middle-class unionism and working-class loyalism was of importance in some loyalists later questioning what they had achieved through engaging in pro-state violence.

Nearly all respondents, loyalist or republican, possessed a localised sense of injustice and understood such injustices as motivational factors. Among IRA respondents it was stated that the knowledge of republican discourse was developed around a more cohesive explanation and coherent ideology. Early violent reaction was not understood as obdurate, psychotic or inflexible, but framed around senses of injustice and both vague and established frameworks of a republican heritage and loyalist defenderism and discourse. With regard to conflict the attachment and development of ideas during violent enactment framed the cessation of politically motivated violence.

The influence of prison experiences

Virtually all respondents were inspired by prison debates within and between paramilitary groups. Such debates were important given that the IRA, INLA and to a lesser extent loyalists challenged the nature of criminalisation and prison authority. For republicans, in particular, their incarceration was rejected as illegitimate and their response to imprisonment was to further develop anti-state policies. It was also understood by republicans that prison debates were not about the imposition of an ideology, but that these debates provided a vocabulary that explained grievances and anti-state actions. The writing of plays, poetry and the learning of Irish (even among some loyalists) were also seen as acts of resistance and the development of a prisoner ideology. Within the prison arena republicans and some loyalists challenged dominant representations of them and also nurtured identities of resistance against prison authority (Corcoran 2006; McKeown 1999).

Prisoners were a part, whilst imprisoned and when released, in the development of styles and strategic and tactical experimentation designed to remove the nature and reproduction of violence (Bean 2007). Given that so many activists understood their activities as being a response to and a resistance against an identifiable antagonist and that many of their demands were based upon social injustices, that could be corrected by housing and fair employment policies, it is possible to see some value in Smyth's (2002: 144) argument that the capacity to move from a military to a political position was generally unproblematic as 'the absence of justice or democracy can be used to justify a reformist strategy, but equally both can be integrated into a justification for armed struggle'.

Smyth's (2005) argument identifies fluidity, especially within republicanism, that was identified and responded to by British state expenditure and policy. The British state's role, although far from perfect, in rebuilding housing stock, developing fair employment strategies and promoting power-sharing and devolution did much to take the 'heat out of' localised experiences of social injustice. Therefore, republicans in prison and beyond were influenced by a changing social order that created space for a non-violent republicanism to develop. Social engineering, the growth in the electoral fortunes of Sinn Fein and the desire to build wider cognition of republican ideas, that would capture an electorate opposed to violence, were factors that encouraged debates among the imprisoned (Munck 1992).

IRA former prisoners were more likely to espouse a mixture of pride in their resistance whilst recognising that their struggle had raised consciousness within the republican movement and facilitated a capacity to critique societal shifts. Articles and summaries of imprisonment, undertaken by former prisoners, consciously presents struggle as having being forged within a comparative international frame. The role of international thinkers was linked to the identification of an internal republican intellectualism that had included 'among their ranks a high proportion of writers, poets, musicians and artists, many of whom endured imprisonment and used those years to further their cultural activities' (Mac Giolla Ghunna 1997: 3–4). The self-presentation of an articulate movement was one of political repositioning and the emergence of transitional republicanism.

Loyalist debates and the reasoning behind them were less structured than in comparison with the IRA, but debates did take place that challenged the value of violence and argued that loyalist violence should aim to be more anti-republican as opposed to sectarian inspired. However, unlike the IRA, loyalists did not have a wider community with which to engage, such as Irish America, and due to public unionist hostility, at times hidden when meeting in private, a significant part of what loyalism was to evolve into was centred around a cadre of those who became political and community leaders within it (Bloomer 2008; McAuley 2005).

A binary sense of being publicly rejected by certain unionist leaders and being encouraged by them in private also furthered a loyalist dynamic based upon relative loyalist independence, from unionist leaders, in the evolution of loyalist group activity. The idea of being 'dupes no more' and the development among some of a leftist notion of political economy influenced intra- and inter-class division and was an important facet of loyalist prison based discussion. Loyalist leaders who emerged from prison did not have the same command and authority within their movement in comparison to the IRA, but their intellectual, social and cultural development has come to dominant the pro-Agreement and conflict transformation structures of contemporary loyalism.

Irrespective of the variant impact of former prisoners upon tactics and reorientation, the organic nature of debate and dialogue within and even at times between republicans and loyalists was significant in bolstering alternative and future practices. Imprisonment also influenced a process that one respondent identified as a time to 'learn a lot of things'. This sense of learning and a commitment to acquiring and developing a discourse and more coherent mode of analysis was understood as a process of developing a post-conflict logic.

Those imprisoned loyalists and republicans who challenged the *modus operandi* attached to violence did so without removing narratives of oppression and resistance, instead developing a repertoire of inclusion that was to be sought by other means (Shirlow and McGovern 1998). The nature of such debates was attached not only to moving out of armed conflict, but also discussing how to produce an alternative political culture within which combatants would no longer be required to act as an armed bulwark. However, neither the IRA nor other groups were to disappear immediately, before the evolution of former political prisoner groups as the new site within which political, cultural and social activism were to be maintained. The impact of imprisonment provided ideological coherence and a recognition that purist ideological explanations needed to be internally reviewed and re-examined in terms of application, feasibility and worth.

As shown in Chapters 3 and 4, there were a series of differences and similarities with regard to understanding how the micro-history of incarceration affected republicans and loyalists. Both sets of prisoners were influenced by internal debates although the numbers involved were greater amongst republicans. Each set of prisoners largely conformed to their respective leaderships inside and outside gaol. Many more republicans understood prison as a site of resistance against British and Irish state hegemony, whereas for pro-state volunteers such activism was undermined by the dimension of being essentially pro-British. One of the more significant differences was that many more republican prisoners, compared with their loyalist counterparts, understood that 'struggle' would continue in a post-imprisonment environment and that the vocabulary and skills needed to perpetuate republicanism required knowledge of how to pursue a non-violent conflict. In contrast, most loyalists thought of the conflict as having ended once they had been released or after the IRA had called a ceasefire, and as a result of this their struggle was to be represented by unionist political parties. For those who were to uptake a role in conflict transformation the emergence from prison had been framed by the experience of debate and dialogue within prison and the capacity to locate that knowledge within a landscape of post-conflict change.

Understanding the 'other' side

The development of cordial relationships between former prisoners at both a personal and group level and the formation of inter-group consortia to deal with interface violence, truth inquiries and social justice is paralleled, at times, by antipathy to the 'other'. Most IRA respondents, as they did in the 1970s, still dismiss loyalism as sectarian, non-progressive, non-socialist, non-autonomous and criminal. Loyalism is thus viewed as misguided, poorly led and self-seeking. Indeed it was also noted that anyone who supported the partition of Ireland could not be deemed to have radical politics despite the clearly labourist-left bent of PUP politics and the social justice agenda pursued by loyalist former prisoner groups. Moreover, IRA attitudes towards the 'other', i.e. unionists and loyalists, remains based upon negative stereotyping and a mode of engagement centred on utilising inter-community contact as a means to persuade those who are pro-union of their ideological 'folly' and the 'incoherence' of unionism. Loyalists and INLA respondents view the IRA with suspicion and interpret them as leadership constrained. Loyalists also view the IRA as continuing their campaign by new means.

What co-joins these groups is that they inhabit similar social worlds of economic exclusion and under-privilege. They have determined a shared role to play in undermining the return of violence which is tied to their sense of status and legitimacy, and a collective belief that the peace process is insufficient regarding the capacity to quell sectarian violence, deliver social justice and challenge their shared experience of criminalisation. Loyalists and the INLA respondents view such engagement as developing shared working-class experiences and values. More generally, former prisoner groups and their related activities are crucial in maintaining structures that allowed groups to promote their legitimacy and beliefs in a structured and non-violent manner (see Chapter 7). Community activism is understood, by former prisoners, as primary in delivering the peace process and also promoting each group's perspectives and identity.

Somewhat ironically, former prisoners suppose that the use of violence has removed the need for violence. The Agreement, which they view in selective ways according to what 'their side' achieved, has created recourse to a *modus operandi* that seeks the same ideological commitments and goals through non-violent activity. Discipline and the capacity of former prisoners to locate a community that recognised their 'sacrifices' helped to pave the way for a smooth transition, especially among IRA volunteers. This transition was furthered by many republican former political prisoners undertaking community-based employment within which the struggle, through civic activism, could be undertaken and in so doing maintain community status and ideological congruity.

Former political prisoner involvement in community work post-1998 not only strengthened their activism as it moved them beyond the confines of their own community, but also created a transition, although hampered by their criminalisation, into civic society and thus removed a political vacuum that may have caused indifference to peace-building initiatives. The hostility between loyalists who supported the Agreement and those who did not was divided between those loyal to former prisoners groups and those 'beyond the pale' of such organisations. The more general trend amongst loyalists to return, if possible, to more normal sites of employment did much to undermine the capacity of loyalism to cope with the tensions caused by the emergence of a post-ceasefire environment. For some loyalists the idea that they were pro-state irregulars and that the war was over meant that a return to 'normal' life appeared rational and sensible.

A complex relationship with the 'other' has emerged. For INLA respondents there appears to be a capacity and desire to work with loyalists and a similar sense of being a minority within a wider, in this case republican, community. INLA respondents seem to object more to the IRA and their 'dominance' of the republican community than they do with regard to working with loyalists. Both INLA and loyalist former prisoners also present the idea that there is a sectarian strain within sections of the IRA and that this is ignored by IRA leaders. Moreover, the INLA feel subjugated by IRA activity and cite cases when their refusal to be served in local bars, in republican areas, has been due to the IRA censuring their activities. Loyalists also appear to have a workable relationship with the INLA and other tiny (non-'dissident') groups such as those affiliated to the Official IRA. In general, there are good working relationships between loyalist and IRA former prisoners, but at times these relationships are strained. However, the relationship between loyalists and republicans more generally is workable and achieves a certain consensus.

One of the obvious dichotomies between the IRA former prisoners and 'other' groups is a higher level of political, cultural and social confidence. These republicans have emerged out of conflict and into a Northern Ireland within which their electoral fortunes and the influence over republican territory is noteworthy and within which their 'sacrifices' have gained them status and influence within their communities. Republican former prisoners are also more likely to be locked into a wider international arena within which their post-conflict role is heralded as successful and valid.

Despite evident tensions it would appear that former prisoners, more so than other sections of society, can work with each other to produce shared social economy schemes and other initiatives around truth, harm and social justice. Unfortunately, the pragmatism of working together is rarely explored and considered as a model of conflict transformation in Northern Ireland more generally.

Beyond conflict

What IRA former prisoners mean by the peace process is articulated around the promotion of republican values and a discourse guided by the eventual achievements of republican goals. It is also understood that republican beliefs have been debated and have secured republican unity and permitted the leadership and the republican grassroots to deny accusations of a 'sell-out', a feature of internal republican discord that has historically undermined Irish republican movements.

The promotion of a non-violent republicanism and loyalism has been influenced by evident identity tapping and/or formation that defined a project that was located in the capacity to weld together disparate forms of Irish nationalism and Ulster/British loyalism. What has unsurprisingly (given the class basis of former political prisoners) emerged is a predominantly class-based notion of identity tied to competing loyalist and republican versions of land, tradition, repression and repelling the violence of the 'other'. However, it is important to note that the evolution of debates undertaken during and after imprisonment has not simply guided mono-cultural enquiry. The terrain of consciousness that is loyalism and republicanism has also explored episodes and political events that do not conform to singular identity constructs (Shirlow and McGovern 1996, 1998).

Loyalists, especially those attached to the UVF, have created a micro-society of ideological identification and dialogue centred upon unravelling the complexities of Irish history (Brown 2007). Thus the Battle of the Somme has been shifted from a selective Orange celebration into an event that is commemorated from a sophisticated analysis that evokes a shared suffering among Irish Catholic and Ulster Protestant soldiers and their families. Emanating from such analysis is an anti-bourgeois discourse that views elite-led unionism as pervasive in its control of Protestant working-class consciousness. IRA former prisoners have produced and written plays that deconstruct the simplistic status of republicanism as unproblematic. Again it is within sections of the former political prisoner community that the challenge to the eulogisation of each respective movement is located.

Developing a path out of armed conflict was aided for both loyalist and republicans as important in the movement out of political isolation and within which political and community dividends could be located. Republicans deemed that they could gain significant concessions from the British state. Loyalists also noted the positive role played by staff and government ministers affiliated to Irish foreign affairs and the sense that the Irish state was lukewarm considering Irish unification. The changing of Articles 2 and 3 of the Irish Constitution and the endorsement of the principle of consent furthered loyalist senses of achievement regarding the Irish state. Moreover, the Irish state has funded and supported a significant amount of post-conflict work by loyalist former prisoners.

The crucially important fact of moving out of conflict was that non-state combatant groups were to maintain their structure and activities via former prisoner groups. The reality that groups would remain intact, although under a different *nom de guerre* has been virtually unacknowledged in the appreciation and understanding of conflict transformation in Northern Ireland (for an exception see Shirlow and McEvoy 2008). The emotional power and resonance of these groups around advice workers, interface workers, elected representatives and community activists was that it removed a vacuum that would, as it has in other societies, undermine demilitarisation. Republican and loyalist former prisoners were not demobilised, as structures remained in which to practise and articulate their political and community concerns. Thus what they viewed as their contribution was not something to be left in the past but instead was to be harnessed into future meaningful conflict-transformation work. The battlefield had been thickened and redirected and this created a sense of mutual reinforcement between the past and the non-violent future.

Conclusion

Amid the broad continuity of political outlook held by former prisoners, however, there have been four specific drivers, which have facilitated changed methodologies. These are as follows:

1 Political (leadership-moral-pragmatic) and ideological acceptance of agreement
The decision to end violence was grounded in pragmatic rationale, based upon an assessment of a utility-futility equation in terms of its continued deployment relative to alternative strategies. The Agreement did not require any formal renunciation of ideological principles.

2 Economic
The second driver has been shaped by the experiences of former prisoners when granted parole from prisons. This became increasingly common during the 1990s and many prisoners commented on their perception of changing economic circumstances within their community. Deghettoisation was underway and the structural basis of conflict was diminishing.

3 Perceptions of the 'other'
We do not find that republican perceptions of loyalists, or loyalist perceptions of republicans have altered markedly in ideological terms. However, shared prison experiences, common class status and support for the concept of peace have allowed cordial personal relationships to develop despite the lack of ideological transformation.

4 Persuasion-experiential in prison
Ideological development in prisons led to an eventual questioning of whether alternatives to armed struggle existed. Again, this did not amount to ideological overhaul, but there were internal discussions over the validity of violence, the position of loyalists/republicans and the changing role of the state. The relaxation of the prison regime was important in developing possibilities of change, in parallel to the relaxation of security measures outside the jails.

In addition, we show that former prisoners still view the conflict via republican and loyalist lenses with the former understanding motivation as being a reaction to state 'oppression' whereas loyalists maintain the ideology of defence and protecting constitutional relationships with Britain. Attitudes on the peace process relate more directly to grassroots and localised experiences of conflict and recovery than they do to external factors such as elite-driven practices of consociation and wider geo-political shifts. The legitimacy of each group remains paramount and the interpretation of moving out of violence is not understood as a process of ideological 'ditching', but of the development of tactics. Violence did not cease solely due to a 'mutual stalemate', but instead owes more to asymmetric perceptions of military success (loyalists) or transformative possibilities (republicans). The shift out of armed conflict is construed along the binary between the 'success' of loyalists bringing 'republicans' to 'heel' and republicans pursuing a united Ireland after 'breaking the sustainability of British authority'. These groups are prepared to co-operate around shared projects. IRA respondents see this work as part of the process of building a united Ireland. Loyalists and the INLA view it as building intra-community relationships between estranged working-class communities.

Interestingly, the capacity and ability to deliver and sustain peace has been developed around a series of both ambiguous and unambiguous relationships among former prisoners. Many of the respondents interviewed have been engaged in long personal and group-based journeys. Virtually all support the Agreement, but have senses that parts of it are ideologically or personally difficult. The remainder of this book highlights how ideological continuity has been juxtaposed with new political tactics. We begin, however, with lesson-drawing from the release of politically motivated prisoners in other conflicts.

2 Former prisoners in a global context

The academic literature on peace processes suggests a considerable amount of borrowing of ideas from previous peace-building (e.g. Darby and Mac Ginty 2003; Ramsbotham et al. 2005). Preparations for peace, its consolidation via ceasefires, negotiations and the marginalisation of ultra spoiler groups and the implementation of peace agreements are all issues common to global peace processes, aspects where policy learning from previous efforts to create peace may be evident. Moreover, ideas concerning the specific – and often most controversial – features of securing peace among former combatants, including amnesties, prisoner releases, decommissioning, demobilisation, institutional and policing reforms, have been transferred and imported from earlier peace processes into contemporary attempts at conflict transformation (Ramsbotham et al. 2005; Sisk 2003; Stedman 2003).

The extent of global influences upon the Northern Ireland peace process has been disputed. Cox (1998; 2006) suggests the international dimension was important, but highlights the geo-political context (the end of the Cold War and diminution of Northern Ireland's strategic significance) as a favourable backdrop, rather than the import of ideas from other peace processes. Dixon (2006) proffers a more sceptical view of the global dimensions to the Northern Irish peace process, suggesting it was a largely home-grown development, one which has distorted supposed rules of management of strong ethnic divisions, including a tendency to turn consociational ideas into whatever is politically expedient at a particular time. Significantly however, Guelke's (2006) consideration of the impact of some features of global peace processes upon Northern Ireland *does* suggest a transfer of ideas to achieve conflict transformation. Aspects of the climax of the Northern Ireland peace process, the Good Friday Agreement ('the Agreement') 'borrowed' items from other peace accords, in terms of prisoner releases, decommissioning of weapons, the demobilisation of armed groups and the reintegration into society of former combatants, whilst tailoring each for the particular circumstances of the end of conflict.

The release of political prisoners is usually a pre-condition of ceasefires and negotiations (Darby and Mac Ginty 2003). Such releases are usually demanded by combatants and their actuality is non-negotiable, although the timeframe and conditions attached to release may be products of bargaining. Although there may be benefits of an all-embracing programme of early release from prison, former combatants cannot be treated as a homogenous group and require different solutions to ensure successful reintegration into society. Key issues involve the reintegration of different types of combatants, issues concerning social mobility, location and the political and emotional impact of prisoner releases.

Prisoner releases have formed an important part of various peace deals, including those in the Balkans, Lebanon and South Africa. The South African case provides the best-known example of how former prisoners created, developed and sustained a peace process. Nelson Mandela's key role in the indirect representations of the African National Congress to the National Party long preceded his release from prison in 1990, as he preferred to wait for release until certain that a deal would hold (Morrow 2005). Prisoner releases may be viewed as an initial step towards acknowledgement of a shared responsibility concerning past events, in that a magnanimous gesture by the state is usually accompanied by changed political conditions and acceptance by non-state combatants that they need to 'guarantee non-repetition' of the past (Hamber and Kelly 2005: 190).

The release of prisoners does not guarantee reconciliation and risks accentuating the hurt of many victims and in some cases retraumatising them. However, the psychological and cognitive harm caused by prisoner release has in many instances been weighed against the impact that such releases will have upon a successful process of conflict transformation and the cessation of violence. In the Northern Ireland context, Mo Mowlam, when Secretary of State, argued that the positive impact upon the peace process that such releases would constitute had to, like other difficult decisions, be measured 'in the round' of eventual outcomes.

There are a plethora of measures which may accompany prisoner releases, including trials, justice, reconciliation or victims' commissions, memorials, reform of the legal system, compensation and reparation. Progress in establishing these accompaniments to early prisoner releases may be conditional upon support from former prisoners. Prisoners are not merely released, but may be expected to involve themselves in further amelioration of the conflict upon achieving their freedom, as ambassadors of peace, selling to sceptics the merits of, for example, disarmament or the reduction of interface violence. Given this, newly released ex-combatants offer the best chance of the type of peace-building from below so often essential in the construction of durable peace processes (Ramsbotham et al. 2005).

Each peace process sets different terms and conditions for prisoner releases and has varied in terms of the extent of reintegration of former detainees into post-conflict policing and security structures. Following the release of 'terrorist' prisoners, states may also begin dismantling aspects of the emergency legal system, such as special, often juryless, courts. The most radical solutions have embraced direct transfers of former prisoners into the police or army, measures which act as 'tangible acknowledgements of past abuses and an effective way to convert a potentially destabilizing armed threat into support for the new structures' (Darby and Mac Ginty 2003: 263).

The release of prisoners is one of the most problematic aspects of a peace process, given the inevitable sensitivities of the families of victims. Recognition of these sensitivities may be as important a reason for the conditionality of release as the risk of former combatants returning to violence; recidivism rates among politically motivated offenders tend to be very low within post-conflict polities (Shirlow and McEvoy 2008). Instead, former prisoners may assist societal reconstruction and dissuade others from engaging in armed combat. The role of prisoners as ambassadors for the process within their communities is often the most persuasive tool in preventing spoiler groups gathering strength.

Prisoner releases and peace processes beyond Ireland

Limits to the benefits of prisoner releases are also apparent. In the Israel-Palestine conflict, prisoner exchanges have been common, but also piecemeal, failing to embed a political process in which territorial disputes endure (Bregman 2003; Fraser 2008: 201). The release of prisoners by the Israeli government is invariably linked to ceasefires by Palestinian armed groups, but the fragility of the overarching political framework means that such ceasefires, such as the three-month Palestinian cessation in 2003, are often violated and the treatment of the prisoners' issue in isolation from territorial questions is unproductive. Released prisoners on both sides enjoy prestige and status within their communities (although the ultimate accolade among some Palestinians has been awarded to suicide bombers, their military effectiveness remains the subject of considerable debate; see Frisch 2006). Almost 10,000 Palestinians remain held in Israeli jails, including nearly fifty parliamentarians, although the number detained since the 1967 war exceeds 500,000. Prisoners, although crucial to a peace process, come second to the issue of territorial ownership (Gormally and McEvoy 1995).

Although the 1993 Oslo Agreement is sometimes viewed as high-water mark of the Arab–Israeli peace process, its basic role was to enshrine mutual recognition of competing sides. In common with the Downing Street Declaration in respect of Northern Ireland (also agreed during 1993) the Oslo Agreement offered a clear statement of principles underpinning the peace process, but lacked detail, which was supposed to follow later. The Oslo Agreement studiously avoided the sensitive issue of prisoners, but the 1994 Cairo Agreement did provide for the release of 5,000 prisoners, although this meant that over 7,000 would remain imprisoned (McEvoy 1998). The release of the 5,000 was conditional upon individual prisoners signing a declaration of support for the peace process, a difficult condition for those objecting to various political aspects of the Oslo accord. Article 16 of the 1995 Israeli–Palestinian interim agreement on the West Bank and the Gaza Strip, a form of 'Oslo-with-details', offered further progress on prisoner releases, declaring:

> Israel will release or turn over to the Palestinian side, Palestinian detainees and prisoners, residents of the West Bank and Gaza Strip. The first stage of release of these prisoners and detainees will take place on the signing of this Agreement and the second stage will take place prior to the date of the elections. There will be a third stage of release of detainees and prisoners. Detainees and prisoners will be released from among categories detailed in Annex VII (Release of Palestinian Prisoners and Detainees).

The first stage of release, as outlined in Annex VII, offered liberation for women prisoners, plus those who had served more than two-thirds of their sentence, or who had not caused fatal or serious injury, or were not held on security matters. These releases were to be followed by a second stage incorporating young (under eighteen years of age) or older (over fifty years old) prisoners and those who had already served ten years or more in prison. The final stage merely promised examination of whether more categories could be released.

Although in many respects bold, given hostility in Israel towards those convicted of attacks upon the country, the conditions associated with prisoner releases in the region created problems. First, the terms lacked time-specificity, either for completion of the plan or its stages. This contrasts with the situation pertaining to the Good Friday Agreement, which made clear that prisoner releases would be completed within two years of the completion of the deal. Second, the Arab–Israeli deal did not distinguish between organisations maintaining or fracturing ceasefires, whereas the Good Friday Agreement and subsequent legislation provided for the return of prisoners to jail under certain conditions, such as the ending of a ceasefire. Third, the Arab–Israeli deal kept open the prospect of some prisoners languishing in jail indefinitely, if not covered by stages one or two, given the vagueness of stage three. Although the provisions highlighted the importance of prisoner releases to a settlement package, the willingness of so many outside prison to continue to use violence (unlike in Northern Ireland, where numbers of armed group volunteers had dwindled and thus there was much focus on those who had already 'fought the war') meant that prisoner releases were not central to an accord. The desire of Palestinian prisoners for release did not dilute the overarching territorial dispute which prevailed and the Oslo accord collapsed because of mutual mistrust over the desire of Israel and Palestine for peaceful co-existence (Dowty 2008).

Despite the regular collapse of political processes, there remains a progressive plan for peace offered by Palestinian prisoners and it remains plausible to contend that greater political progress might have been made if those incarcerated had assumed primary negotiating positions. The essence of the 'prisoners' plan' is the establishment of a Palestinian state in the West Bank, Gaza Strip and East Jerusalem; the right of return for refugees and reform of the Palestinian Authority (Lesch 2008). The two-state solution offered by the prisoners is popular among the majority of Palestinians as a realistic outline of what is attainable (Smith 2007). However, with the majority of prisoners drawn from the more secular Fatah organisation, it is hindered by a perception that other prisoners belonging to Islamic fundamentalist groups declining to recognise Israel, notably Hamas and Islamic Jihad, prefer a much stronger set of proposals. Indeed internal division between Palestinians, allied to lack of confidence, has hampered negotiations with Israel (Dajani 2005).

Where early release of prisoners has been thwarted or refused, such as in the Basque peace process, political progress has been halted. The Irish and Basque peace processes invite comparisons in terms of the similar efforts of militants to force governments to concede their demands for the principle of self-determination, but the treatment of those who have prosecuted the 'wars' has been markedly different. A combination of the unreliability of ETA (Euskadi Ta Askatasuna, the Basque separatist movement) ceasefires and the unwillingness of successive Spanish (and French) governments to go beyond autonomy for the Basque country and concede the legitimacy of Basque self-determination, as outlined by Basque nationalists in the 1998 Lizarra Forum and 2003 Ibarretxe Plan, has prevented a Good Friday Agreement-type deal emerging, despite the links between Sinn Fein and Batasuna, the political wing of ETA. Sinn Fein advised Batasuna on the construction of the Basque peace process. The Lizarra Forum was labelled the 'Irish Forum', given its status as the outworking of a pan-nationalist emphasis upon self-determination (Gillespie 1999). Co-operation between the moderate Basque nationalists of the Partido Nacionalista Vasco (PNV) and the militants of Batasuna mirrored that between the Social Democratic Labour Party (SDLP) and Sinn Fein which fed into the 1993 Downing Street Declaration of principles underpinning the Northern Irish peace process.

In the Basque peace process, however, there was a marked reluctance by the state to acknowledge the need to accommodate ETA and Batasuna within meaningful political dialogue, a problem exacerbated by internal divisions within ETA over whether to sustain ceasefires, dissent which has dissipated the credibility of the organisation's cessations of violence. With no large-scale prisoner releases on offer, there remains a dearth of credible ambassadors for peace among Basque ethnic militants, and young Basques within ETA's youth movement, Haika, have attempted to escalate violence (Alexander et al. 2001; O'Broin 2008). The main Spanish parties, the Conservative Popular Party (PP) and the socialist party, the PSOE, have episodically attempted to grant rewards to ETA prisoners in the hope of eliciting a permanent cessation of the separatist group's violence. These concessions have included transfer of prisoners to the Basque area, generous remission for inmates serving sentences for lesser offences, invitations to 'on-the-run' suspected ETA members to return to Spain and even hints of an amnesty (Gillespie 1999). However, these developments have been set against considerable political pressure for a tougher line against prisoners led by the pressure group the Association of Victims of Terrorism (AVT), and the sympathetic ear offered to the AVT – and outright rejection of negotiations with ETA/Batasuna – by the PP is similar to the stance of the DUP prior to the Good Friday Agreement.

The strength of this countervailing force has strained bipartisanship on the Basque issue, with the PP, particularly when in opposition, taking an uncompromising line on prisoner releases and instead offering support for victims. This counter-balancing has included substantial financial support for the families of victims, whilst the most generous pardoning and early prison releases were awarded to those convicted of organising counter-terrorism *against* ETA (Woodworth 2001). In 1988, the constitutional Basque nationalist party backed the Mesa de Ajuria Enea, a common front against terrorism, but broke with the PP and PSOE in the Lizarra Declaration in order to advance Basque nationalism (Magone 2004). This has created a broader Basque nationalist movement with the level of pan-nationalist support for Basque politically motivated prisoners, extending beyond ETA's core, with the PNV supporting better treatment and location near home for ETA convicts. This sympathy, reminiscent of the mobilisation of nationalists in Northern Ireland during the republican hunger strikes of 1980–81 and revived during the peace process, was extended by the arrest and imprisonment of dozens of members of Batasuna, in 2002 via the law of political parties, which banned parties associated with terror and prohibited their representatives from contesting elections.

With half of ETA's 1,200 prisoners incarcerated in French jails, bi-national agreements on prisoners between the Spanish and French governments would be required within a sustained peace process, but neither government appears willing to embark on this course, given the propensity of ETA ceasefires to collapse. The Basque case thus remains one of the most striking in terms of the need for delicate sequencing, involving durable ceasefires, political engagement by governments and staged prisoner releases.

The limitations of state 'terrorism' to defeat ETA's 'terrorism' were exposed by the revelations concerning the Spanish government's use of GAL (Grupos Antiterroristas de Liberacion) mercenaries (Woodworth 2001). However, the failure of that extreme strategy has not softened attitudes towards ETA. There remains a belief – far from confined to government circles – that imprisonment rather than prisoner release is the better way to deal with the problem of Basque terrorism. By the 1990s, arrests of ETA and IRA members were outstripping new recruits and both organisations were damaged as a consequence (Sanchez-Cuenca 2007). The decimation of ETA, a smaller organisation than the IRA, is thus still viewed as a possibility, seen as preferable to any legitimisation of its campaign signalled by premature prison releases.

Moreover, the limited offers made by the state to prisoners thus far have been rejected by ETA, which has taken a strong line against its own members who have been signed up for early release on the Spanish government's terms (McEvoy 1998). For ETA, prisoner releases without an accompanying satisfactory political solution are viewed with derision, seen as a means of dividing Basque militants and weakening the struggle for an independent Basque homeland (see Marguiles 2004).

Demilitarisation, Demobilisation and Reintegration (DDR)

A basic definition of the wider development of DDR is that of 'a process introduced following a conflict and directed primarily at ensuring the transition of combatants to civilian life' (Muggah 2005: 242). DDR is one strand of the post-conflict peace-building that has 'become in some ways the "core business" of the international humanitarian and development community' (Krause and Jutersonke 2005: 447). As peace processes embed, government and non-government actors support the reintegration of former combatants into society, with the aim of ensuring that peace is permanent and that previous fighters become peaceful assets for the communities to which they return. This literature is relevant to the study of paramilitary prisoners in Northern Ireland because it provides an international context for the issues that these prisoners and their communities face.

When a new government has been formed after a period of conflict, DDR can be fully implemented. During this process, governments and their non-governmental organisation (NGO) partners are crucial. Successful DDR is dependent on political will and planning (Kingma 1997). Active participation of ex-combatants in DDR programmes is also highlighted as an indicator of success (Rolston 2007). However, as Kingma notes, this reintegration of combatants is highly contentious:

> In most efforts to support reintegration, policy makers face a dilemma on whether or not to treat the ex-soldiers as a special target group. Support programmes have to strike a balance between dealing with the specific needs of these people and not creating discontent among the rest of their often poor communities, which would actually jeopardize true reintegration (Kingma 1997: 162).

Özerdem (2002) elaborates on this dilemma. Giving former combatants a defined role provides an alternative to the options of crime or antisocial behaviour. It also means that leaders can sell a peace agreement to their fighters because there are tangible benefits for them and they can return home and demonstrate that they have been rewarded for their efforts. However, it can enrage non-combatants who have suffered during the war, but do not receive special attention and it encourages ex-combatants to continue to see themselves as fighters and as a group apart, which retards the process of reintegration.

Disarmament as part of the overall DDR process represents another dilemma for governments. A large numbers of weapons in circulation after a war can lead to a crime wave, as happened in South Africa after 1994. Despite the successful reintegration of combatants into society, including within the 120,000 police force, and even greater hostility towards criminals due to the new broad legitimacy enjoyed by the reconstituted police force, crime flourished because the number of guns available tempted others to take them up for the purpose of robbery (Butler 2004; Gamba 2003). In South Africa, the integration of former African National Congress (ANC) combatants within state policing structures was accompanied by the establishment of a Truth and Reconciliation Commission, which although difficult for victims, created unthreatening space for all previous 'sides' in the conflict for analysis of what occurred.

There were three elements to the South African Truth and Reconciliation process: violation of human rights, amnesties and reparation, which, combined, accounted for over 20,000 witness statements and 7,000 applications for amnesties (Whittaker 2007). The purpose of the Truth and Reconciliation Commission was to establish *why* events took place and to produce some form of understanding and comfort for the families of victims. Repudiation of tactics or renunciation of deed was not required. Indeed the ANC rejected the Commission's position that the armed campaign in any way violated human rights, arguing that killings could not be regarded as such in a just war of liberation. The ANC extended the message to Irish republicans that acceptance of early release and support for a political deal need not involve any repudiation of previous political positions (McKeown 1999).

Ex-combatants can use weapons to reignite conflict, as seen in border clashes between Eritrea and Ethiopia during the mid-2000s, or in the involvement of the former Kosovo Liberation Army in conflict in Macedonia (Knight and Özerdem 2004). However, whilst leaving weapons in circulation carries clear dangers, it does not follow that disarmament is the key method of ensuring future peace and stability. Buy-back schemes designed to encourage the handover of weapons have, in countries such as Angola, led to people handing in rusty or broken guns and there is no guarantee they will not use the cash to purchase more sophisticated weaponry (Gamba 2003; Knight and Özerdem 2004). Instead of assuming that disarming combatants is the first step to permanent peace, policy makers would be better to view it as part of a programme of reintegration and to remember that 'because combatants are likely to become highly fearful and insecure as they demobilise, they can gain an added sense of safety if they are not forced to disarm fully, especially not before the political terms of an agreement have been fulfilled' (Walter 1999: 154–5).

Prisoners and other combatants often form part of the newly reconstituted armed forces, as has happened in Namibia, Tajikistan and Cambodia, among other countries (Darby and Rae 1999). However, the decision to disarm combatants or rearm them as part of a new legitimate military is part of a difficult process of reacclimatising the population to deal with life after civil war. The 1989 Ta'if Accord (Document of National Reconciliation) in Lebanon provides an example of how asymmetrical disarmament can create ongoing problems, with Hezbollah declining to accept the deal's terms and continuing to arm. The Ta'if Accord insisted that all armed groups were to disarm, with weaponry to be held only by a reconstituted national Lebanese Army. Yet the permission granted to neighbouring Syria to oversee this process ensured that Hezbollah's growth in Southern Lebanon proceeded largely unchecked. Its members held no intention of integrating into regular Lebanese forces, believing that Shiite representation within the state was inadequate and that a continuing military presence and close links with Iran would assist (Harik 2005; Milton-Edwards 2006).

Hezbollah's support base among Shiite Muslims allows its resistance wing to operate with minimal internal interference within Lebanon. This support provides the clearest example of an organic community in which combatants, former prisoners, political activists and support base are largely indistinguishable, with a cohesive social background, common religious outlook and political programme which fuses social and welfare activity with religious fervour. The role of former prisoners, many of whom were released after Israel abandoned its 'security zone' in the South of Lebanon, has been instrumental in linking the 'Party of God' to its local support base, oscillating between political and military activity and selling compromises, including campaigning across sectarian divides. Although Lebanon's political system is confessional at representative level, the electoral make-up of many constituencies requires parties, including Hezbollah, to seek support beyond its 'natural' religious base. Moreover, whilst Jihad and religious fundamentalism remain core components, Hezbollah has also campaigned on secular issues and participated in governing structures, factors which have encouraged minimal interference from the Beirut government, despite the effective maintenance of a state-within-a-state (Saad-Ghorayeb 2002). Overall, reintegration in a Lebanese context has meant the reabsorbing of combatants and prisoners within their community, whilst Syrian influence remains strong within the polity. As such, as the former President Amin Gemayel conceded, there is scant concept of Lebanese citizenship compared to the sense of community belonging (Gemayel 1992; Kerr 2005; Russell and Shehadi 2005).

Following the end of conflict in Bosnia-Herzegovina, the 1995 Dayton Agreement required the scaling down of warring Serb, Croat and Bosniak armies, which in total amounted to over 400,000 combatants. The Dayton Agreement required the reconstitution of a Bosnian army from the local population, a provision designed to exclude Croats and Serbs based outside the territory, but also designed to prevent non-local Muslim groups, including those linked to Al-Qaeda which had participated in conflict, becoming involved in new state structures (Kohlmann 2004). However, the creation of effectively two states-within-a-state, the highly autonomous Bosnia and Herzegovina and the Republic of Srpska, within a single federation meant that building up a Bosnian army had limitations and was overshadowed by a large international protectorate, initially of over 60,000 troops, placed within the country to prevent any return to conflict (Bideleux and Jeffries 2007).

The Dayton Agreement desired the influx of former combatants into newly constituted armed forces and policing structures, whilst those associated with genocidal acts and charged with war crimes were barred from political or military activity. The reconstituting of the armed forces has 'accomplished little with regard to helping unify Bosniak and Croat forces', but Serb forces have been considerably demilitarised and foreign Muslim forces removed (Cousens and Harland 2006: 90). Whilst refugee returns were a much larger problem, prisoner releases became entangled with post-Dayton bargaining, the Bosnian government attempting to delay releases to ascertain more information concerning the fate of Bosniaks captured or executed by Serbs.

The size of the various combatant armies was reduced to a mere 5 per cent of their strength at the head of the conflict, but the 'new' Bosnia-Herzegovina was one based upon ethnic separatism, in which post-conflict 'reintegration' has been within separate armies which continue to exist within a supposedly unified state (Ramet 2005). War crimes indictments were pursued with gradually increasing vigour against war leaders, despite protests against such prosecutions within Serbia and Croatia, where some regarded those indicted not as war criminals but war heroes (Bose 2002). Meanwhile, the transfer of some combatants into criminal activity rather than political action, most notably via corruption and drug-trading, has provided considerable problems in post-conflict Bosnia-Herzegovina.

In the Arab–Israeli conflict, many Palestinian combatants were integrated into the 30,000-strong armed police force in autonomous areas on the West Bank, following the 1993 Oslo Accords and the 1995 updating. However, this reintegration of combatants into 'regular' forces was not a success. During the 2001 Intifada, the return of Israeli troops to 'autonomous' areas diminished the local police, many of whom sympathised with the uprising. This sympathy rendered irrelevant the 1998 Wye Memorandum, in which, in return for Israeli concessions, the former Palestine Liberation Organisation leader, Yasser Arafat, agreed to take action against groups continuing to use force against Israel. In a further attempt to reduce the impact of hardline 'spoiler' groups, the much vaunted 'roadmap to peace', proposed by the United States and first outlined in the 2001 Mitchell and Tenet plans for political progress, has stressed the need for the confiscation of 'illegally held' Palestinian weapons in the first stages of a ceasefire, as a precursor for Israeli demilitarisation. This requirement overlooks the severity of rivalry between Palestinian organisations, making internal control or regulation almost impossible, even allowing for some movement by Hamas from Jihad towards a more cautious, evolutionary approach to change (Hroub 2005).

The success of disarmament and demobilisation may be conditional upon the clarity of requirements and the effectiveness of supervisory teams. In Sierra Leone, for example, these processes were only concluded successfully in 2002, with over 70,000 combatants stood down and shorn of weapons, after the UN took on a major role in overseeing even-handed demilitarization (Berman and Labonte 2006). In Congo, the UN enjoyed less legitimacy in terms of its disarmament role, as some of the warring parties wished to continue the battle and the newly integrated state army proved slow at the task (Roessler and Prendergast 2006).

The end of a civil conflict seems to have a particular impact on women whether they have been directly involved in the conflict or not. Pearce's (1998) analysis of the post-conflict situation in Central America found that, as managers of the domestic sphere, women had to deal with the sudden return home of their male partners and relatives. These men returned to peace and often to unemployment and Pearce draws on survey data to establish that this situation led to an increase in incidents of domestic violence. When it comes to the experience of female combatants returning home, profiles of different countries produces different views. Spear (2002) says that women returning home in Zimbabwe were stigmatised. By taking up arms they had violated deeply held beliefs about a woman's place and so were shunned and criticised. However, Humphreys and Weinstein (2005) argue that in Sierra Leone, traditional views of women aided their reintegration as the units in which women fought were less likely to be associated with egregious methods of combat. For female combatants themselves, there is evidence that they experience depression and frustration when the war is over and they find themselves expected to take up their former domestic roles, leading to phenomena such as increasing divorce rates (Colletta et al. 1996; Kingma 1997).

Class and social mobility is another area of difference. For those from poorer backgrounds, reintegration is a problem as lack of education means they have limited skills to offer to potential employers or business schemes (Spear 2002). Those with limited education or health problems are less likely to be retained in any new security force set-up as commanders of new forces look for the best recruits (Kingma 1997). However, focusing on the poorest and assuming that the skilled and educated can cater for themselves can have unintended consequences. Alden (2002) points out that former army leaders in Mozambique, who had received a high level of training and education from their Soviet allies, were not catered for in that country's reintegration programme and this led to many turning their talents to organised crime.

A final cleavage to be noted is the rural-urban split. Returning to a rural community can be an advantage, as the older style of extended family networks and agricultural economy provides a ready framework for reintegrating former fighters (Knight and Özerdem 2004). However, it is often easier for NGOs and governments to organise official reintegration programmes in urban areas, which means those who want to settle in the countryside are often forced to return to the city to seek help (Alden 2002). Those from rural backgrounds can face the added challenge that their urban counterparts are more educated and able to take advantage of the schemes offered (Shafer 1998).

Government involvement in the reintegration of former combatants varies enormously in terms of attitude, sustained commitment and finance. At worst, it can be as malign as official neglect. AMODEG (the Mozambican Assoc- iation of the War Demobilised) represents former soldiers from both sides of the civil war in Mozambique. The organisation's initial brief was concern for the socio-economic status of members, with campaigns on issues such as pensions. However, the government has steered AMODEG towards programmes of 'civic education' which mainly involve radio broadcasts urging ex-combatants to get involved in the reconstruction of communities, without any acknowledgement of the special problems and stigmatisation they have faced. AMODEG have also had to deal with the fact that different regions and levels of government view their existence and role in very different lights (Shafer 1998).

DDR: implications for former prisoners in Northern Ireland

Not all non-state combatants served prison sentences and, obviously, the process of DDR applies to all combatants, not just those who were incarcer- ated. However, the literature reviewed above does provide some useful inter- national examples of how those returning from imprisonment or combat to a situation of supposed transition and possibly peace can be affected by, and affect in turn, attitudes towards their reintegration. In shifting the focus from the international to the level of Northern Ireland itself it is necessary to provide some information on the conditions that prisoners found themselves in during their time inside, before moving on to consider the basis and impact of prisoner releases and demobilisation.

The majority of paramilitary prisoners were held in prisons in Northern Ireland. Here they were, for the most part, physically separated from other prisoners and often further segregated according to the organisation to which they belonged. However, whilst there was not a similar categorisation in jails in Great Britain the prisoners were still viewed as a 'class apart' by both prison officers and fellow prisoners and this served to keep them isolated from the general prison body without actual physical separation (Borland et al. 1995). The majority of literature written about paramilitary prisoners focuses on Northern Ireland and particularly the H Blocks of the Maze Prison, usually referred to by its former inmates by its previous title of Long Kesh.

For republicans, the plight of prisoners served as a rallying call, a symbol of suffering that could draw people to the wider republican movement. The rejection of criminal status by political prisoners aroused the sympathy of many nationalists otherwise indifferent or hostile to the republican 'armed struggle', but nonetheless cognisant that those incarcerated were not 'ordinary criminals'. Bew et al. (2002: 201) note that 'as early as November 1980 the Provisional-led campaign supporting political status was turning out parades comparable in size to the great civil rights marches'. Prisoners as an icon represented republican suffering and self-sacrifice, maintained by a British security system which alienated nationalists. The climax of this suffering, the republican hunger strikes of 1980–81, proved decisive in opening a political avenue for republicans, with Sinn Fein contesting elections unbroken from 1982 onwards. The prisoners' hunger strikes also raised global awareness of the republican struggle and facilitated a major import of arms for the IRA from Libya shortly afterwards, one which, had it continued without interception, contained the potential to alter the balance of forces in the 'war' (Moloney 2002).

Until the Northern Ireland peace process took route, it was difficult to demur from O'Duffy's (1993: 148) assertion that 'the overemphasis upon security policy at the expense of substantial social and economic reforms has not been successful in promoting consociationalism'. A new approach from the British government, accompanied by political change among republicans, ensured that a security-oriented policy was replaced by relaxation inside and beyond the jails, and engagement in negotiation. This more productive approach was followed by the clinching of the Good Friday Agreement and the implementation of certain aspects of DDR. The change of attitude from the British government was reciprocated, indeed partially initiated, by embryonic new approaches from prisoners, who began facing up to political realties and prepared for release into a post-conflict Northern Ireland.

Nonetheless, Rolston's comparative study of Northern Ireland and other examples of DDR finds that the Northern Irish case study is something of an anomaly, arguing that 'in some ways the Irish case provides a lesson in how not to conduct DDR' (Rolston 2007: 274). He argues that an obsession with decommissioning meant that removing weaponry took precedence in the process at key periods and therefore hampered the reintegration of former combatants within society, amid uncertainty over the *bona fides* of paramilitary ceasefires. From the outset, the Labour government elected in 1997 attempted to 'park' decommissioning away from the other issues to be negotiated (O'Brien 1999). The IRA did not state, contrary to popular myth, that it would never decommission and indeed former members began to indicate from 2000 onwards that decommissioning would form part of the process (Tonge 2005). However, what was ruled out was first, any requirement for decommissioning in advance of a settlement and, second, any linkage of the pace of decommissioning to progress on the release of prisoners. Decommissioning, so far as republicans were concerned, was a matter for the IRA and the Independent International Commissioning on Decommissioning (IICD) to resolve. The Good Friday Agreement did not require decommissioning, merely urging political parties to exert maximum pressure to secure it as an outcome, a form of words so vague that it appeared to be ignored entirely by loyalist paramilitaries for over a decade.

Accompanying release, there were difficulties for prisoners in adapting to changing circumstances. Spear (2002) argues that membership in a fighting force confers status in society, one threatened by a peace agreement. She claims that this explains the phenomenon of punishment beatings in Northern Ireland, because such a task allows paramilitaries to continue defining themselves as defenders. Therefore, 'any reintegration of these former combatants into society will have to provide them with a role of equivalent status to the one that they had in the conflict, or at least positively recognize the role they played in the conflict' (2002: 145). She acknowledges that such a task has to be squared with the sensitivity arising from the families of victims seeing perpetrators assume prominent positions in public life. Some aspects of republican prisoner reintegration, in particular, have been very prominent. Of Sinn Fein's thirty-five elected representatives in Dail Eireann, the Northern Ireland Assembly and the Westminster and European parliaments at the beginning of 2005, it was claimed that fifteen had been IRA members or held convictions for politically motivated offences (Breen 2005). Candidates seeking election to the party's *ard chomhairle* still tend to mention prison 'experience' in campaign literature. The PUP's two elected members in the first post-Good Friday Agreement Northern Ireland Assembly had both served prison sentences for UVF activity.

Beyond these 'headline' reintegrations, Rolston (2007) notes that programmes of reemergence within society were organised largely by former combatants themselves, with the help of voluntary organisations, and that government responsibility in this area was lacking. Traditionally, republicans had been suspicious of government assistance. Such scepticism diminished markedly during the 1990s, contrasting with the position during the 1970s when plans for a Belfast office that would assist loyalist and republican prisoners and their families were shelved because republicans were suspicious of the possible strings attached to Northern Ireland Office funding. During the peace process, selectivity over sources of funding diminished and alternative sources became available via EU peace and reconciliation projects. From 1998 until 2004, former prisoners' groups received over £17 million of public money (Gallaher 2007: 117). However, as peace has embedded, the level of funding has declined and the work of former prisoner organisations has broadened into more general community projects rather than issues concerned directly with the welfare of their 'clients' (ibid.).

The search for a meaningful role for released prisoners is based upon a combination of development of prisoners' self-help skills, education, political work and, perhaps most significantly, the manner in which 'they have been centrally involved in local conflict transformation and indeed cross-community activities' (Rolston 2007: 206). For some, post-imprisonment has meant a resumption of former domestic life, bereft of political or community activity. For another sizeable group, reintegration has signalled continued efforts at political transformation via political work in Sinn Fein, the PUP or Ulster Political Research Group (UPRG) in which the continued struggle for the attainment of longstanding political objectives is juxtaposed with substantial working relationships with opponents from the rival community. As the conflict endured, Gormally et al. (1993) noted that former life-sentence prisoners who were released from prison were not expected to do military service because they had done their time for the movement and because they were too well known. These and other former prisoners concentrated their energies into campaigning for Sinn Fein, or engaging in community work, rather than volunteering for the IRA. Their dynamism and experience, therefore, powered the development of Sinn Fein as the dominant branch of the republican movement through the 1980s and 1990s. For others, reintegration has meant engaging in local cross-community work or other localised projects, such as restorative justice programmes.

Several variables affect processes of reintegration. For republicans in particular, the experiences of female prisoners (a much larger category compared with loyalist former prisoners) and the challenges they faced returning to the 'home front' were in some ways particularly acute, ranging from an inability to rear children to social marginalisation. Alternatively, the support network for prisoners in jail provided by women often strained family budgets and families faced continuing hardship beyond release (Ward 2006). The educational attainment of prisoners before, during and after their prison sentences affects their reintegration. There are also differences between rural and urban backgrounds and the social class composition of those areas in terms of attitudes to reintegration, opportunities for community activity and treatment by the communities to which they return. Whilst republican former prisoners had strong supportive networks across many working-class nationalist areas and sympathy in some middle-class neighbourhoods, loyalist former prisoners commonly report greater isolation and exclusion outside a limited number of enclaves. Moreover, there remain institutional barriers to reintegration. Although support for policing now permeates loyalist and republican communities, former combatants may not join the reconstituted police force, a position which contrasts with several other peace processes. The Independent (Patten) Commission Report (1999: 92) declared: 'we emphatically do not suggest that people with serious criminal or terrorist backgrounds should be considered for police service.'

Prisoner releases and the evolution of peace

Throughout the 1980s and 1990s prison continued to be constructed as a vital site of resistance to British rule among republicans, for whom imprisonment has long been 'an accepted part of the republican struggle' (Maillot 2004: 157). For loyalists, the confusions and dilemmas imposed as a consequence of imprisonment by their 'own' state may have impinged initially upon political development, but did not inhibit contributions to the resistance of criminalisation and the development of a peace process. Prisoners served as consultants within prison walls and as activists on the outside. However, there was a sea-change after the hunger strike. Prison was an alternative power base for the development of a northern leadership within Republicanism. Once that leadership established itself towards the end of the 1970s, the prisons did not produce a coherent or damaging challenge to that ascendancy.

Within the jails, there was some co-operation between republican and loyalist prisoners in respect of organisation, conditions, releases and changes, with compounds holding joint loyalist-republican representative membership in some circumstances (Gormley-Heenan 2007: 53–4). The representative functions accorded to prisoners honed leadership skills which were readily deployed on the outside. Prisoners acted as think tanks and as debating agencies during the peace process. English (2003) records how republican prisoners debated among themselves the case for a united Ireland, often discomfiting each other by the stridency and logic of a rival case. The prisoners debated the nature of British colonialism and imperialism, the extent of support for republicanism and the links of republicans with other 'oppressed' groups. Loyalists also engaged in considerable introspection from the 1970s onwards, their prisoners being asked by loyalist leaders within the jails why they were there, in an ideological, not factual quizzing (Sinnerton 2002).

Von Tangen Page (2006) highlights the positive approach of prisoners to the 1993 Downing Street Declaration as one of the most important aspects of the development of the peace process. The arrival home of prisoners on Christmas leave in December that year played a vital role in facilitating a republican response to the document and provided an early indication of the concessions – in terms of prisoner releases – that could be accrued from a future political deal. Whilst holding reservations on the Declaration's definition of Irish self-determination, IRA prisoners ensured that the document remained intact as a framework for a more detailed future agreement. The release on parole of republican prisoners with serious credentials by the Northern Ireland Office, as part of Sinn Fein strategy to secure support for the peace process, was evident in the run-up to the August 1994 IRA ceasefire declaration (see e.g. Feeney 2002). The ceasefire was bolstered by the willingness of the United States administration under Bill Clinton to grant visas to former IRA prisoners, including the veteran Joe Cahill, to tour the United States to 'sell' the process to republican sympathisers and fund-raisers (O'Clery 1997). Loyalists such as David Ervine and Billy Hutchinson also received visas to attend peace conferences in the United States. Loyalist perceptions that the IRA had lost were prompting debates among their prisoners that new tactics were required of pro-state irregulars and the US and British governments were anxious to facilitate this revised thinking.

Prisoner releases and the Good Friday Agreement

Academic literature has focused on the factors that explain the success or failure of attempts at DDR, but the release of prisoners as an essential component of post-conflict reintegration has received surprisingly little attention. Many conflicts end with the combatants still at liberty, whilst in officially 'recognised' wars, captives are covered by the internationally recognised conventions associated with prisoners-of-war. For combatants captured in non-official conflicts however, their position as prisoners is far less certain. State responses to non-state political violence vary enormously even among neighbours (see, as one set of examples, Omelicheva 2007), whilst there is no template in terms of prisoner releases as violence subsides.

The early release of politically motivated prisoners may be based upon the perception of them upon holding sufficient 'clout' in peace negotiations to secure recognition from government(s) to obtain premature release. Clearly this was the case in Northern Ireland, where previous non-inclusive deals had failed and where a settlement which attempted to omit republicans was famously described by the Irish government's adviser, Fergus Finlay, as 'not worth a penny candle' (*Independent*, 27 May 1996).

Moreover, prisoners, once released, were useful agents in terms of 'policing the peace' in terms of dealing with spoilers. Darby and Mac Ginty (2003: 267) argue, 'spoiler groups can only be neutralized with the active involvement of ex-militants'. The denunciation, threats and violence pitted by the Provisional IRA's members and former prisoners against the republican ultras, the Real IRA (RIRA) after their 1998 Omagh bombing killed twenty-nine civilians is testimony to this, even if infiltration, policing and lack of community support were perhaps of greater salience (Tonge 2004). Despite their functionality, the requirement for inclusion of prisoner releases in the Northern Ireland peace accord was nonetheless, alongside policing changes, the aspect of the Good Friday Agreement which upset Unionists more than the deal's constitutional provisions and, as such, held the potential to destabilise the settlement (Kerr 2005). The 'mainstream' loyalist paramilitary groups also took strong action against ceasefire 'refuseniks', notably in the UVF-UDA feud of the early 2000s, when a section of the latter group attempted to undermine the peace process, and also in UVF activity against the anti-Agreement Loyalist Volunteer Force (LVF).

Whilst early releases of prisoners are often highlighted as one of the novel aspects of the Good Friday Agreement, such a feature was not new in a Northern Ireland context. The formal ending of the IRA's Border Campaign (Operation Harvest) in 1962 was *preceded* by the release of internees by the unionist government at Stormont, as the republican effort faded. The last batch of internees among the 256 interned without trial during the IRA campaign were freed 'into an unwelcoming and indifferent world' in April 1961, with over one-third obtaining premature release by formally renouncing violence (Bishop and Mallie, 1987: 47). Such a renunciation was a not a requirement for those released under the Good Friday Agreement and the IRA did not formally sign the Mitchell Principles of non-violence subscribed to by Sinn Fein. Nonetheless, in terms of precedent, the British government reminded unionists hostile to early prisoner releases of the willingness of previous unionists to engage in similar practice at the end of an earlier IRA campaign (Powell 2008).

For the non-state combatant groups and their political representatives, the early release of prisoners was negotiable only in respect of the timetable, not the actuality, as Sinn Fein's President, Gerry Adams, made clear to his party's supporters (Adams 1998). Adams requested full prisoner releases within one year; the British preferred three years and the compromise reached was release within two years. The benefits to republicans were made visible by the Sinn Fein leadership at the party's 'double' *ard fheis* (conference) in April and May 1998 (two conferences were staged soon after the Good Friday Agreement was concluded to allow the movement to fully 'debate' the deal). The life-sentence prisoners known as the 'Balcombe Street gang', responsible for bombing various supposed 'establishment' targets in London during the mid-1970s, were paraded before the May *ard fheis*, to a rapturous standing ovation, as an indication of the 'comrades' who would be freed if Sinn Fein backed the Agreement. The PUP, particularly in its work in the East Antrim Conflict Transformation Process (EACTP) was instrumental in persuading the UVF to become essentially a 'comrades' association' (Edwards 2007). Within the PUP and the EACTP, the presence of former militants who had served long sentences for 'fighting the war' urging peace-oriented moves and the decommissioning of paramilitary mindsets was crucial in persuading the UVF's membership that continued violence was bereft of utility.

Predictably, a negative unionist reaction followed Sinn Fein's highlighting of the IRA prisoners who would secure release (Powell 2008). Indeed loyalist paramilitaries were anxious about the implications for the release of their prisoners. According to Gary McMichael, the leader of the short-lived Ulster Democratic Party (UDP) associated with the UDA (until the party's post-Agreement electoral failure and disbandment) loyalists had 'decided not to argue for more than we got on prisoners because we knew we also had to bring the general Unionist population with us' (quoted in Spencer 2008: 178). Given this, it was unsurprising that the Agreement's language on prisoner release was low-key, almost sheepish, in tone.

Of the five paragraphs in the Agreement on 'Prisoners', the final two dealt with the legislative timetable and vague, non-specific promises to assist the reintegration of prisoners, whilst only three paragraphs dealt with the substantive terms of releases (HM Government 1998: 31). The first promised 'accelerated release' for those incarcerated, whilst the second made clear that ultras or 'spoilers' would be marginalised, as those 'prisoners affiliated to organizations which have not established or are not maintaining a complete and unequivocal ceasefire will not benefit from the arrangements' (ibid.). The third paragraph promised that the review of release dates would permit 'account to be taken of the seriousness of the offences for which the person was convicted' (ibid.). This was a curious statement, given that it was overridden by the next sentence, which declared that 'any qualifying prisoners who remained in custody two years after the commencement of the scheme would be released at that point' (ibid.).

For republicans, the early release of prisoners was tantamount to recognition of the IRA as a 'proper' army and its members as prisoners of war. The IRA's portrayal as mere criminals by the Conservative government under Margaret Thatcher during the 1980s was confounded by an internationally recognised peace deal, which recognised conflict participants as military and political entities with whom governments had negotiated and whose ceasefires were formally respected and rewarded. Republican paramilitaries appreciated the new legitimacy and utilised it to engage in international comparisons with other guerrilla armies struggling for justice. The most favoured comparison was with the ANC in South Africa, although the linkage was rejected by political and academic opponents. According to O'Malley and McCormack (2004: 6) 'any attempt on the part of militant republicans to equate the IRA's actions with the actions of Umkhonto we Sizwe [the military wing of the ANC] is both politically and morally indefensible. The former lacked political legitimacy and moral standing: the latter had both'. Such arguments are grounded in the lack of extensiveness of Sinn Fein's electoral mandate and the reformability of Northern Ireland. For republicans, the occupation of part their country remained illegal and mandates for violence are not necessarily reducible to quantitative support. Given this, even the cessation of conflict did not require repudiation of the previous struggle. Thus the IRA's announcement of the ending of its armed campaign in 2005, made by the former prisoner (of twenty-one years) Seanna Walsh, included the following: 'we reiterate our view that the armed struggle was entirely legitimate'.

As many former IRA prisoners articulated views via Sinn Fein upon release, their immediate primary tasks were to secure 'depoliticised' policing and ensure that the British government's promises of demilitarisation were implemented, demands that are common across peace processes (Ramsbotham et al. 2005). In this respect, former republican prisoners tended to view themselves as part of an organic resistance community rather than as agents of reintegration during the early post-release years (Bean 2007; Cassidy 2005). With Sinn Fein now firmly entrenched in government and former prisoners now sat on policing boards, the emphasis has moved from physical resistance, which is concluded, to continued societal transformation, via action within reformed state institutions in the interim. Loyalist former prisoners have struggled to articulate their views (which are strongly supportive of the extension of restorative justice schemes) on policing boards, given their lack of presence on local councils. Moreover, an early study suggests that outside the areas with a substantial Sinn Fein presence within district policing partnerships, there is a preoccupation with middle-class policing issues at the expense of other concerns (Ryan 2008).

A key role of former prisoners has been to increase contacts across the communal divide. The aim of agencies in supporting such projects is that increased cross-community cooperation will diminish inter-communal hostility, a belief for which there is longstanding evidence (e.g. Allport 1954). Although there is no simple 'bridges diminish bigotry' equation, the ability of former prisoners to co-operate across boundaries, evident whilst incarcerated, has been extended outside the jails. This should not be equated to societal reconciliation or acceptance of the 'other side'. Republican former prisoners, for example, have encouraged residents to *protest* against Orange parades under 'Make Sectarianism History' banners whilst working to ensure that such protests are non-violent, whilst loyalist former prisoners have co-operated with their republican counterparts in ensuring peace whilst marshalling Orange rights of parade.

The release of prisoners in Northern Ireland was particularly stark because it was not accompanied by a plethora of 'equalising' measures in terms of victims. Peatling's (2004) critical account of the peace process exaggerates its shortcomings and erroneously labels the political agreement as a failure. Nonetheless, he has a point in claiming that, in respect of prisoner releases, the 'associated dimensions of bereavement, forgiveness, trauma and remorse remain among the thorniest and most poorly addressed issues in the peace process' (ibid., 67–8). However, he does not discuss how former prisoners discuss and debate these issues in a manner that promotes peaceful co-existence and in some cases even apology.

Conclusion

On the announcement that Long Kesh/Maze Prison was to be considered for status as an 'International Conflict Transformation Zone', the former IRA prisoner turned Sinn Fein councillor, Paul Butler, welcomed the proposal and declared that 'Events in Long Kesh have helped shape the recognition and understanding of the political nature of the conflict here' (*An Phoblacht*, 24 February 2005). Prisons are indeed 'sites of struggle' during conflicts and the broader changes in security apparent during the peace and political processes were first apparent in more relaxed regimes within the jails from the late 1980s onwards. Prisoner releases were also an essential part of the peace process. Although political agreement involved dissembling from political leaders and governments, Sinn Fein's president, Gerry Adams, was not bluffing in insisting that a deal would have been impossible had early prison releases not been included. The Good Friday Agreement constituted an acceptance of a longstanding republican argument that those incarcerated were political not criminal prisoners (see English 2006). This plea, also entered by loyalists, is common to many global armed groups existing beyond state armies.

Although hugely controversial, the management of prisoner releases avoided mistakes made in other processes. First, unlike the South African case, republican and loyalist prisoners were not required to engage in detailed individual pleading for release according to the circumstances of their offence. Instead, blanket releases afforded to those belonging to an armed organisation on ceasefire, irrespective of the deeds perpetrated by individual members, provided clarity and comprehensiveness, avoiding prolonged appeals to tribunals or commissions. Whilst eliciting some public outrage, in that individuals regarded by some as 'mass murderers' could qualify for release within a few years of their offence, the treatment of all such offenders as politically motivated ensured there was no hierarchy of crimes. Second, the focus upon groups on ceasefire, rather than individuals, avoided the problems of the Middle East peace process, where prisoners have been obliged to sign documents supporting the process. This creates difficulties for prisoners no longer supportive of violence, but for whom aspects of the political process remain problematic. Moreover, a requirement to individually sign is more likely to fragment groups and encourage spoiler organisations to recruit those prisoners uncomfortable with the process, given that such prisoners are not benefitting from their current membership of a particular armed group. Third, the timetable for prisoner releases was short. Its rapid implementation, amid the brief 'honeymoon period' following the Agreement, facilitated the process.

Had the beginnings of prisoner releases been delayed for years after the Agreement, the deal might have collapsed. Fourth, prisoner releases were not conditional upon any other aspect of the peace process, other than one obvious measure; that the armed groups whose members were freed remained on ceasefire.

The process of prisoner releases in Northern Ireland also benefitted from bipartisan political co-operation between the main political parties at Westminster and inter-governmental symmetry between the British and Irish administrations. Amid rows over the apparent lack of progress on paramilitary decommissioning of weapons, bipartisanship became frayed, with the Conservative opposition threatening to link prisoner releases to progress on decommissioning, outside the terms of the deal. Any such movement from freestanding prisoner releases (ceasefire conditionality apart) would have endangered the process. The speed of releases and the marginalisation of political opponents of the deal contrasts with the Middle East and Spanish cases, where inter- and intra-party political rivalries have inhibited progress. In the Northern Ireland case, with most prisoners released within two years of the deal, political objectors could only rage from the sidelines at the manner of an Agreement which 'puts terrorists in government while releasing their convicted "blood-brothers" from the jails' (Robinson 1998). Whilst lamenting his party's eclipse by the DUP, the Ulster Unionist Party (UUP) leader, David Trimble, could sardonically ask, knowing the impossibility of the feat, how the DUP intended to return republican prisoners to jail (Tonge 2005).

The handling of the prisoners issue in Northern Ireland provided a model form of conflict management, one in which policy export is likely to be greater than the policy-learning from other global processes. Early prisoner releases did not, of course, provide closure for victims, nor even an apology for those relatives of the security forces, who the IRA and INLA had perceived as 'legitimate targets' during the conflict. Nor was the release of prisoners accompanied by other mechanisms of conflict resolution, such as a Truth and Reconciliation Commission. The lesson gleaned from global peace processes was to ensure that prisoner releases were not linked to potential 'deal-breakers'. Instead, the released of politically motivated offenders merely symbolised that the armed conflict was over. Reconciliation and communal healing could wait for less charged political climates.

3 Political views and understandings

> In real terms the phenomenon of paramilitarism was created in the 1970s, and therefore the question I would have for ... those who believe themselves not to be complicit in the circumstances that gave shape to Northern Ireland, is what on earth went wrong in the time when there were no paramilitaries? What actually happened when there was no rampant UDA, UVF or IRA? What was so wrong in our society that the circumstances of explosion were created? (David Ervine, former loyalist prisoner 2001: 1)

In engaging with the narratives presented by former prisoners we seek to capture the complexity of combatant lives and experiences. Whilst drawing upon the interpretations of events and life histories we aid the contextualisation of some broader arguments presented elsewhere in the book. Such personal points of reference reveal much about the nature of the social fabric and social changes across time. Broadly, it considers the extent to which former prisoners draw upon established understandings of 'the past', and how these have been reinforced, reinvented or even abandoned. More narrowly, it examines the extent to which former prisoners and the organisations representing them have questioned certain ideological assumptions, which seemingly underpinned their conduct and 'justified' their actions in the conflict and post-conflict phases.

The narratives presented are structured around past events that shaped the views of combatants; whether 'combatants' engaged in 'military' activity primarily because of strongly held personal beliefs, deeply held ideological perspectives, or some combination of both. It also outlines how particular beliefs and actions have been framed by specific cultural, social and political interpretations. We focus on several key phases: the reasons for becoming involved in a non-state combatant group; the degree to which prison experiences and education (both official and unofficial) shaped the view of the past; the extent to which communal and individual views developed in prison; and how this set in a politics transposed into the post-conflict landscape.

The approach outlined above allows former prisoners to frame, interpret and analyse their involvement in key events. In one sense it is possible to regard all those former prisoners interviewed as a cohort, in that all were born within the same time period, were (roughly) at a similar life stage, and faced the same set of historical events within the same social context and political structures. In response they drew upon similar (if competing and contested) cultural forms and community resources to become active in non-state combatant organisations. However, the motivations of those who joined non-state combatants cannot be explained in terms of a simple continuity with Ireland's political history; the actions of those who became active in such groups cannot be seen in linear terms; and their views and understandings developed and changed over time. In turn, we also consider whether those who did so feel their membership affected social and personal change and if such change in turn altered the political views of former combatants and politically motivated prisoners.

In this and the following chapter we also consider the longer term political and social effects of those who became non-state combatants. To begin to understand this we introduce briefly the concept of 'turning points' as first projected by Strauss (1959) and use the data accessed in interviews to identify these through experiences of personal involvement in some of the main events marking out the contemporary political history of Northern Ireland. Such turnings are accomplished when the person's self-conception alters, or when he or she takes on a new set of roles, or enters into fresh relations with a people experiencing the same political and cultural situations (Mandelbaum 1982: 150). Individual biographies change over time and it is important to introduce a further concept of 'adaption' as individual life histories also involve 'continuous adjustment and periodic adaption [where[personal adaptations are both the source of social adaptation, and also responses to it' (Mandelbaum 1982: 150).

It is, therefore, also important to link an individual's life story and actions 'with their collective behavior as part of an ongoing continuum of historical change' (Hareven 1982: 7). This involves processes of transformation, adaptation, individual and societal change. All life courses have identifiable dynamics, punctuated by 'key events', which give specific meaning to the life stories of individuals. Such events can be normative, everyday, perhaps in truth even rather mundane: experiences of formal education, marriage, parenthood or divorce. Other events are more exceptional, for example, in the context of this work the joining and subsequent activity in a non-state combatant organisations, imprisonment, release and reintegration (Shirlow and McEvoy 2008). Much of what follows in this and the next chapter highlights these turning points and seeks to place these in the context of individual and political change in Northern Ireland.

By this approach we move from 'thin' descriptions involving who did what and when (of which there are many concerning the Northern Ireland conflict), towards 'thicker' accounts that describe and seeks to understand why certain actors undertook the actions they did (Geertz 1973). In other words, we seek to explain and understand the subjective social worlds of former prisoners as constructed in specific situations. First, therefore, it is important to outline briefly the broad social context within which such experiences took place and the social frames within which the decision to become active in non-state combatant organisations was made.

Political socialisation

As in other societies (Billig 1995; Inglehart 1977, 1980, 1989; Inglehart and Rabier 1986) Northern Ireland is characterised by specific and identifiable political and cultural attitudes, or more accurately, by dominant sets of competing and contested attitudes. These are bounded and reinforced by patterns of political socialisation, through which process sets of values and dominant frames of thought are transmitted from generation to generation. Central to understanding the nature of Northern Irish society are these conflicting value systems, which rest primarily on competing senses of national and not religious identity.

These conflicting identities 'acquire significance, meaning, and value within specific contexts and cultures' (Cook-Huffman 2008: 20). The strength and development of such strong common communal values are historically bound and socially constructed and further underpinned by each group's ignorance of the other's life patterns and perspectives. Together these patterns of social bonding and exclusion give rise to a distinctive worldview based on attitudes and knowledge that are learned and transmitted from generation to generation. This results in what Calhoun (1994: 3) describes as identity being established before participation. Core here is the social construction of the 'other'; that is a set of processes through which various forms of 'us' and 'them' are created, reinforced and perpetuated (Miles 1989; Potter and Wetherell 1992).

The determining of such perceptions remains core to understandings of politics in Northern Ireland, where such processes of political socialisation are restricted almost exclusively to respective political communities and transmitted through a wide array of self-generating values, myths, norms and 'traditions' passed on through distinct discourses, and competing historical reference points. As with any long-term conflict, this involves the social construction of oppositional groups and an awareness of social and political differences that is deeply located as is an understanding of the categorisation of the 'other'.

Indeed, Connolly and Maginn (1999) suggest that social difference finds expression and is understood from early infancy (although not necessarily using the terms 'Protestant' and 'Catholic'). Certainly by the time they reach adulthood most citizens 'have already absorbed one or other of the two communal views of the history and legitimacy of Northern Ireland and of British involvement in Ireland as a whole, both through formal teaching and through their families and friends' (Boyle and Hadden 1985: 56). The process is reinforced by construction of discourses drawing distinctions between 'legitimate' and 'illegitimate' political aspirations (Laclau and Mouffe 1985; Howard et al. 2000).

The baseline political identities of 'Irishness' and 'Britishness' are consistently reproduced, in both formal political arenas and through everyday relations and popular cultures (Cairns et al. 1998). There are many examples of this; the political commentator Eamonn McCann once described how, growing up in a Catholic nationalist household: 'One learned, quite literally at one's mother's knee, that Christ died for the human race and Patrick Pearse for the Irish section of it' (McCann 1993: 65). In opposition, the poet Gerald Dawe recounts of his own upbringing that: 'protestantism was like the air one breathed, [and] the ground one walked on was assumed to be *British*' (Dawe 1998: 26, emphasis in original). The construction of difference also rests on the strength of consensus within each community, where both working-class Protestant and Catholic communities draw upon deep-rooted folk memories, and highly structured patterns of political allegiance that are seen to shape and represent distinctive groups.

This gives rise to conflicting understandings of the past and competing visions for the future. Irish nationalism and Ulster unionism drew on competing understandings of history, collective and personal memories, and experiences of conflict to justify and structure their reactions to contemporary social and political events. These interpretations underpin and support their respective visions of future political and social structures (see McBride 2001; Walker 1996, 2000). This sets the ideological boundaries of the wider imagined groupings of 'Protestant/unionist/loyalist' and 'Catholic/nationalist/republican' and the context for the history of political violence between those that Boyce (1995) once characterised as the suffering people and the threatened community.

While recognising that the motivation for social and political activism is always likely to rest within a variety of complex socialisation experiences (Jordan 2002; Klandermans 1997; Tarrow 1994; Tilly 2003) the identities that are constructed within conflict situations are most often based on the delegitimisation, demonisation and depersonalisation of the opposite group. High levels of physical and social segregation, where the perspectives outlined above are reproduced within geographically tightly knit and self-perpetuating communities, amplify the social reproduction of difference, which in turn maintains the desire for continued physical separation (Shirlow and Murtagh 2006).

Framing conflict

While many who joined non-state combatants drew on constructions of the 'other' in particular ways to explain and 'justify' what they did, it would be wrong to suggest that the strength of political cultures made people act in some preordained way. Processes of socialisation shape people's actions and beliefs, but they are also influenced by subjective orientations and material conditions. While individuals can draw on common reference points, these are used to interpret circumstances and to construct interpretations of the broader social dimensions of the divisions in different ways. Political action is structured both by differences reinforced by patterns of cultural learning and also in response to external circumstances and structures.

These explanations are framed by boundaries that define the situation, while at the same time offering a set of explanations concerning the events taking place. Hence, Arena and Arrigo (2006: 106) suggest the broad worldview constructed by the IRA as follows:

> the problem centers on the marginalization and disenfranchisement of the minority Irish Catholic community in Northern Ireland by an alien, tyrannical government. This subjugation began with the occupation of Ireland by British imperialists, continued with an oppressive Northern Ireland regime, and has manifested itself in events like the Battle of the Bogside, the Bloody Sunday massacre and the deaths of beloved comrades in the 1981 hunger strikes.

On the other hand, the corresponding perspective from loyalism is encapsulated in the following:

> The UVF and UDA were both formed supposedly to 'defend Ulster' from its enemies, the IRA. The desire to keep Northern Ireland in the United Kingdom was expressed through a willingness to kill known republicans or, more commonly, members of the Catholic community from where the IRA drew support from 1970 onwards. … loyalist paramilitarism retains a political dimension … the sense of siege, suspicion of the British government's intentions, and fear of republicanism (Tonge 2006: 153, 166).

The above contextualises the historical and social boundaries within which individual political responses including non-state combatant membership and activism, were made.

Those interviewed had a number of different motivations for joining non-state combatant groups. Most sought to find some collective expression to a society in conflict. For some it was the manifestation of longstanding family traditions, while for others it was a highly personalised emotional reaction, perhaps motivated by an identifiable crucial event. Some respondents were cultivated into organisations, others succumbed to peer pressure, while others merely thought themselves as reacting to either defend their community or take the war to the enemy. For the majority interviewed, however, the decision was based upon events occurring daily around them. Most often the decision to become involved emanated from antagonism towards an identifiable 'other'. Only much later was there a questioning of deeply held beliefs and the emergence of a more specific ideological direction.

Family histories and traditions

The ease with which these occur is sometimes determined by what is termed 'anticipatory socialisation', that is learning that prepares us for roles that will be adopted in the future and drawing on the above frames. The exact patterns and forms of socialisation and the functions of 'militarianism' within both republican and loyalist communities has been increasingly recorded in a growing number series of biographies and autobiographies (Adams 1996; Anderson 2002; Clarke and Johnston 2001; Collins 1998; Crawford 1987; Gilmour 1999; Lister and Jordan 2003; Morrison 1999; McGartland 1998; O'Doherty 1993; Sinnerton 2002; Stone 2004).

While we must take seriously Hopkins' (2001) point that all must be read with a cautious eye for idealised presentation and self-censorship, the above works nonetheless provide important information regarding the formation of socially and politically bounded communities within which group membership is made real. One set of explanations that emerge concerning non-state combatants suggest that the forces of socialisation may be so strong that those who join are simply reproducing traditional roles within their working-class communities. The notion of the ideological reproduction of communal values within particular families is found within both republican and loyalist districts.

For some this brings with it a 'generational obligation' whereby traditions of conflict (Boyce 1995) are handed on from generation to generation linking past events to the present day to provide historical legitimacy for contemporary activities. This notion is perhaps most deeply located within republicanism, where a hereditary tradition is widely recognised, whereby 'certain families exert a domination influence on its history' (Bishop and Mallie 1987: 14) It is possible to be taught the expectations of what it is to be a republican. In his biography of Bobby Sands, for example, Dennis O'Hearn suggests that if you 'lived in a Nationalist/Catholic ghetto and your father and your uncles and brothers were IRA volunteers, you joined too' (O'Hearn 2006: 18).

Among interviewees, however, this seems to have been true in only a limited number of cases. Certainly amongst the republicans there were those who felt that they were drawing directly on family continuities in becoming active in republican non-state combatant groups. The following gives clear examples of this:

> You know, it was tradition in the family … me mother's father, he'd been in the
> IRA in 1916 … So I was aware of all that connection and also there was, there

would've been a history of it in relation to when I was growing up 'cos I used to live with my aunt in Ardoyne at the weekends ... what would've happened ... I would've sat with me granny while my granddaddy and uncle went out so you were getting ... wee bits and pieces ...... stories and stuff what he would tell you and different people would tell you and then also Republican songs and stuff 'cos, you know, I used to learn Republican songs from being a child and I had to sing them for him on the way up to Mass on Sunday ... . (IRA male)

A similar narrative emerged from an INLA male former prisoner, who declared that 'family connections had that sort of background ... an IRA background ... mostly on my mother's side more than anything else ... that's what led me down that road'.

A UVF male member offered a similar structure of family influence and the projection of micro-history: 'I was seventeen and I became involved with the UVF when I was fourteen. I would have had a strong sense of being an Ulsterman or being British because of my father and the war and stuff.'

With former prisoners the transmission of the ideological and political through the family was not a uniform factor, nor a universal experience. Indeed, as shown in following quotes family members may have been politicised, but the political values and beliefs of parents did not match those of their offspring who were influenced by unfolding events or complex peer relationships. For many former combatants, there was no direct inter-generational transmission of ideas that influenced group membership. As one IRA activist, in a common aside, declared, 'there wouldn't really have been a massive historical thing of republicanism in the house. My family would have been republican but they wouldn't have been members of the movement. I think that was more to do with their offspring rather than them coming to it.'

For a female IRA former member the notion of being from a Catholic nationalist background was important but for her there was no 'political awareness raising in the house, none whatsoever ... certainly not about republicanism'. Similarly, for another IRA male activist there was an emotional and verbalised sense of republicanism, but within a context of a family that had 'no real republican family ties. I had republican records in the house, I heard songs at parties, but there was no real strong republican history in the family'.

Although they were made, references to the family as a focus for direct socialisation were much less frequent amongst those who joined loyalist organisations, reflecting the general sense that loyalism did not have a communal background as coherent and accepted as that located and evolved within republicanism. It is important to recognise such differences between non-state combatants and their respective communities. As the work of Shirlow and McEvoy (2008) indicates, loyalist family members were likely to condemn the actions of their children in being involved in loyalist groups more so than was the case for those who joined the IRA. There were, of course, other conjugates for socialisation within the Protestant community, such as the Orange Order and associated flute and accordion bands (McAuley and Tonge 2007; Tonge and McAuley 2008) as well as Tartan gangs and loyalist social clubs.

More frequent were references to friends and peers, particularly from those joining the UDA, as one recruit, in a common response, made clear: 'The main reason for me joining the UDA was my big brother was in the UDA, so he was, family and friends were all in it. And it was kind of like more peer pressure than anything to join.' Another member spoke of peer influence as his motivation for joining:

> I couldn't turn round and say a member of my family was killed or anything like that there. It was just that my mates were in it so I joined up. It was as simple as that there. One thing led to another, imprisonment and everything else. The reason I joined the UDA was more or less because my friends was in it and that's as simple as I can get. (UDA male)

It is important to note that within loyalism the capacity to join either the UDA of the UVF often differed. Membership of the UVF was usually culti-vated; they regarded themselves as an elite organisation within loyalist combatant groupings, and as a smaller organisation the emphasis for recruit-ment was often upon family ties or direct acquaintances. The structure of the UDA was very different; it emerged as a broad movement with membership of up to 40,000 in the mid-1970s (Elliott and Flackes 1999: 474). Membership was based more upon willingness than established *bona fides* and throughout its existence it retained a loose federal structure compared with the centralised leadership of the UVF.

Turning points and transitions

Any life course involves change, and at different periods the reinforcement or abandonment of existing views and roles and the adoption of new ones. This is as true of those who became involved with non-state combatants as it is of others. Most of those who became members, and certainly those who joined in the initial years of the conflict, drew on socialised understandings and broad ideological positioning. In Northern Ireland, however, such broad ideologies are at the core of political life: 'because they establish the range of common-sense understandings' (Cash 1998: 228) and provide 'a motive and framework for action' (Drake 1998).

Although the broad patterns of political socialisation identified above were established and solidified following partition, and despite the strength of political socialisation, there is no claim that this negates the role of individuals in actively shaping their own biography. While almost all in Northern Ireland draw on competing understandings of difference, not all joined the non-state combatants, or even felt motivated to respond in this way. So why did those interviewed join such organisations? What were the key motivations for what Ferguson et al. (2008) term as 'crossing the Rubicon'?

Social norms and particular circumstances may well frame life choices, but the quotations that follow often reveal how those who became non-state combatant members evaluated and made active decisions within those frameworks. In their explanations former prisoners draw on different reasons, including: personal history or experiences; direct responses to localised circumstances; as an individual in reaction to wider political events; or sometimes because of specific worldviews or ideological beliefs. None of these were exclusive and often they were overlapping.

One set of explanations given for involvement in the non-state combatants was because of a highly personalised, even emotional response to what was happening immediately around them. Take, for example, the following:

> Well, like most people at the time it wasn't an ideological thing it was more a gut reaction to something that was happening at the time. I was 17, 18 so I wasn't like very aware of stuff, but it was more like a gut reaction to what was happening …it was more like a, a general sense that something was wrong and something needed to happen. (IRA male)

The young age at which others chose to join and the relationship between that desire to join and the activities of British soldiers was also presented. Interestingly the following quote surmises that the respondent had no political thoughts, although their motivations are influenced by a highly politicised conflict:

> I think I was about 11. I hadn't a clue why I was joining it [the republican movement]. Basically because I just hated the people that shot [named person] and hated the Brits and didn't think they should be in our country and just had a notion how an 11-year-old would have and things just got worse then from then on, you know, you get older and you, you're seeing what was going on and the brutality and, all, I wouldn't have had any political thoughts. (IRA female)

As for the following loyalist the sense of being a defender or protecting 'The People', itself a highly politicised notion (defined by both loyalists and republicans) was also presented as a motivational factor: 'I joined the UDA because I saw people in the area so frightened that they couldn't even go out at night without republicans coming to the area so I joined the UDA to protect that area … to defend the area against these people' (UDA male).

In essence joining up was not necessarily framed by distinct political ideology or clearly defined by political discourses. Rather the desire to become active was set against broad concepts of group togetherness and the 'right' (itself a complex term) to defend or attack an identified 'other'. Commonly, former prisoners explained their choice in terms of a reaction to what was seen as a society in turmoil. The following is typical of such stories:

> It was personal reasons. It wasn't anything to do with politics really, it was just people that I had went [sic] to school with who had chosen careers in the security

forces and a few of them had been killed. At that time it had appeared to me that republicans were killing people with sort of impunity that security forces didn't seem to have a handle on the situation. And one of the options I looked at was joining the security forces on a part-time basis, but I decided that wouldn't be a good idea because you would only be setting yourself up as another legitimate target, so that's why I joined the UVF. (UVF male)

Of particular interest in the above quote is the idea that the covert nature of being an UVF member produced measured risks and that anonymity was important in pursuing a military reaction to events. The issue of risk and anonymity points to an interesting sense of motivation. As with other former combatants the impact of events is important but as in the case outlined above joining up was also influenced by other decisions.

Likewise, the following quote from an INLA former prisoner points to how events such as Bloody Sunday were important, but also central is the constant reference to age and the reality that riots that became a prominent site within which to articulate and practice defenderism and group loyalty:

When I joined the INLA I was 17 years of age in 1975 and prior to that I was a member of the Provisionals and prior to that I was a member of *Fianna Eireann* in the Official IRA. So basically I joined the Official IRA *Fianna* at 13 just going on 14. I think I was roughly around 13 in 1972. I joined because of events on ground. There were heavy riots at the time; there were killings just a hundred yards away from here during the riots, there were civilians killed. There was Bloody Sunday for example and that was very strong in people's minds, even though I was a very young age at that particular time I was aware of it on the streets. (INLA male)

As with other combatants it was the breakdown in civil order and the growth in defender groups on the ground in which individuals could operate in a manner understood as reacting to 'the shootings and bombings and indiscriminate attacks' (UVF male) or in response to the 'violence in the streets that was day and daily – every night' (UVF male). Others responded directly because they saw the conflict directly affect 'people in our [school] class' (IRA male) or daily events witnessed 'raids, houses getting searched, people getting arrested, all that type of stuff' (IRA male). In reply many people felt 'powerless' and enacting violence 'gave you some sort of strength' (IRA male).

Some former combatants offered more exact circumstances regarding their decision to join the conflict:

I remember sitting in a bar, I was about sixteen and a half, seventeen, I was sitting in a bar with my mates, and I just wanted to have a drink a laugh. But something came on the news and it was roughly about the time of all the bombs in Belfast City Centre and people being killed and what do you call it, Bloody Friday. And I remember an older person … turned round and said 'somebody should do something about that' and I remember sitting and thinking maybe it was drink, maybe it was that man saying somebody should do something about it. And at the moment I decided that person would be me. (UDA male)

Further specific catalysts for involvement were revealed. A loyalist former prisoner explained 'one of my best friends' father was shot dead. I went to the funeral … his young sister was screaming for her daddy to come back. I can remember crying. I left that, but swore if I ever get the chance for revenge then I would so it was mostly a human response to what was happening around me' (UVF male). A female former IRA prisoner told a similar story behind her motivation for joining: 'I very clearly mind [named person] being shot. He was shot out at the front of the house and being a nosey wee girl … I looked out the back window and I see him being carried out with his comrades and, and that was, I knew he was dead and, and I never forget that sort of sight.'

In many instances those interviewed conveyed the sense that joining was 'very idealistic, not ideological, but idealistic in that you tend to simplify things in terms of right or wrong, black or white' (IRA male) or that they had done so because they saw their community 'as basically left defenceless'. This former IRA prisoner claimed at the time he had an 'idealistic sense of injustice and stuff' (IRA male) while one loyalist suggested it was more 'excitement than anything else to be truthful' (UDA male).

Two things stand out from these series of interviews. First, the number of times interviewees claimed their initial motivation 'wasn't anything to do with politics really', or that a direct response to events around them caused them to turn to the non-state combatants to find some form of expression. Second is the early age at which many of those interviewed became involved with non-state combatant organisations. Most commonly people joined these groupings because they saw it as some kind of collective response to concrete or perceived danger, or an expression of a shared collective identity as community boundaries, real and ideological, become more clearly demarcated through conflict.

Although joining up was expressed through a sense that the motivation that led to involvement was 'not political', this was based on a somewhat peculiar notion of what is, and what is not political. Reactions to daily events co-joined with existing group localities and the intimate geography of segregated living to produce shared responses to what was deemed as transgressive and unacceptable behaviour by the identified 'other'. Understandings by non-state combatant groups are framed by group dynamics, senses of group suffering and by perceived achievement of the move towards the unification of Ireland or the defence of Northern Ireland's constitutional status. These are overtly political constructs that may be understood as a motivational politics that was to evolve into a more defined political discourse. Politics was important as context, but more central was the reinforcement of a sense of collective identity, which set such incidents in a broader framework, often by the determining of the other through frameworks of understanding that heighten ideas of difference, division and adversarial activity. Also important is the reinforcement of the other side as pernicious, duplicitous, violent and perverse.

Important here is the recognition of the strength of unity constructed through notions of 'imagined communities' (Anderson 1991) and in relation to other identities, and senses of difference. Put simply, such identities are based on some notion that there are others with similar social, economic and political senses of self. This base for the expression of social solidarity often finds expression through what people believe they are not, as much as through strongly held beliefs of what they are. Moreover, identity is positioned through both its social and symbolic aspects (Hall 1997). The political dimensions of the construction of the other are paramount, not least because the categorisation of outsiders and the other is central to determining those who are included and excluded in the right to participate in the polity, and to exercise political power (Marshall 1950).

These constructions of otherness present as differing understandings and interpretations of conflict. For republicans the casting of the 'other' centred primarily on the British state and its imperialist role in Ireland, which in itself fused the notion of a legitimate anti-colonial struggle. The following is representative of such views:

> Going right back through our history all the struggles against the British and the realities in Ireland it legitimised our actions, it allowed us to make that big moral jump from, we're totally opposed to killing, but everybody else in the world has had to kill people in order to gain their freedom. And Ireland's no different. (IRA male)

A contrary loyalist position aims to delegitimise the anti-colonial position through endorsing the idea that republicans 'were wanting to kill us. It didn't matter what sex we were or what age we were as long as we were Protestants. The people who were bombing were wanting to blow us all up' (UDA male). Thus, joining loyalist combatant groups was seen as a way to 'defend my own area against republicans' (UDA male) or to 'fight against republicans' (UVF male).

Prison experiences

Increasing involvement and organisation of non-state combatants in everyday life and state reaction to organised violence quickly resulted in the swelling of the number of political prisoners held in Northern Ireland's gaols. Reactions differed between loyalists and republicans, not least because, as some of the above quotations illustrate, there was little or no history of wide-scale imprisonment of those involved in pro-state violence, while republicans had both ideological and communal experiences, especially a history of imprisonment, to draw upon in order to structure a response.

Moreover, the central motivation for engagement with non-state combatants was very different between loyalists and republicans. Most who joined loyalist groups perceived their actions in terms of 'active defence'. Many regarded their actions to be just as legitimate as those undertaken by the legal forces of the state, and claimed to be doing so because their government was 'not acting with sufficient resolution' (Bruce 1994: 199). Loyalists were unified in their perceptions of the state's inability or unwillingness to 'protect' their community (Corcoran 2006: 141; McAuley 1998a) leading Schulze and Smith (2000) to conclude that many who joined saw themselves as filling a vacuum left by the state security forces in defending the Protestant unionist community population against militant Irish republicanism.

One UDA former prisoner made this clear in his determination that he saw himself 'as a defender not as offender, but as a defender' who had been 'prompted ... to defend my community' (UDA male). Bruce (1994) identifies the essentially paradoxical position for loyalists, who while acting illegally believed they were doing so to defend the state that then imprisoned them. Given this the shock of imprisonment by the state, especially among those imprisoned in the early phase of the conflict, was paramount, but despite a growing awareness of the complexities of their relationship with the state, loyalist prisoners were only able to produce a limited oppositional identity to the British state.

For republicans the situation was very different. While their actions initially were also expressed in terms of community defence of nationalist communities, they quickly began to see themselves engaged in another phase of the 'long war', a campaign of 'attrition against enemy personnel' and the forces of British 'occupation' in Ireland. Indeed, in many ways their relationship with the state was more straightforward than for many loyalists, as they simply refused to recognise the legislation and jurisdiction of a 'foreign state' that was imprisoning them. In response to this they set about constructing a set of ideas that took as their reference points ideological and practical links with the past.

This had direct consequences for their behaviour and attitude of those imprisoned through the stressing of perceived continuities with previous generations of republican prisoners. Thus, writing in the 1950s, Sean MacStiofain, later the first chief-of-staff of the Provisional IRA, made clear that in the republican movement: 'a political prisoner did not just vanish into jail to be forgotten. The jails and camps themselves were an important sector of the revolutionary front' (MacStiofain 1974: 66). Such links with the past were overtly stressed by the new generation of prisoners. This is clearly seen in a statement made on 21 October 1980 by Brendan Hughes, the then IRA Officer Commanding in the Maze, in which he claimed:

> The repeated prison battles of republicans to gain their rights as POWs have been a focal point through successive liberation struggles of the past three centuries ... who proudly bore the standard of Tone, Lalor, Pearse and Connolly, and stood in open defiance of the tyrannical oppressor of our nation. (Cited in English 2003: 192).

While it is beyond the parameters of this chapter to trace in detail the history of politically motivated imprisonment in Northern Ireland (instead see Chapter 4), two broad points are, however, worth making. First, beginning with internment in 1971, the circumstances under which a growing number of republican and loyalist prisoners were held created an environment where group identity could be quickly reinforced and where 'shared political idealism … instilled in the various paramilitary factions a sense of purpose and group loyalty' (Bates-Gaston 2003: 250). Second, the situation also set in place the foundations for heightened debates within and sometimes between all of the non-state combatant groups, which in turn allowed for parallel political developments amongst both republican and loyalist prisoners.

It is important to highlight several possible turning points surrounding the prison experience. As one republican prisoner stated 'the reason for joining and then sustaining commitment wasn't the same' (IRA male). The period of imprisonment can be thought of as a clear time of transformation, both individually and collectively, for the non-state combatants. Most commonly this meant a growing engagement and involvement with education, both formal and informal. In his biography of Bobby Sands, for example, O'Hearn (2006: 52) describes the increasing politicisation of younger republican prisoners from the mid-1970s onwards. He suggests how as 'they became politically aware, differences with other prisoners from other organisations began to matter. … Soon, other prisoners saw them reading and debating on political themes and more of them joined in'. This was a common experience amongst those interviewed. One recalled his involvement as follows:

> in those days, we did read Irish history and we did go to political lectures; we did learn more about everything. It was your first chance to read books on communism, books on revolution, Che Guevara, [James] Connolly, all the things that you wouldn't have read when you were a teenager and probably wouldn't have read. But in Long Kesh, all these books were being passed around, everybody's talking about them, everybody's debating them. So you naturally want to be informed about it. You want to understand it … So they were all forming some form of political understanding of what was happening. (IRA male)

Following the hunger strikes, the culture within the republican wings of the H Blocks was reassessed (Walker 2006: 146). One consequence was that debates concerning the validity of armed struggle as a sole tactic were increasingly aired (Hennessey 1997). Certainly by the mid-1980s the Sinn Fein leadership was articulating a realisation that armed struggle on its own was 'inadequate' as a strategy (Taylor 1997: 336). Former IRA hunger striker Tommy McKearney has highlighted some of the discussions taking place at the time, suggesting that prisoners felt a re-evaluation was necessary, because: 'the military campaign was not really bearing fruit' and they 'had to consider what the options were' (cited in Walker 2006: 73). These debates provided republicans with an ideological vocabulary and new forms of cultural expression (Whalen 2007), while not challenging the efficacy of violence. Input from prisoners became central to the debates that evolved and to the development of a long-term political strategy for the republican movement (see Chapter 4).

Although the process was less pronounced, loyalists, who from the early to mid-1970s had begun to be imprisoned in sizable numbers, also began to review their longer term strategies. Increasingly this politicisation meant recognition that their position in relation to the state was far from straightforward. Meanwhile, supporters increasingly organised and agitated around issues, both within the prisons and beyond (Shirlow and McEvoy 2008). These included the formation of support groups for prisoners and their families, opposition to the 'supergrass' system (PUP 1985c), protests against treatment within the prisons (Shankill Bulletin 1986) and support for the segregation of prisoners according to political allegiance, which occurred '*de facto*' in 1982, following the destruction of loyalist cells in an organised protest (Ramsbotham 1998).

Overall, however, the political representation of loyalist prisoners remained restricted (certainly compared with their republican counterparts). This reflected the continued distance (and sometimes open conflict) between the political representatives of the non-state combatants and other factions of unionism, most notably the DUP (McAuley 2004). It was also an indication of the poorly developed political and historical awareness of many loyalists (McAuley 1991; McEvoy 2001). Two of the loyalist prisoners interviewed explained the difficulty they faced in these terms:

> For myself and other young people of my generation growing up, politics wasn't, it never entered your thought. One, you were never taught it in school, you, you never knew anything about your own, your own history, Irish history, in school, you weren't taught it. It wasn't until a lot of us went to gaol that we realised … I was the same. I thought Northern Ireland was shaped from day one. (UVF male)

A UVF male explained that he 'had only turned seventeen a couple of weeks when I was arrested and what seventeen year old has an ideology or a political sort of thought? I didn't see it at the time in that sense.'

Moreover, the processes of political transformation amongst prisoners were extremely uneven across loyalism, in part explained by differences between the UDA and UVF leaderships, the culture of different organisations within prison and the military campaign they sought to pursue without. For those associated with the UVF the process was directly influenced by the personality and political perspective of Gusty Spence, in his role as Officer Commanding within the prison structure, where he called for a 'universal ceasefire' and argued that 'Loyalist and Republican must sit down together' (Spence 1977). Central to Spence's leadership was an emphasis on education and self-questioning. As a consequence, UVF prisoners: 'who had never reflected on

why they had become involved, were prodded into serious political thinking'
(Howe 2002: 8).

While those within the remit of the UVF had at least the possibility of a
reasonably structured approach to political learning, the approach within the
UDA was much less structured. Their experience tended to be much more
isolated and individualised. This was made clear in the following: 'I always
pushed for education. ... But I found that in the loyalist wings nobody had any
interest. Then the authorities didn't show any interest in generating classes. I
was one of the ones that pushed them.'

A male former UVF prisoner described the broad attitude of some fellow
loyalist prisoners in the following terms:

> The point was that it wasn't over when you went inside. For me we had to struggle
> to remain as a military organisation. Have discipline and construct ideas. The
> conflict was changing so you needed to have ideas. It was hard to convince people
> that we needed ideas as they saw themselves as irregulars. So for me the point was
> to ensure they thought of themselves that way, but that they had made sacrifices
> to build a better Northern Ireland and that had to continue on the outside. People
> were political but didn't have the language.

The engagement in political debate was not universal, however, amongst
loyalist prisoners and certainly not all were involved in such processes. Bruce
(1994: 281) cites one journalist who told him 'that when he was interviewing
IRA men he had trouble keeping up with their thinking; when he was interviewing loyalists he had trouble finding any'. Nonetheless, political thinking
did evolve amongst loyalists and a deepening political awareness was central to
the story told by many of the former prisoners interviewed. Take the following:

> You have more time to read and digest things, to put your own swing on things.
> Politically, you'd be more astute ... You learnt more and you digested more and you
> retained more because you had the time. ... That's how I got into it. And once you
> get a wee bit more intellectual, you form your own ideas. It does mould you into
> getting more political. (UDA male)

Again, for this male former UVF prisoner:

> I think prison introduced me to an arena whereby I could explore those things if I
> wanted to. Now I know some people wouldn't go near it with a barge pole but in
> some way I was drawn to certain things. I think on my release from prison I have
> reflected on that experience and tried to apply it in some way to my further study
> and education and that type of thing and working in the community and stuff

Such ideological innovation or (re)discovery was attached directly by those
involved to structural and experiential contexts and marked identifiable
turning points in the life courses of many prisoners. Moen (2000) suggests that
the strategies of resistance developed by republican prisoners included the

development of the 'consultative and collective nature of republican strategy and the subordination of individuality to group identity and need'. Laurence McKeown, a former IRA prisoner, records how the notion of resistance was broadened as republican prisoners became increasingly 'engaged in a cultural, literary and dramatic struggle' (McKeown 1999: 191), as culture and education became increasingly politicised areas of prisoners' day-to-day activities. The outputs of the 'struggle through education' are recorded by Whalen (2007:169) as a means of 'inspiring active solidarity among the population outside'. One republican prisoner spoke of how when he was reimprisoned in the early 1980s, he 'went straight into the educational system because it was part of the struggle' (IRA male). The effects of this perspective on republican prisoners were widespread:

> I remember going to prison and people saying Brits get the hell out of Ireland and whatever united Ireland develops that's good enough me. And I remember thinking that wasn't good enough for me. And I was thinking why should we fight and lose friends and that? It has to be a better type of Ireland, a red socialism. And personally, how does it reflect on me? I would have a more social outlook from going into prison. (IRA male)

The following is worth quoting at some length, as it traces in some detail not only a key turning point in the biography of one former prisoner, but also the group of which he was part:

> The prison was breaking up into those who were conservative and who were revolutionary. And there were those of us who dove into it, learning what Marxism was and Engels and all the rebellions – Mao Tse Tung in China. You had this interest and that was kind of frowned upon. … I remember one incident, I won't mention his name, but actually somebody was caught passing *Das Kapital* from one cage to another and that person was put under arrest. He was grounded as you would call it, in his cell because he passed this on. I remember one time I wore a Che Guevara shirt, which is more pop art than anything. And I was asked by the commanding officer of the cage not to wear it and I just refused. I wore it until it actually fell off. … They'd say 'that's a communist thing'. And I'd say it's not communist, it's a sense of who Che Guevara was as a young person.

He continued by outlining some of the changes:

> I resented that that reactionary element that ran the camp wouldn't let us broaden our mind. So any time you went to education you certainly learnt the Irish language and the history of Ireland. But you were never taught to analyse. And it wasn't until there was a group came in, Gerry Adams and Patrick Hughes and that was the first time, he actually sat in the room, he put the chairs in a circle and he gave us the book I think it was the Orange State. He asked me and a few others what did I think of the chapter? He said 'what do you think about that?' and we were going 'I don't know, you just asked me to read it'. 'No. Analyse it critically, youse are politicians. You have to understand that you're politicians rather than

soldiers. You have to think for yourselves. You have to think what the struggle is, that it has – there can never be a military end to this. It has to end in politics. Youse are in prison, you've got the opportunity to learn. But not only learning and reading, but to critically analyse everything about you.' And that was, given the direction we were going in, the first time of 'oh, they're telling us to actually think'. Rather than the early days of the camps from 1971 to say 1972 – you weren't taught to think. You were just told how many pikes were used, how many cannons were used in 1790 and all these things were certainly very interesting, but we weren't told this is the politics of the Orange State. Michael Farrell's book was one of the books that looked in-depth at the sectarianism of the state. (IRA male)

While there were formal channels for prisoners to express themselves within Sinn Fein, the above passage demonstrates the depth of informal links available through frequent meetings between prisoners and the party leadership. English (2003) has clearly demonstrated how the political thinking that developed amongst republican prisoners increasingly informed the peace process through arguments for alternative means to pursue the goals of the republican movement.

Albeit to a lesser extent, parallel processes occurred within loyalism, where critical thinking also deepened amongst important elements of loyalist non-state combatants (McAuley 2002, 2004). For some, imprisonment gave the first opportunity of contact with a range of social and political ideas and the tools to question 'some of their assumptions and beliefs' (Fitzduff 2002: 114). As a consequence, a fuller political analysis emerged (Green 1998) developing from what Von Tangen Page described as non-state combatant 'think-tanks', and suggesting that they 'were a vital ideological force' behind the increased politicisation of the loyalists in the late 1980s and early 1990s (Von Tangen Page 2006: 95). Eventually, this discursive framework found political expression in the 'new loyalism' of the PUP and UDP (McAuley 2005). With the PUP the regime initiated by Spence in the prisons took a meaningful form on the outside (Stevenson 1996) with Spence playing a pivitol role in eventually bringing about a loyalist ceasefire (Taylor 2000).

Both the UDP and PUP were to become central to the outcome of the peace process. The willingness of the PUP in particular to engage in dialogue with political opposition, including Sinn Fein, marked a sea change within loyalist politics. Although there were differences in the strategies and tactics adopted by the UVF and UDA during the conflict and peace process (some of which are discussed in the next chapter), there was a common recognition that prisoners should be seen as making a vital contribution to strategies during political negotiations (Garland 2001: 282; Spencer 2008: 115–18, 164–5, 212–13; Wood 2006).

Overall, the journalist David McKittrick neatly encapsulates the consequences of political change when he says:

The tabloids used to call it 'the academy of terror', but behind its walls and barbed-wire fences valuable changes of mind have taken place. In the IRA H-Blocks the idea of a peace process took route at an early stage as long term prisoners contemplated both their own futures and the prospects for the republican movement in general. Most of those who have emerged from the Maze in the 1990s have lent support to the peace process, giving an influential form of endorsement of the IRA ceasefire. Something similar was happening in the UVF and UDA H-Blocks, where the first generation of imprisoned loyalists had time to ponder on whether a better alternative to violence was possible. (McKittrick 1997)

Gains and losses

Part of that introspection referred to above involved consideration of themes of gain and loss, at the level of both the individual and the political. The level of personal trauma suffered by former prisoners has begun to be recognised, as are the negative experiences on family and relations with home and relationship break-ups as a result of imprisonment being reasonably commonplace (McEvoy et al. 2004; McShane 1988). Moreover, former politically motivated prisoners also report confidence loss, introversion, restlessness and paranoia (McEvoy 2001).

Almost all those interviewed recognised some sense of loss at a personal level (or that of friends and family). Notably, however, in the interviews about 'gains' and 'losses' former prisoners consistently projected their answers in particular way and through an identifiable structured discourse. This emerged in a form that most often sought to give primacy to the communal over the individual. Individual hardships were recognised, 'I lost a lot of really good years because I was in gaol (IRA male), or as another put it, 'a lot of losses, a lot of friends were killed in the conflict itself and a lot spent a long time in prison with 20 year sentences (INLA male). Even more telling in personal terms perhaps was the declaration from a former UDA prisoner: 'I have one child and my wife wouldn't have any more children until I guaranteed her that I wouldn't go back to prison and I couldn't ever do that. So I've only got one child and I love children and I've lost lots of very good friends. So I mean, personally I lost a lot' (UDA male).

A male former INLA activist outlined the level of his personal loss as follows:

> Personally, I joined the IRA at a very early age and I've paid a very high price for it. I've done a total of 18 years in prison and I lost almost all youth and the trauma that my family went through, in relation to when I was in prison. I came from a big family, four or five sisters. They suffered greatly financially, psychologically because of my being in prison.

One former republican prisoner summarised his feelings in the following terms:

> Obviously there's a lot of personal loss for people. That has to be seen as nothing other than a negative thing. People have lost people; families have had people go to gaol and all that there. It's harder for families whose sons or daughters went to gaol than it is for people who went to gaol. (IRA male)

Most often, however, these considerable personable losses were positioned in the stories told as being secondary to communal or group gains brought about by the actions of former prisoners. These 'positive' features of imprisonment were largely seen to take two forms. First were the bonds developed around personal relationships and comradeship. The following is typical of such responses: What did I gain personally? I gained a lot of friends, long-term friends. I don't think, if it wasn't for the UDA and the conflict, I don't think I would have had those friends' (UDA male). Such views were by expressed by members across all the non-state combatant groups as with the following from this former INLA prisoner: 'Because of prison I have gained a lot as well. I've lost a lot but I've gained a lot as well. Like the friendships. There's a lot of bonds that have been created through the conflict, for me that's personal gain' (INLA male).

Second was a widespread recognition of the political aspects of imprisonment and the role of prisoners in achieving the broader goals of the non-state combatant organisation. Such views are encapsulated in the following from a male former IRA prisoner: 'I gained loads of experience because of gaol. Personal experience and you gained a better self-awareness ... You can go through really crappy, shitty, brutal times, but you realised that you could cope ... I think it was because I knew what was happening, because it was politically driven.'

This loyalist former prisoner suggested that his 'personal gain was being part of an organisation that put the IRA on their backs and that's what they did. The organisation that I'm involved in made these people go the way, they're going now. Because they knew there's no way they're going to beat us. Yep, they knew they were never going to beat us and they never would' (UDA male). Another member of the same organisation suggested 'politically ... to me it's now cast in stone that there will not be a united Ireland. The shame of it is that there had to be lives lost to prove that' (UDA male).

Broadly, most former prisoners argued that what they had done had been necessary, although occasionally they questioned the worth of particular actions. As this former loyalist prisoner argued 'there were losses, but as well as that I wouldn't change anything. Well, I wouldn't like – if the same circumstances prevailed I would do the same again' (UDA male). A male IRA former prisoner summarised his position as follows:

> Personally, I don't feel any loss. I don't feel any negatives of it, or very few. Obviously, it would have been better not to have some of that stuff happen, but in

general terms no negative feelings about the struggle. No negative things about decisions I made or what happened to me or anything.

These comments do not always fit easily with the dominant construct of those involved in political violence as driven by a particular set of psychological traits or a terrorist personality (Arena and Arrigo 2006: 3) nor in Northern Ireland, the presentation of non-state combatants as merely ruthless and atavistic (McEvoy et al. 2004; Walker 1984).

What is certain is that as memorial and commemoration become more centre stage in contemporary Northern Irish society the life histories of all those involved will become increasingly important. This is contentious ground. The casting of blame and the positioning of non-state combatants as the root cause of conflict reflects not only the emotional residue of thirty years of conflict, but also deeply held ideological positions. Initiatives such as the formation of a Victims' Commission have failed to reassure those who see the release of political prisoners as an unfair cost of political settlement, while unionist politicians in particular have been critical, the DUP claiming that 'all decent people recoil with moral contempt at the prospect of the mass release of those who have murdered and maimed the innocent' (DUP 1998: 6). The Orange Order declared the scheme as yet another in a long list of concessions designed to appease gunmen and bombers (*Orange Standard*, December 1998, June 2003).

Former non-state combatants are neither unaware nor immune to such criticisms, but it should be recognised that for almost all involved in the conflict extreme violence 'holds little allure' (Shirlow et al. 2005: 23). As one UVF spokesperson put it recently, the contemporary UVF now regard themselves as 'fourth generation' of volunteers, but see one of its key tasks as the prevention of a 'fifth generation' (cited in *Combat* 2006, issue 38). Such views were mirrored almost directly by Declan Arthurs, one of the last IRA prisoners to be released from the Maze. As he put it: 'I was in gaol to prevent my children, and other children, having to suffer as we did, that this would be the last generation of Republicans who would become political prisoners and that we would see a united Ireland at last' (cited in Cadwallader 2000; 16).

Release and transformations

Release marks a momentous event in any prisoner's life (Wolff and Draine 2004). This is no different for politically motivated prisoners, although the occasion most often occurs in a particular context, involving not just the individual, but also the community. Those released from prison faced further turning points in their political biography most notable in the extent to which former prisoners were willing to continue to play a role in promoting the transformation of conflict.

While it has been argued that latent support for non-state combatant groups is widespread throughout Northern Ireland (Hayes and McAllister 2004) and that the conflict itself was sustained by 'the popular ambiguity that exists towards the use of political violence' (ibid. 2004: 12), debates concerning legitimacy remains core to the relationships between former prisoners, non-state combatant organisations and their respective communities (Mitchell 2008).

The early release of politically motivated prisoners was by far the most difficult and unpalatable part of the accord (Von Tangen Page 2006). The level of its unpopularity can be gauged by the Northern Ireland Life and Times Survey (2000), which indicated that a minority of Catholics (31 per cent) and a tiny number of Protestants (3 per cent) supported the schedule for early release. The Conservative shadow secretary for Northern Ireland, Andrew MacKay, declared 'there could be no excuse for releasing such evil men so quickly' and that it was 'a sad day for the rule of law when terrorist bombers who so recently killed totally innocent victims are released back on to the streets' (cited by Foster and Woolf 2000). Even Tony Blair, who played a central part in negotiating the deal, described the releases as 'hard to stomach' (*Guardian*, 23 June 1999).

Not only did former prisoners encounter a climate of hostility to their release outside of their immediate communities, they also faced socio-economic problems within them. While Bruce (1992: 198) asserts that loyalist non-state combatants are more proletarian than their republican counterparts, arguing that the IRA was able to recruit from across a much wider class spectrum than were loyalist groupings, both were primarily working class and disproportionately drawn from deprived working-class areas of Northern Ireland. Upon release the vast majority returned to the areas from which they originated, hoping to find cultural and physical support. That also meant, however, that they experienced the high unemployment rates and levels of deprivation experienced across working-class communities in Northern Ireland.

While there are clear parallels in the practical issues that both loyalist and republican former prisoners faced around reintegration, there was much variation in the ideological and political space they occupied within their own communities. Féron summarises these differences as follows, for former republican non-state combatants:

> there are many possibilities for reconversion: either as activists in the main, fast-growing Republican party Sinn Fein, or through the dense networks of community activity in the Catholic community ... [whereas] on the Loyalist side, where community activity networks have always been less developed ... the volunteer and community sectors receive fewer demands in Protestant neighbourhoods, even the most working-class ones (Féron 2006: 451).

The continued public distancing of mainstream unionist political grouping. from former combatants is deeply felt by former loyalist prisoners groups and former prisoners constantly feel forced to engage in legitimacy-seeking processes within the wider unionist community. As one former combatant put it:

> even today, in fact we're getting more isolated now than what we were when we first come out. When we come out, we were probably, you know, accepted within the small minority communities within the protestant working class from where we come from, but once you go on to the wider community we're treated just the same … marginalised. (UVF male)

However, as Fitzduff notes, by the mid-1990s 'there were an increasing number of meetings between activists on both sides, arranged mostly by community workers and mediators … in some areas, former non-state combatants began to cooperate on common social problems, as they increasingly realised their collective social disadvantage' (Fitzduff 2002: 113). Former prisoners played an increasing role in preventing a drift back towards conflict and in developing confidence in political futures within their respective ethnic blocs. In so doing they developed contacts across civil society, and met with statutory agencies and political adversaries. In what follows we consider not only the consequences for politics, but also the effects this had on their sense of self-identity and the core constructs of what it means to be a loyalist or a republican.

Conclusion

It is always important to recognise that when people recount their life histories in the present it can be subject to distortion, addition or memory loss (Brewer 2000: 69–71). The stories told above, however, remain central to an understanding of the recent political history of Northern Ireland; not least because as Féron points out issues concerning the status and future of former prisoners relate directly to 'the political and ideological struggles over the more general meaning and purpose of the Northern Ireland conflict' (Féron 2006: 448).

Those interviewed had a number of different motivations for joining non-state combatant groups. For some it was the manifestation of longstanding family traditions, while for others it was a highly personalised emotional reaction, perhaps motivated by an identifiable crucial event. Most sought to find some collective expression to a society in conflict. Some respondents were cultivated into organisations, others succumbed to peer pressure, while others merely thought of themselves as reacting either to defend their community or take the war to the enemy. For the majority interviewed, however, the decision was based upon events occurring daily around them.

Most often the decision to become involved emanated from antagonism towards an identifiable 'other'. The conflict in Northern Ireland made weighty demands on both republican and loyalist combatants, including lengthy prison sentences, dramatically reduced life chances and ultimately perhaps death. Structural violence brought with it a culture of social exclusion and deionisation of the 'other'. The experiences of 'fighting the war', imprisonment and the emergence of new leaders brought changes and this chapter has identified some of the major points of transition undergone by former prisoners throughout their political life histories. Only much later was there a questioning of deeply held beliefs and the emergence of a more specific ideological direction.

Former prisoners and their representatives and groups occupy core ground in the transformation of Northern Ireland's polity, particularly given the lead of many, from both loyalist and republican backgrounds, in breaking with political dogma associated with particular historical interpretations of the past. Although cross-community and conflict resolution processes driven in many cases by former prisoners have begun to be embedded in the polity of Northern Ireland, high levels of social distance between loyalist and republican communities continue mirroring the strength of community bonding within such districts (Cairns 1989; Cairns et al. 2003).

4 Imprisonment, ideological development and change

> While republicans in Long Kesh discussed and analysed (and loyalist paramilitaries did body building) unionist politicians waited to return to Stormont. Lacking the educational advantages of the prison cell, they were not ready for the new world of government in which political power came in a cultural wrapping (*Irish News*, 31 March 2003).

Writing in the *Irish News* on the occasion of the donation of republican former prisoners' books to the Linen Hall Library in Belfast, Patrick Murphy managed to touch in one paragraph on two assumptions about non-state combatants imprisoned during the Northern Ireland conflict. The Long Kesh library was a collection of books amassed by IRA prisoners during their time incarcerated in the Maze prison. The donation of the collection to the Linen Hall was a succinct way of reiterating a popular view that time in prison had not put them on the sidelines of the conflict. Rather it had allowed them to prepare for the future in way not afforded to mainstream politicians. In one throwaway line, Murphy's article portrayed loyalist prisoners as a less cerebral grouping, seemingly devoted to toning their muscles rather than stretching their brains whilst imprisoned. This chapter examines whether the prison caricature of republican scholarly endeavour versus loyalist narcissism withstands scrutiny.

Non-state combatants on both sides 'played little part in the onset of the current troubles in Northern Ireland: they were its products rather than its creators' (Guelke 1995: 185). Many who became involved with these groups were reacting to rising inter-community violence rather than consciously taking action based on a philosophical position. The UVF came into being in 1966, and that year also saw the fiftieth anniversary of the Easter Rising, which attracted new people to republicanism. However, the Provisional IRA was not really resuscitated until after the tensions stirred by O'Neillism and the civil rights movement had turned into an explicit conflict, and the UDA was the coalescence of a number of smaller defence associations formed in response to violence on the streets. UVF members have also carried out activity under the name of the Red Hand Commando (RHC), whilst violent activity associated with the UDA was attributed to the Ulster Freedom Fighters, in part to preserve the UDA's legal status. The INLA emerged in 1974 after a split in the Official IRA.

Given the reactive nature of early non-state combatant activity and organisation, prison provided a space for self-reflection and debate for many, although not all prisoners, as well as access to a range of educational opportunities (Bishop and Mallie 1987; Fitzduff 2002). Politicians associated with non-state combatants have often sought to establish that prison was a profoundly important experience and that prisoners developed a store of wisdom and knowledge that would have a positive impact on their communities. For example, a policy document for the PUP, associated with the UVF, argued: 'If the "troubles" have done nothing else they have "wised up" the ordinary man and woman in the street and equally important, those men who were prepared to fight for what they believed. Long years in Crumlin Road Jail and Long Kesh prison camp certainly provided the solitude for deep contemplation of those things political and otherwise' (PUP 1998).

The presentation of the prison experience by non-state combatant organisations and their political affiliates has laid stress on the legitimacy of the prisoners as political and their role within their respective movements, both in terms of the acts that led to their sentences and their continuing importance to their organisation whilst within prison walls. A quarterly journal produced by IRA prisoners assured readers: 'The gaols have been the arena for a different struggle – the struggle through education. Time and a common purpose have enabled us to study the nature of the world in which we live and to educate ourselves to become better able to bring about change in the Ireland of today' (*An Glor Gafa*, Autumn 1989).

Discussions of the prison experience and prisoners' thoughts have often featured in the papers and magazines associated with non-state combatants organisations and their political associates. After conflict emerged in the late 1960s two rival publications emerged which both purported to represent the thinking of the republican movement. *An Phoblacht* and *Republican News* were both published from 1970, but while *An Phoblacht* was produced in the Republic of Ireland and was close in thinking to the southern leadership of the Provisional IRA, *Republican News* was Belfast based. By 1976 these two news sheets became noticeably divergent (Bishop and Mallie 1987), but merged in 1979, becoming *An Phoblacht/Republican News*. This reflected the increasing dominance of the Northern leadership within the provisional republican movement, although the paper's office was located in Dublin to keep it away from raids by British security forces. In 2005, the *Republican News* element was dropped from the title after a relaunch.

The Derry-based *Starry Plough* represented the INLA and its political affiliate the Irish Republican Socialist Party. Compared with *An Phoblacht*, publication of the *Starry Plough* was not consistent and other publications, such as the Belfast-based *Saoirse*, only lasted for a few years. The UDA also lacked a single continuous publication as its official voice: different newspapers and newsletters surfaced and there was a proliferation of them in the early 1970s when the UDA was could claim with credibility to be a mass membership organisation, with an estimated 40–50,000 joining up (Bew and Gillespie 1999: 39). In the end, titles such as *Ulster Loyalist*, *Ulster Militant* and *Magilligan's Outpost* sank without trace, reflecting the decentralisation (or fragmented, even) nature of the group. The UVF, on the other hand, maintained *Combat* in one form or another from the early 1970s until 2007 when it became *The Purple Standard*.

Within these publications, prisoners have been presented as the martyrs of their movement, suffering on behalf of others and embodying the plight of their people. However, their activism has also been celebrated, making prison an alternative battleground. This has made the prison experience central to the legitimacy of non-state combatant organisations. This legitimacy has been augmented by claims that the years of education and debate in prison provided and/or shaped ideological developments in that incarceration provided the space required to explore and debate ideas and offer advice and leadership to those on the outside. The development or otherwise of these four roles – as icons, fighters, ideologues and leaders – in the years before the inception of the peace process that led to the signing of the Good Friday Agreement are of importance.

It is apparent that prisoners did have huge symbolic importance for their organisations and that prison walls created a space for debate. However, prison was also a place where one could be marginalised, ignored or manipulated. One of the INLA prisoners interviewed left the Provisional IRA in part because of his prison experiences.

> During those years in prison I more or less learnt through my time of mixing with Provisional members that they were not the type of people that I ever expected them to be. Most of them were non-political for a start. Most of them hadn't a clue where republicanism came from. Most of them were in prison because they got involved with the IRA because their friends were in the IRA and I was treated as an outsider in prison because of my socialist beliefs. (INLA male)

McKeown's interviews with fellow former IRA prisoners highlight how in the early years education was part of an autocratic system that focused on discipline and loyalty and that many prisoners were alienated by this.

> These people in jail a longer time had done some reading and it was they who became the education officers. But the classes were compulsory, which created a lot of resentment and there was an unwritten law that you didn't ask a question because if you did the lecture would last longer and your mates would kill you later. (McKeown 1999: 42)

The militaristic nature of the IRA's regime within prison relaxed after its initial establishment, which meant that education was something that could be embraced by those who wanted to engage in debate about why they were in prison and what the future could hold. However, given the negative experiences of some prisoners and others' antipathy towards classes, it is not enough to proclaim that 'the whole history of the jails has been a process of learning. Thirty years of struggle have given us, and the people, the confidence to have no fear of developing another way' (*An Phoblacht*, 16 December 1999).

Imprisonment and special category status

As noted in the previous chapter, the majority of those convicted of scheduled offences were imprisoned in Northern Ireland itself. Huts at the old Long Kesh airfield were pressed into service in the early 1970s as prison compounds after the introduction of internment. A new prison was constructed on this site and prisoners were transferred to the new blocks of the Maze from 1976. This held the majority of male non-state combatants. Women were initially held in Armagh gaol, which was an old prison noted for poor conditions. These facilities were replaced when a complex of new prisons was completed in 1987 at Maghaberry. Generally, the facilities at the Maze and Maghaberry were of a much higher standard than the main prison for non-political prisoners (known within the system as ordinary decent criminals or ODCs) who were generally held in the Crumlin Road gaol, though some acted as orderlies in Long Kesh.

Prisoners affiliated to a paramilitary organisation were usually based within a community with fellow members. However, there were differences between republicans, who favoured a communal and highly co-ordinated style of living than the 'less organised, less disciplined and more individualistic culture of loyalist prisoners' (McEvoy et al 2004: 653). With the introduction of internment came the categorisation of prisoners associated with the conflict as special category. Special category status had been introduced by the then Home Secretary, William Whitelaw, as a matter of expediency (Hennessey 1997). However, it was taken as evidence by the prisoners that they were in fact political prisoners or prisoners of war rather than criminals. The categorisation was the basis of organising prison life by segregating prisoners into groupings based on group affiliation and the prisoners had privileges compared with ODCs, such as the freedom to wear their own clothes. Removal of special category status in 1976 was part of the Labour government's strategy to 'depoliticise' the conflict and promote a normalised view of the violence in Northern Ireland, part of an argument that violence was the outcome of unjustified lawlessness and that anyone imprisoned for paramilitary offences was therefore a criminal. After the end of the hunger strike of 1981, following the deaths of ten republican prisoners, this category was tacitly reintroduced at the Maze.

The symbolic importance of prisoners

The struggle to re-establish special category status highlighted the importance of recognition of paramilitary actions as political rather than criminal. The idea that special category status equated to political status was important for both loyalist and republican non-state combatants. Resisting criminalisation fitted with republican rejection of the state and imprisonment was depicted as the inevitable outcome for an honourable patriot rather than criminal acts which were committed out of greed or malice. The author of the article 'Political Prisoners' argued that if anyone were to question the political status of those incarcerated 'we who live under the might and power of the oppressor believe that the answer will be the same as that of their forefathers. The felon's cap is the noblest cap an Irishman can wear' (*Republican News*, July 1971). McEvoy (2001: 19) argues that resistance to criminalisation through the hunger strikes and no-wash protests was a means not just of establishing the legitimacy of the prisoners by asserting their political status, but 'an attempt to abrogate power from the prison authorities and publicly diminish the authority of the state that had sentenced them'.

Legitimacy has always been seen as a more complicated issue for loyalists, although resistance has a long history. As Rolston (2006: 660) notes, 'from the Nineteenth Century on, loyalists have shown that where they believe that the state is unable or unwilling to defend them properly, they will organise paramilitary groups outside of legitimate state forces'. The UDA and UVF continued in this vein of conditional loyalty (Miller 1978) and pledged support for the existence of the state and the legitimacy of its forces, whilst claiming legitimacy from the state's inability or unwillingness to pursue defence of Northern Ireland's constitutional state to the hilt:

> Our future role will be to help the security forces by keeping peace among the people unless the security forces fail to get a grip of the situation in Northern Ireland … The UDA will take the offensive against the IRA and do our level best to eliminate and destroy them as Mr. Whitelaw and the Heath Government should have done a long time ago. (*Belfast Telegraph*, 12 July 1972).

However, although many in the loyalist community shared UDA and UVF frustration at what they saw as the weak commitment of constitutional security forces, what the majority hoped for was a relaxation of legal restrictions on state combatants in order to get the job done, rather than non-state combatants taking on the job. A former prisoner acknowledged this viewpoint:

> Within the Protestant Community, it was seen that security forces' hands were tied and they should have gone and basically shot people. It was a hard line, you'll always hear that phrase, 'they should take the gloves off'. There was that type of opinion in all shades, where you saw security forces defending loyalism or Protestantism. Prior to 1969, loyalists or Protestants would have joined the B

Specials or they would have joined the police force. As long as they had a badge of authority they felt, if I shoot a Catholic or a Republican, that's OK. (McGlynn 2004)

Republicans were fighting the British state and imprisonment by that state seemed the inevitable action of an enemy government. The imprisonment of loyalist non-state combatants was more complicated. They found themselves in the unusual position of committing illegal acts to defend the state and then being imprisoned by that state (Bruce 1992) in prisons they accepted as legitimate institutions (Gormally, McEvoy and Wall 1993). McEvoy (2001: 32–3) argues that the loyalist promulgation of 'their only crime is loyalty' was a reaction to their inability to demonstrate the same 'clear oppositional resistance' to the British state and that this meant that 'their capacity for resistance was correspondingly muted'.

Loyalist prisoners nonetheless defend their political status and often copied republican techniques in order to resist criminalisation. For example, they made use of the European Convention on Human Rights to challenge government penal policy (McEvoy 2000). However, the continuous following of republican strategies brought the danger of accusations that they were becoming too close to the IRA, a charge that had a strong influence on the decision to abandon loyalist blanket protests against special category status (Crawford 1999). Another problem for loyalist prisoners in comparison with republicans was that they had 'a considerably smaller political constituency in the community' (McEvoy 2001: 32). Instead, the DUP leader Ian Paisley acted as the voice of militant loyalism whilst condemning the actions of the UVF and UDA. In an article entitled 'Paisley hits out at "Loyalist Killers"', David McKittrick pointed out that 'as recently as two months ago, Mr. Paisley made a call for Protestants to band together for "the defence and preservation of our country". He did not, however, spell out specifically what form such defence would take' (*Irish Times*, 20 March 1975). The success of the DUP in implying the legitimacy of extra-constitutional action in defence of Northern Ireland, without actually engaging in such action or offering public support for those who did, left loyalist non-state combatants little room to appeal for community solidarity.

Reconciling defence of the state and imprisonment by the state was a difficult task for loyalists. UDA and UVF publications complained about poor treatment at the hands of prison staff with allegations that 'there are more crooks among the prison service than there are among the prisoners' (*Ulster*, October 1986) and 'let me tell you without fear of contradiction, there is no such thing as a loyalist Screw' (*Combat*, December 1977). However, very little explanation was offered as to why 'young Protestant patriots' were subject to beatings and intimidation by 'mercenary jailers' (*Combat*, August 1975). That said, although the ambiguities and contradictions of having the status of British prisoner rather than British soldier were hard to square for loyalists, the plight of prisoners was something that could be drawn upon as evidence of loyalist suffering. For example, a plea to support the loyalist prisoner welfare group, the Orange Cross and 'help to alleviate the discomfort and tedium of the long hours of imprisonment' came with the admonishment that 'if we had all stood shoulder-to-shoulder in 1969, they wouldn't be there now' (*Ulster Militant*, 30 September 1972).

Loyalists and republicans sought to prick the consciences of those on the outside through near constant reminders of the prisoners' plight. Letters from jail talked of poor conditions and brutal staff, whilst Christmas was noted as 'a time when the prisoners and their families torn apart by war are remembered' (*An Phoblacht*, 21 December 1982). For republicans the idea that prisoners were martyrs for their cause and the embodiment of wider suffering was something that was easier to present, not least because the policy of internment swept up far more Catholics than Protestants.

Between the introduction of internment in August 1971 and the end of the policy in December 1975, 1,981 people were detained, of whom 1,874 were Catholic (cain.ulst.ac.uk/events). The disparity reflects the differing levels of involvement in extra-constitutional action against the state between the communities, although 'many of those interned had no connection with the most active of republican organisations, the Provisional IRA. This was a reflection of the RUC's outdated intelligence, as well as the youth of most of those involved in the violence' (Guelke 2007: 279). However, even after internment ended and the number of prisoners declined, the idea that the prisoners were a potent symbol of a legitimate struggle was easier to pitch for republicans than for the loyalists imprisoned by their own state.

Undoubtedly the plight of being imprisoned for political actions was symbolically important for organisations. They were evidence of the injustices of a state that loyalists accused of selling out Northern Ireland and republicans decried as an illegitimate occupier. Political rather than criminal status was demanded as recognition of the legitimacy of the actions of these individuals and their wider movements. The political status of prisoners and their suffering at the hands of an 'unjust' state fed into narratives of loyalism as a noble cause betrayed and republicanism as an idea that had been forcibly repressed by its enemies. They could be used passively to invoke sympathy, guilt and indignation elsewhere. However, prisoners were not portrayed merely as victims, but also as activists.

Prison as an alternative battleground

It has been argued that the Provisional IRA dealt differently with prisoners, as compared with previous incarnations of the IRA who wrote them off as an isolated grouping in enemy hands. If the war was being fought outside then those incarcerated could not contribute and they could actually prove a liability if the experience of interrogation and imprisonment had led them to betray information to the security forces. However, in the 1970s prisoners became 'volunteers arranged on a different front' (Bowyer-Bell 2000: 10). Taking the war inside the prisons was in part a pragmatic response, as government policies of normalisation meant that the 'IRA was hemmed in on the outside', with the abandonment of special category status representing an opportunity to change tactics and 'take the war inside the prisons' (Smith 2002: 115). This alternative battleground also had the moral advantage over the arena of the street where casualties of the tactics favoured by the Provisional IRA during this period such as car bombs were often civilians (Hayes and McAllister 2001). In the gaols the IRA were unarmed prisoners who were pitted against the might of a coercive state institution.

Battling the justice system became another means of taking on the British. McEvoy (2000) argues that the policy of not recognising the court was dropped in 1976, after the Long War strategy was formulated, in response to the realisation that British withdrawal was not imminent. If the conflict was going to be protracted then volunteers should co-operate in their defence and aim for an acquittal. If they were not successful they could draw comfort from the fact that a full trial had been an expensive process, which fitted with the idea of an economic war that would drain the British exchequer. Constant challenges to prison rules and procedures, which were often supplemented by judicial review, were a way of checking the power of the prison authorities and, by extension, undermining their legitimacy.

Confronting the prison authorities and flouting their rules was a way of demonstrating that the prisoners could not be broken by British pressure. The tenth anniversary of the mass escape from HMP Maze in 1983 was marked with celebrations by republicans, amid the claim that it 'broke the illusion that the prisoners were powerless within the prison, at the mercy of the jailers, and was a most fitting response to the British government's futile attempts to imprison the Irish will to be free' (*An Phoblacht*, 23 March 1993).

The blanket and no-wash protests and the hunger strikes that followed the withdrawal of special category status were highly publicised campaigns by republican inmates and their actions were celebrated as a well-evolved strategy against the state. *Saoirse* (6 May 1983) argued that the death of the hunger strikers underlined 'the price to be paid for the winning of national liberation: the struggle of the prisoners cannot be divorced from that struggle'. On the tenth anniversary of the strike Bik McFarlane, the Officer Commanding at the time, wrote from prison:

> In the wider political arena the Hunger Strike reshaped the nature of the liberation struggle. Traditional strictures were shed as the Republican movement found a new political vibrancy, demolishing the British myth that we had little or no support, and moving forward with the people into a new era of struggle. (*An Phoblacht*, 2 May 1991)

The risks of a hunger strike meant such a strategy was a difficult one for the leadership outside prison to endorse initially, especially after the death of Frank Stagg in Wakefield Prison in 1976 brought no concessions on the policy of denying special category status to prisoners serving their sentences in Great Britain. Those in HMP Maze were determined to press on, believing that the 'IRA leadership was out of touch with the intensity of feeling in the prison' (Coogan 1995: 229). Subsequently, it has been claimed by a former prisoner that it was the leadership outside the prison which extended the hunger strike unnecessarily despite the offer of a deal (O'Rawe 2005). However, republicans within and beyond the gaols were sceptical of the value of British offers given that the 1980–81 hunger strike had been stopped once amid a government offer which subsequently proved unacceptable (Beresford and Maas 1997).

The differences between the prisoners and the leadership outside is something that will be explored further, but it is important to note that despite the complexities of the impact of the hunger strikes on the Provisional IRA and Sinn Fein, its role in the ideological development of the movement has rested in part on its construction of the foundations of the way the movement is now. The perception of the prisoners as leading the way in the activism that would lead to victory tapped into a narrative of unbroken morale and organised determination and a sense of unstoppable momentum.

Loyalists were also keen to stress that prisoners remained active and committed to the cause. This was a difficult task during the protests against the withdrawal of special category status. The UVF wanted to highlight the fact that they too had men 'on the blanket' but a letter from the commander of the H Blocks stated: 'I wish to make it absolutely clear that in no way whatsoever do we the UVF align ourselves with any forms of republican protest here in "H" Blocks' (*Combat*, 22 March 1979). A journal proclaiming support for the UDA celebrated the 'brave brothers' on blanket protest in a 'courageous stand for segregation and political status' (*Ulster*, 5 May 1979). The 'dirt-infested republicans' on the other hand were viewed as revolting and a condemnation framed in racist discourse raged, 'even the savage in darkest Africa observes their toilet instincts and what kind of animal fouls its own nest?' (*Ulster*, July 1978).

There was palpable frustration for loyalists protesting for political status, because of the belief that to the outside world the protests were the preserve of the republican movement, as evinced by a picture of HMP Maze on a front cover, accompanied by the question 'Long Kesh 1980 – Did you know this place contains loyalists too?' (*Ulster*, May 1980).

After the protests in the Maze subsided, loyalists always sought to stress that, far from suffering passively at the hands of the prison system, they were people who could 'let the world see that their spirit of resistance is not diminished by the long sentences meted out to them by a regime they fought to protect' and for whom the benefits associated with special category status were 'the fruits of many long years of deprivation by hunger strikes, blanket protests and fights for segregation, which were not the domain of the Provos regardless of what popular public opinion might think' (*Combat*, December 1990).

The problem was that resisting a legitimate prison service was a complicated task for loyalist prisoners. Allowing republicans to attack loyalists and forcing visitors to wait for excessively long periods were charges that were frequently levelled at prison officers. However, although peaceful protest against prisons conditions was presented as ineffective because 'heavy-handed prison warders' would use this as an excuse for violence (*Combat*, September 1993), the tactic was still employed.

'Prison reports' in the March 1994 edition of *Combat* informed readers that loyalist prisoners had refused to lock up on the previous New Year's Eve in protest at their treatment, but that they had done nothing more aggressive than engage in a karaoke competition. *Combat*, claiming to speak for the UVF, was clear that their prisoners were being unfairly punished by the state for crimes committed in its defence; that the conditions and treatment within gaols were unacceptable; and that prison officers who enforced this regime were not loyalists. However, beyond justifying flashpoints of violent protest or taunting individual prison officers judged to be particularly reprehensible, articles did not seem to resolve the issue of how to deal with imprisonment and poor treatment by one's own country without breaking out into full rebellion. However, it should be noted that of the twenty-nine prison officers killed during the conflict, two were casualties of loyalist violence (McEvoy 2001: 114). In both cases these deaths followed disturbances within loyalist wings.

As well as criticising the staff and procedures of the Maze, loyalists also had the option of stressing that they had a positive relationship with those running the prison, therefore implying that staff members were tacitly sympathetic to their cause. For example a UDA prisoner in 'Loyalist Prisoners' Page' compared the compounds at the Maze with the experiences of those imprisoned elsewhere. Being treated like an ODC meant poor morale and limited access to educational and recreational facilities, whereas the system practised in the H Blocks 'encourages both self-discipline and responsibility towards others, which leads to mutual respect for each other. In this way we gain respect from the prison authorities' (*Ulster* September 1987). 'The end of another era' was a historical overview of UVF prisoners' time in the Maze, printed after the announcement that prisoners were to be transferred to Maghaberry. The article informed readers that when loyalists were transferred to the Maze 'to begin their fully recognised political status' they ran their compounds as a disciplined military unit:

> Even when the republicans burned down the camp on the evening of Tuesday 14th October 1974 the LOYALIST POLITICAL PRISONERS lined up in full military formation and in full parade dress, handed over their compound intact to the army.

Indeed, it brought a response from one officer who remarked 'GIVE ME TWO BATTALIONS OF MEN LIKE THOSE AND THE IRA WOULD BE OUT OF BUSINESS IN A FORTNIGHT'. (*Combat*, October 1991)

Education and debate within prison

The idea that prison was a unique learning environment that created the leaders of the future is a particularly important feature of the Provisional IRA's and UVF's understanding of their role in Northern Irish political life. English argues that after the hunger strikes 'the culture of the jails remained one of dynamism and of activist energy and IRA prisoners saw themselves as very much still involved in and connected with the war being prosecuted by their comrades outside' (English 2003: 228). This fits with the view that in the long-term 'the prisons became a research department for the republican movement' (Bishop and Mallie 1987: 275).

It has also been argued that loyalist prisoners 'became a form of think tank for their organisations outside the prisons and were a vital ideological force behind the increased politicization of the loyalist paramilitaries in the late 1980s and early 1990s' (Von Tangen Page 2006: 95). The pivotal figure of UVF debate was the group's original leader, Augustus 'Gusty' Spence. Spence had been in prison since 1966 and he set himself up as a welcoming committee for the influx of prisoners in the early 1970s. His method 'was to foster an atmosphere that kept men alert by encouraging them to think about themselves, about why they were in prison, about ideas to improve their conditions' (Sinnerton 2002: 42). During the 1970s both *Republican News* and *Combat* broadcast the results of prison dialogue through the respective columns 'Long Kesh Notebook' and 'Behind the Wire'.

One important element of the prison experience for non-state combatants was access to education. It must be noted that Rocks (1985) found that these prisoners were not actually significantly more disposed to education than ODCs. Irwin (2003: 477) built on this study and argued that the difference for the paramilitaries was that their leaders 'carried out a training needs analysis on the prisoners and were given the autonomy to negotiate with the authorities over the curriculum on offer and pedagogy employed'. In addition to securing official prison education tailored to the prisoners' interests, leaders also organised classes on history, politics and cultural subjects such as the Irish language. This echoed the experience of republican internees at the Curragh during World War Two, who held their own language classes whilst imprisoned by the Irish government (Willis 2007).

Two important elements of ideologically coherent policy were developed in prison during the 1970s for the Provisional IRA: the Green Book and the Long War strategy. The Green Book outlined that the IRA were not just fighting for the withdrawal of the British, but for a specific type of united Irish state – a democratic socialist republic. However, the phrase 'greenbooked' referred to the training of recruits to withstand interrogation (Moloney 2002). The Green Book, therefore, outlined what republicans were fighting for, but its central importance came from its role as a tactical manual that complemented the cell system and allowed the IRA to withstand state pressure.

The idea of the Long War strategy was thrashed out by the internee Gerry Adams, and he rehearsed the main ideas in a series of articles in *Republican News* published under the pen name 'Brownie'. It seems prison gave Adams the space and time to formulate this ideological approach to resisting the British, which was founded on the notion that there was no imminent British withdrawal. However, 'the long war doctrine was really just a statement of the obvious' (Moloney 2002: 150). The Secretary of State for Northern Ireland during this period was Roy Mason who, in his own words, 'had been harassing the IRA with as much vigour as was legally acceptable in a liberal democracy' (Mason 1999: 174). The strategies and tactics that came out of cages nine and eleven, where future republican leaders such as Adams were held in Long Kesh, were the product of debate and analysis by the prisoners. However, it was not the case that prison gave Adams et al. a vantage point that allowed them to predict the future actions of the British: rather it gave them space to work out how to react to their current policies and find ways of insulating non-state combatants against their tactics.

Whilst the Long War and the Green Book were developing in Provisional IRA cages, UVF prisoners were subject to the attentions of Gusty Spence. His aim was to ask provocative questions that would prompt self-examination of motives and aims amongst the prisoners. Spence sought to establish that common cause could be found between republicans and loyalists in Northern Ireland if loyalists could acknowledge both an Irish element to their identity and a critique of the previous Stormont regime. He argued: 'In so far as people speak of fifty years of misrule, I wouldn't disagree with that. What I would say is this, that we have suffered every bit as much as the people of the Falls Road or any under-privileged quarter in many cases more so' (cited in Boulton 1973: 172).

Within prison Spence's ideas were translated into Irish history classes and, for a few prisoners, learning Irish. Negotiation and debate with republicans was also a key feature of the era, although in the Spence era it was members of the neo-Marxist Official IRA, on permanent ceasefire from 1972 onwards, who acted as intellectual sparring partners. Spence was dismissive of the Provisional incarnation of the republican movement, opining that 'the Provos didn't have a political agenda' (Garland 2001: 120). On a more practical note, the only real place to meet and debate with others was within Open University courses and the protesting Provisional IRA were absent from these classes from 1976. Therefore, the few UVF prisoners who enrolled for

Open University degrees only had the opportunity to thrash out their ideas with Official IRA inmates.

UVF compounds were run on military lines and prisoners lived within a structured and autocratic environment so there were definite opportunities for them to be schooled and trained. Literature on the development of UVF political thought within prison concentrates on the 1970s when Spence was the Officer Commanding with the authority to impose his programme on new arrivals. He assured his men that 'when the history of loyalists and Ulster comes to be written I am confident that the unbending Ulster Volunteers of Long Kesh shall rate a mention alongside the heroes of the Somme, Thiepval and Passchendale' (*Combat*, August 1975). Many of the inmates seemed to respond to this programme and articles appeared, such as 'A critical appraisal by a UVF prisoner of war' articulating the Spence-esque position that 'polarisation of the loyalist and republican communities plus the absence of dialogue between them' were causes of conflict (*Combat*, August 1975).

However, when Spence stepped down as Officer Commanding in 1979 due to ill health, his successor, Billy Hutchinson, was swiftly overthrown by a coup organised by newer members who were more militant than Spence et al. and favoured a more clearly military path for the UVF (Crawford 1999). The idyll of debate and self-analysis was diluted but remained active among several prominent loyalist prisoners.

The UDA did not have an equivalent of Gusty Spence on the inside. Within prison, the UDA's structure was looser than that of the more hierarchical UVF (Crawford 1999) and the UDA were less likely to engage in organised activities such as education. Whilst the UVF claim that 60 per cent of their prisoners gained qualifications in prison, the UDA figure has been recorded as 20 per cent (Irwin 2003).

The UDA were feted at different periods of the Troubles for producing the documents *Beyond the Religious Divide* (1979) and *Common Sense* (1987) under the auspices of the New Ulster Political Research Group. These were blueprints for a civic Ulster government (initially within an independent state) that would accommodate Catholics and Protestants (see also Chapter 6). The prime movers in these developments were not serving time. Political activists who had come through the trade union movement, such as Glenn Barr, and UDA leaders on the outside, including John McMichael and Andy Tyrie, were the driving force. For the UDA, the key 'achievement' beyond the defence of the constitutional position, its role in the Ulster Workers' Council strike of 1974, which brought down Northern Ireland's first devolved power-sharing government, and the publication of two important political documents, did not have much input from Long Kesh.

It must also be noted that policy documents and political activity such as the foundation of the Ulster Loyalist Democratic Party (later UDP) were only one element of an amorphous organisation which included many members who were completely hostile to such political activity. Given the diffuse nature of power within the UDA, which was reflected in the loose structure of UDA prisoners, the scope for prisoners to organise themselves into a think-tank and then transmit those ideas outside was limited.

The cells occupied by INLA prisoners were not feted as a place of evolving debates and strategising either. This is because neither the INLA nor the Irish Republican Socialist Party's (IRSP) position on politics or tactics changed significantly during the conflict. The original leader of the IRSP, Seamus Costello, presented his split from the Official IRA as the inevitable outcome of ideological differences. He 'was in constant touch with his colleagues in the Official IRA leadership, but still could not find common ground for his ambitions and analysis and direction of the politically minded and so withdrew to found the INLA' (Bowyer-Bell 2000: 220). He took with him members of the Official IRA in Derry, who were exasperated by the Dublin leadership's continuing progression towards complete non-violence (O'Dochartaigh 1997). The INLA stuck to a Marxist view of the conflict as the result of an imperialist power oppressing the Irish and creating a 'rotten little neo-colony' (*Starry Plough*, June 1988) on the island. Pronouncements from prison such as a letter from 'republican socialist POW [Prisoner of War]', Gary Adams, stuck with the need for a strategy of national liberation as 'this is of course one of the main tasks facing the revolutionary vanguard' (*Starry Plough*, February 1990).

Prisoners and leadership

Crucially, the INLA did not develop an established master plan either inside or outside jail for increasing support or achieving the group's aims. In academic discussions of republicanism, there is consensus that the INLA suffered from poor leadership. Costello himself has been depicted as an intelligent and able leader (English 2003; Holland and MacDonald 1994) but after his murder by the Official IRA in 1977 there was no-one of equal quality to succeed him. The foundation of the IRSP had attracted the support of Bernadette McAliskey who acted as an articulate and high-profile spokeswoman. However, she left within a year. The assassination of Thomas 'Ta' Power by the Irish People's Liberation Organisation (IPLO) in 1987 cost the INLA another significant political mind.

The INLA co-operated with the IRA during the hunger strike, with three of the ten dead being INLA men, and they generally enjoyed more cordial relations with them than with other republicans (Bowyer-Bell 2000; Kennedy-Pipe 1997). However, despite taking part in this seismic shift within republicanism, the INLA outside prison were not in a position to try to exploit it for political or tactical gain. During this period there was an influx of new members and some electoral success at local government level. However, Thomas McGlinchey, whose power was in the ascendancy within the INLA leadership in the period after the strikes, was someone with a commitment to action rather than political strategy (Coogan 1995) and the following years of murderous feuding, supergrass trials and informer infiltration meant that it was Sinn Fein who were able to build something of greater substance out of the legacy of the ten dead strikers. The INLA's membership was down to approximately one hundred by the mid-1980s (Arthur and Jeffery 1988) and so volatile that there was no leadership structure with which prisoners could join forces or gain influence.

The situation was different for the Provisional IRA. The broad sweep of internment meant that whilst the IRA's southern leadership were for the most part on the outside, northern members were much more likely to be in prison. The prisoners of cages nine and eleven, including Adams and Brendan Hughes, both interned in 1973, came up with plans to restructure the IRA and resist infiltration by the security services and these cages 'provided the nucleus of the Provisionals' Northern Leadership' (Taylor 1997: 198). The period of internment for Adams, from 1973 to 1977, demonstrated that prison could be a site of debate and strategising and showed that ideas could be produced within prison that could influence the tactical organisation of the IRA and provide ideological context for the movement, in this case the end goal of a socialist thirty-two county republic and the Long War necessary for its achievement. It could also act as an alternative power-base, giving the internees and prisoners of the mid-1970s the credibility and experience to challenge the current leadership.

The southern leaders' influence on *An Phoblacht* meant that what was happening in the Republic of Ireland gaols received as much attention as what happened in Long Kesh and Crumlin Road. 'Limerick and Portlaoise – Horror and Shame' alleged that unless there was a public inquiry, it would not be long before republicans were murdered in jail, as had happened in the civil war era (*An Phoblacht*, 12 December 1975) and the letters page documented horrors such as 'Torture in the Bridewell' (*An Phoblacht*, 16 April 1976). This difference in focus suggests a need to assert that those in the Republic of Ireland were witness to their fair share of suffering and to argue that the struggle was as much about overthrowing the 'collaborationist' southern government as it was driving the British out of Ireland.

Northern Ireland was the focus of *Republican News* and the prisoners were not just victims, they were an authority. When the journal urged a boycott of the constitutional convention elections of 1975 this was backed by a petition signed by the women of Armagh Gaol and a supportive letter from the prisoners of Long Kesh, advising 'remember Stormont' (*Republican News*, 26 April 1975). In addition, articles such as 'The British Strategy' by 'Solon' were part of a regular analysis of British intentions and policies in Northern Ireland coming directly from the prisons (*Republican News*, 27 March 1976). As Adams's successful ousting of conservative southern Provisionals from positions of power showed, prisoners were not just researchers for their movement: they could use their time in prison to challenge those in charge and prepare to take the reins themselves.

It was prisoners again who pushed for action during the hunger strikes, against the caution of those on the outside. In terms of motivation, hunger striking has been a tactic that republican prisoners made use of at different points of the movement's history. Sweeney (1993) argues that the roots of hunger striking as a symbolic act stretches back much further. He argues that it fits in with a long-held Irish cultural understanding of the power of self-sacrifice dating back to the pre-Christian era. McGarry and O'Leary argue that 'far from being victims of Ireland's cultural legacies they [the strikers] were exploiting them' (1995: 247). They criticise more romanticised views of the strike, where emotive language details how 'the hunger strikers died for a cause more ancient than the grey walls of Long Kesh Prison' (Beresford 1987: 430). They point out that Beresford's own study showed the prisoners only picking up Irish language and culture once they were inside those grey walls.

Aided by the implacability of Mrs Thatcher and the coincidence of a by-election in Fermanagh and Tyrone that resulted in the striker Bobby Sands becoming an MP shortly before his death, the strike gained international attention. It has been argued that the election of Sands changed the leadership's view on elections and that 'when they saw the masses of nationalists prepared to go to the funerals of hunger strikers and the thirty thousand who voted for Sands, they realised that the basis existed for a sizeable mass movement' (Mallie and McKittrick 1996: 20). Wichert (1991) argues that once this strategy of electioneering was in place, the republican movement was inexorably driven further from the military path because elections used up resources and activism was downplayed to broaden the potential pool of support. Therefore the consequences of the strike were unforeseen and possibly unintended.

Moloney points out that the decision as to whether or not republicans should stand for election had always been a pragmatic issue so it was the fact that the result of the hunger strikes was a strategy of permanent electoralism that was the real change: 'the scale of the flip-flop was huge' (Moloney 2002: 202). However, English argues northern leaders had already decided that the purely military approach to the situation was not the best way to advance their cause. Therefore, according to English, the hunger strike was 'an unintended *accelerator* of a process already favoured by the leadership' (English 2003: 206). He contends that the prisoners opposed this strategy: to them the thousands following coffins and voting for Sands were thousands of people who the British government had blithely ignored. English's view does seem to be corroborated by the 'comm' (prison letter) smuggled out from the Maze to the outside leadership signalling their acceptance that the strikes had run their course, arguing: 'One of the primary lessons to emerge from this phase of our protests is that the nationalist minority in N. Ireland [sic] are politically incon-sequential and impotent in the context of the six county statelet. That point is very important despite the electoral successes.'

When the tenth anniversary of the strike was marked in *An Phoblacht*, the editorial declared that as a result of the strike 'Britain lost. The British offensive was turned back; republicanism rose again' (*An Phoblacht*, 2 May 1991). Many of those who served sentences for IRA activities would agree, but it is notable that an article in the prisoners' own journal argued that the electoral path the strikes opened up had not been the right one to take because 'reliance upon electoralism as our primary political thrust has shown up its limitations' and had in fact prevented mass mobilisation north and south (*An Glor Gafa*, Summer 1991). Republicanism was now obliged to seek its mandate from the living rather than the dead of 1916–19.

The prison issue that replaced political status in the period after the hunger strikes was strip-searching. There were other campaigns, notably against extra-dition of prisoners, but strip-searching was the most constant source of outrage as regarded the prisoners and it was seen as a particular issue for female prisoners, though not exclusively so. It was presented as another way in which the British authorities exerted control and used their own procedures to oppress republicans and a form of 'institutionalised sexual abuse' (*An Phoblacht*, 11 January 1990).

However, whilst the campaign against strip-searching was a constant, it never dominated republican rhetoric in the way that the campaign for political status had. For example, in a 1985 issue of *An Phoblacht*, the article 'Abhorrent searches in Magilligan' which detailed the use of strip and anal cavity search as a tool of humiliation and control, was half the size of the piece on 'Sectarian Threats at Shorts', deploring the intimidation of Catholic factory workers (*An Phoblacht*, 12 September 1985).

The period after the hunger strikes showed the change regarding the importance of prisoners and the struggle in prison in another way. Their authority on prison matters was firmly established, but compared with the 1970s, where *Republican News* had referred to the prisoners as arbiters and thinkers on many matters, they were not often called upon to pronounce on matters outside prison walls. 'Prisoners Refute Faul' reported that female prisoners would continue to refuse to co-operate with the Lifers' Review Board in direct contradiction to claims by the prison chaplain Denis Faul, the priest who many prisoners blamed for encouraging parents to take their sons off hunger strike (*An Phoblacht*, 17 April 1986). 'Magiligan Visit Protests' covered prisoner boycotts of the new visiting system, which they said denied them privacy. The article stated 'the protest may prevent prisoners from seeing their families for a considerable time but the republican prisoners believe it is their only option' (*An Phoblacht*, 15 January 1987). The prisoners were therefore the authority on prison matters and the official organ of the provisional republican movement reported on their decisions and strategies. However, these related for the most part just to what went on in prison, the two key issues being strip-searching and extradition.

In terms of leadership potential, the prisoners showed in the hunger strike that they did not need the permission of colleagues on the outside to implement their chosen tactics. The genesis of the Long War strategy during internment marked prison out as an alternative power-base from which Adams et al. developed a successful challenge to the existing leadership of the provisional republican movement. However, that challenge was not repeated after the southern leadership had been defeated. Prisoners retained their moral authority within the movement, but their leadership role seemed limited to managing resistance to policies that affected them directly and to rising up the ranks, using the fruits of prison debate and education, through Sinn Fein after their release.

The scope of prisoners' authority also diminished during the 1980s for the UVF. Bruce contends that the era of political debate and education in prison had a limited impact on the ideology and strategy of the UVF and that even at the height of Spence's pre-eminence, the leadership outside 'was dominated by people who thought he had gone soft' (Bruce 2001: 73). The 'Behind the Wire' column faded into obscurity and replacements such as 'Prisoners' Viewpoint' and 'Prison Principles' focused more on prison conditions and issues such as the campaign to segregate HMP Magilligan. Nelson (1984) contends that the indifference of the UVF leadership did not stop the prisoners viewing their organisation as a socially progressive force who could undertake a war that would be just and legitimate. Spence's programme only had a genuine impact on a select number of individuals and did not appear to alter the aims or strategy of the UVF on the outside. However, the basic thrust of Spence's belief in the scope for common ground between working-class republicans and loyalists would be the template for the ideological path pursued by political representatives of the UVF once the peace process steered the organisation towards a ceasefire.

The decentralised nature of the UDA both inside and outside prison meant that it was difficult to channel support for ideological change or to offer an alternative leadership to the organisation. The key shift in the UDA's presentation in the 1980s of its political philosophy was the diminution of its commitment to an independent Ulster. When the UDA leader John McMichael launched the Ulster Loyalist Democratic Party in 1981 he argued that 'more and more of our people will realise that they've a separate identity from being Irish and from being British' (*Marxism Today*, December 1981). However, the party's manifesto committed Northern Ireland to a position within the United Kingdom and therefore represented a retreat from the demand for independence, a policy that had laid the UDA open to criticisms that it was a 'prod Sinn Fein' (Bruce 1992: 233). This change came about because UDA leaders such as McMichael and Andy Tyrie gauged reaction outside their group to their ideas about an independent Ulster, rather than because they faced a challenge to their leadership from an organised coterie of prisoners.

Ideological development and imprisonment

The eruption of conflict in Northern Ireland at the end of the 1960s led to many men and women serving time, either as convicted prisoners or internees, in Northern Ireland and Great Britain. Christmas appeals in publications associated with non-state combatants underlined the personal sacrifices made by those inside and poems by prisoners were a means of expressing the misery of separation from loved ones. 'Visit', for example, includes the verse 'stolen life/bitter pain/of a loving wife/and poor wain' (*An Glor Gafa*, Spring 1993).

Time in prison also carried the danger of political, as well as personal isolation, and there were no guarantees that an imprisoned member of a non-state combatants group would not be cut off from the decision-making processes of his or her group. However, isolation from the mainstream of events had definite advantages. The IRA's truce of 1974–75 ended with the southern leadership of the republican movement being discredited (Bew, Gibbon and Patterson 2002). The truce had been called because of confidence that the British would soon be on their way out of Ireland. When it became apparent that this was not the case it was easier to accuse those in the south of being out of touch. Part of Adams's prison rethink was a blueprint for a Northern Command that would carry out military operations while the Southern Command would deal with supplies. Isolated from the mistakes being made on the outside, prison gave Adams time to design a new IRA structure that would protect the organisation from the British and wrest control of the IRA from the Southern old guard.

Isolation also allowed prisoners to say and do things that would have earned them swift condemnation or worse in a more public arena. Reaching out to nationalists was a dangerous business for a unionist politician. William Craig, head of the Vanguard Party, ended up crushing the life out of what had been an increasingly popular movement when he suggested an expedient alliance with the SDLP during the Northern Ireland Constitutional Convention of 1975. Away from the public eye, Gusty Spence and other members of the UVF felt free to engage with republican prisoners in dialogue as an aid to the development of ideas.

The first years of imprisonment provided a rich array of images of both suffering and resistance that could be used as emblems of the cause being fought. Prisoners were presented by their groups as victims and martyrs, but also as resilient and committed to continuing activism. This early period also made the prisons central to the struggle by non-state combatants to establish the legitimacy of their goals and methods because the expedient introduction of special category status and its subsequent withdrawal opened up an opportunity to define non-state combatants activity as explicitly political and as the expression of valid aims and aspirations.

The four groups that are the focus of this study were non-state combatants groups who espoused extra-constitutional violence as a justifiable means to an end. However all four of them had developed a political party by the end of the 1970s. The Provisional IRA was complemented by Sinn Fein and Seamus Costello's split from the Official IRA in 1974 was signified by the foundation of the IRSP, with the INLA's existence revealed only months later. UDA members articulated the viability of Ulster nationalism firstly through the New Ulster Political Research Group (NUPRG) and then a political party, the Ulster Loyalist Democratic Party (ULDP). The UVF made three attempts to maintain a political party. Although the Ulster Loyalist Front and Volunteer Political Party were short-lived, the Progressive Unionist Group (formed in 1977) became the Progressive Unionist Party that guided the UVF through the peace process. This commitment by all four groups to political activity suggests that the groups were not just reacting to events and were interested in ideological development. However, this evolution and the role of prisoners within it varied between organisations.

Education and debate were both clear features of the IRA prison experience. In the first years of imprisonment prison was a place where strategies were formulated and long-term plans made. Despite its common status as a training manual, the Green Book produced by the prisoners did serve as a primer for republican politics. In articulating a vision of a democratic and socialist Republic of Ireland, this document gave members a clear understanding of what they were fighting to achieve. It served as the template for the manifesto that would replace the federalism of Sinn Fein's previous Eire Nua policy and in so doing was part of the successful plan to wrest control of the provisional republican movement from the old guard in the south.

From within the prison, the campaign to reinstate special category status developed a momentum beyond that which those on the outside were initially prepared to risk. Prisoners took the initiative and stuck to their strategy. The capability of prisoners to organise protest and challenge prison authority meant that those in jail could present themselves as soldiers fighting on a different front. However, the sympathy and broader support the strikes engendered encouraged the determination of the leadership on the outside to pursue the 'republican opening of the 'second front' of electoral politics from 1982 onwards', a change of tactics that reflected 'a recognition of the need to diversify tactics and mobilise a wider section of Irish nationalists than the small number of supporters of outright militarism' (McAuley, McGlynn and Tonge 2008: 95). The leadership was committed to fighting on this battleground, despite the reservations about the implications of this from some members of the movement, including prisoners.

It is clear that within the provisional republican movement a process of defining goals and redefining tactics took place after the IRA's negotiations with the British government in 1972 failed to secure any indication of intention to withdraw from Northern Ireland. Many prisoners were central to this project and the struggle within prison was a touchstone for the movement in the 1970s and early 1980s. However, this acceptance of the need to broaden support, prepare for a longer campaign and designate activities other than military operations as an equally important part of an overall war was driven by the reality of British military strength and the political will of successive governments to maintain the integrity of the United Kingdom.

The INLA did not carry out the same process of redefinition. The group started out with a Marxist analysis of the conflict and stuck to this viewpoint. What was happening was a war of national liberation, the successful conclusion of which would be followed by implementation of a socialist state. The INLA looked for a broad front within republicanism and the campaign for political status was seen as the highpoint of republican unity by members because 'The H Block Committee demonstrated the benefits of broad front activity. There is no reason why such broad front committees cannot be formed again' (*Saoirse*, 6 May 1983). However, the INLA remained a tiny grouping, and despite a stated commitment to Marxist ideology, academic literature on the INLA tends to records their deeds rather than their thoughts. Atrocities, such as the murder of churchgoers in Darkley, or the no-warning bomb at the Droppin' Well Bar in Ballykelly, loom larger than policies and publications. Arthur and Jeffery (1988) argue that the IRSP were always a minor element of the organisation and that the emphasis was clearly on the military. There is a definite consensus that the organisation suffered from poor leadership and without the ability to maintain unity within the organisation or the willingness to adapt or scale down aims, there was little desire for ideological evolution.

The UDA was an amalgamation of many smaller groups and even after its official inception it was 'still very much a set of local organisations that lacked any clear strategy' (Bew and Patterson 1985: 64). The defining event of those early years for the UDA was not the protest for special category status but the Ulster Workers' Council strike of 1974. The UDA appeared to gain political coherence through the NUPRG's proposal for an independent Ulster and a civic Ulster nationalism which would 'encourage the development of a common identity between all of our people regardless of religion' (NUPRG 1979). However, the UDA remained a decentralised grouping and included many people with no political motivations or interests. The structure of its compound in the Maze reflected this loose arrangement and there was arguably less scope here for a programme of education or a commitment to debate.

The UVF also contained many members who saw military action as the sole *raison d'etre* for a paramilitary group. However, both inside and outside prison there was political activity related to the championing of the common interests of working-class people in Northern Ireland and a critical appraisal of the role and worth of mainstream unionist politicians. Political activity remained an optional extra for the UVF, but the 1970s did provide a training ground for the political representatives of the organisation in future years.

Conclusion

Special category status was brought in as a matter of expedience by the British government, but was seized upon by the INLA, IRA, UDA and UVF as proof of the political status of those imprisoned for paramilitary activities. These organisations all sought to stress the legitimacy of the actions undertaken by those who ended up in jail. Legitimacy was also proclaimed by presenting the prisoners as martyrs for the cause whose suffering was emblematic of the pains of the wider community. Prisoners themselves were keen to show that they were not marginalised by their sentences. Instead, they were engaged in education and debate that allowed them to visualise the society that would emerge from their struggle. In this way they could act as a research department for their leadership or become leaders themselves. However, not all prisoners engaged in this process and there were tensions between those on the outside and those in prison.

In the early years of the conflict, as internment swelled prison numbers and then hunger strikes made events in prison the focus of international attention, all four groups remained officially committed to the idea that they could achieve an outright victory. Common identities, based on class or the civic citizenship of an Ulster or Irish nation-state, were proclaimed as a means of reconciling a divided society once that victory had been achieved. However, some elements in the thinking of the UVF and IRA did lend themselves to later ideas of conflict transformation. Spence's commitment to dialogue with republican prisoners signalled the possibility of pursuing political ends through means other than violence and of recognising to an extent the legitimacy of opposing aspirations. For the IRA, prison became a different battleground and the republican movement then espoused electoral politics as another front in the campaign against the British. These alternative arenas allowed for a shift and the reconciliation of opposition to the British presence with the growing realisation that violent conflict was not going to achieve republican goals in the near future.

5 Political and tactical change among former prisoners

The contribution of paramilitary prisoners to conflict transformation remains a surprisingly under-stated aspect of the Northern Ireland peace process. Amid the focus upon an ambitious consociational deal between nationalist and unionist politicians and examination of the roles played by the British, Irish and American governments, the actions of those who 'fought the war' in bringing about its end have attracted far less analysis. Yet prisoners played a significant role in creating conditions for peace.

Republican prisoners moved away from the 'self-inflicted theological inertia' which had impaired durable political progress (Adams 2005: 122) whilst loyalist political leadership emerged as a consequence of prison experiences (Gallaher 2007; Garland 2001; Gormley-Heenan 2007). Having played constructive roles in developing the peace process, former prisoners have subsequently demonstrated an ability to defuse inter-community tension and, on the republican side, have radically altered their relationship with the British state. Former prisoners have utilised the organisational capacity and structures of paramilitary groups and developed these as agents of conflict transformation. 'Management systems' and structures evidently mobilised to engage in violence were reoriented towards developing positive community roles in respect of restorative justice, opposition to violence and reducing sectarian tensions at interfaces. Concurrently, former prisoners and their representative groups have developed client relations with the local state, in the search for funding for local conflict transformation and reconciliation projects (Shirlow and McEvoy, 2008).

These radical developments have been facilitated by dialogue initiated by former prisoners, on an inter-communal basis through meetings with former prisoners on the opposing side and via intra-group dialogue. Former prisoners have attempted to persuade militants of the need for conflict transformation and peaceful methodologies. This chapter traces the evolution of ideological and political development among former prisoners during the peace process, beginning with an assessment of their curious frequent omission from analyses of conflict transformation in Northern Ireland.

Written out of the script? How the role of prisoners has been overlooked

Subjective and objective reasons exist for the near-exclusion of prisoners from analyses of the development of the peace process. Subjective factors include hostility to combatants; opposition to violence and a reluctance to attribute credit for ending the conflict to those regarded as instigators. Objective reasons for the concentration on other aspects of the peace process include the startling nature of the power-sharing deal between long-term opponents; the importance of the British-Irish inter-governmental axis and the exogenous contributions of the United States government and the European Union. Indeed, there is a lack of academic consensus over whether the primary causes of the peace process were mainly internal to Northern Ireland, based either upon carefully orchestrated choreography by the British and Irish governments working with local political parties (Aughey 2005; Dixon 2008; Tonge 2005, 2006), or influenced by a wider global contexts which diminished Northern Ireland's strategic value (Cox 2006; Ryan 1994; 1997); or shaped by policy learning from international peace processes (Guelke 2008).

Existing explanations of the peace process, even when rooted in internal causes, tend to look beyond the contributions made by prisoners, instead exploring elite-level inter-governmental brokerage or government-party relations (e.g. Dixon 2008; O'Kane 2007; Peatling 2004); or party change (Tonge 2005) or military fortunes (e.g. Moloney 2002; Taylor 1997, 2000, 2002). The exclusion of prisoners from narratives of the peace process is particularly surprising given the importance of their release within the terms of the Good Friday Agreement and the significance of earlier events in the gaols (Shirlow and McEvoy 2008). Most prisoners developed their political ideas within the gaols having entered as novices. The majority of those incarcerated were between the ages of nineteen and twenty-five at the time of their arrest (Crothers 1998). The lack of emphasis upon former political prisoners is also contingent upon other factors such as the constant media engagement that prioritises criminal elements, the limited focus of academics who studied such groups from afar (if at all) and also the issue of trust required to access such groups. Despite issues of confidentiality, former prisoner groups feel aggrieved that studies of them by academics have been based more upon the building of academic careers rather than offering analysis, even critical evaluation, which aids the wider process of conflict transformation. It could also be argued that the fascination of some writers with non-state combatant violence has meant that an evaluation of post-conflict activities and conflict transformation has been overlooked.

The organisation of prisoners into their own wings of the gaols during the early years of the conflict; the formulation of the republican Long War and Left Turn strategies; the ousting of the 'old guard' conservative original IRA leadership and the rejection of criminalisation amid prolonged struggle for special category status, with its seismic impact upon the electoral outlook of republicans, were all developments which fermented within the prisons and impacted upon ideological development. Given the authority and respect afforded to prisoners within areas of core republican and loyalist support and the status of prisons as sites of struggle, it appears improbable that prisoners could fail to be crucial agents of the peace process. Whilst the peace process was developed by political elites, the insistence, as one former IRA inmate put it, that there has 'always been a tendency from ourselves in the gaol not to accept at face value whatever leadership people may say' indicates the need to avoid one-dimensional, top-down accounts of the development of peace. This does not rule out the possibility of a movement's leadership outside prison duping the prisoners in terms of the essential components of the peace process, as claimed in two accounts of republican change (McIntyre, 2008; Moloney 2002), but makes such duplicity a formidable task. The process aspect of peace required a sustained commitment from former prisoners in the buying of the consequences for themselves and the selling of the advantages of conflict cessation to those still inclined to sustain conflict. Negotiating skills acquired through bartering with prison authorities were transferred to alternative areas after release, such as interface work or defusing the potential for violence during contentious parades.

Prisoners were obvious beneficiaries of the Good Friday Agreement and their release was instrumental to the deal being clinched. The pace of prisoner releases increased during the peace process. In demanding the freeing of the remaining 380 Irish republican prisoners in the year prior to the Agreement, Sinn Fein (1997: 14) stressed that 'international experience shows that is imperative for the issue of political prisoners to be addressed during the process of conflict resolution'. Of these prisoners, seventy-three were serving life sentences and eighty were serving sentence of twenty years or longer. In April 1998, as Sinn Fein's *ard fheis* debated the Agreement, one-in-seven of the motions concerned prisoners, or 'political hostages' as they were termed; in 1999 this figure fell to a mere three of the eighty-seven conference motions and by the 2000 event, with the gaols emptied and republican former prisoners having been released to warm receptions within their community, there were no such motions and the party's 'Prisoner-of-War' department closed soon afterwards (Sinn Fein 1998, 1999, 2000). Many IRA prisoners were to maintain their 'struggle' via the offices of Sinn Fein.

Intra-group ideological change – from what sort of ideology?

The former republican prisoner, Anthony McIntyre (1995, 2001, 2008) suggests that the leadership compromises of the peace process were facilitated by a lack of ideological depth among the Provisional republican movement. His interpretation suggests the prisoners were part of a predominantly situational rather than ideological organisation, most of them incarcerated in response to the political circumstances of 1969–72, rather than through fidelity to the Easter Rising of 1916 or the First Dail of the Irish Republic of 1918–19. On this assessment, mass recruitment to the Provisional IRA (the growth of which surprised even its leaders) was primarily as a response to the excessive force of, initially, the B Specials and the Royal Ulster Constabulary (RUC), soon followed by the British Army, with IRA numbers increasing steadily until the nadir of British security policy, the killing of fourteen civilians on Bloody Sunday, in 1972. Loyalism has been seen as similarly reactive phenomena, constructed originally as a defensive reaction to the rise of republicanism at the beginning of the 1970s (Wood 2003).

Provisional IRA prisoners may indeed initially have been influenced far more by the immediacies of hitting back at perceived oppressors than by the Holy Grail of the indivisible Irish Republic. Moreover, the ideological justification offered by IRA prisoners for participation in the conflict may have been retrospective and flimsy, was theoretically under-developed (Alonso 2006) and, as such, 'might not have had all the isms on it' (IRA male). Nonetheless, the IRA's armed campaign continued for over two decades beyond Bloody Sunday, longevity surely unattainable if commitment was lacking, or if violence was mere reaction to security force excesses. The accounts of McIntyre and Alonso both tend to conflate the republican leadership (who were committed to the ideals of 1916 from the outset of IRA) with the led (who developed their commitment) and also minimise the extent of ideological development which occurred within prison. Loyalist paramilitarism was also bereft of 'isms', but was based upon a strategic view that only by 'terrorising' republicans would the IRA's war cease. Whilst an ideological lack-of-depth and lack of political sophistication were apparent, the enduring nature of the conflict, despite the possibility of cessation during the mid-1970s, suggests that situational explanations are necessary but insufficient explanations of the Long War. It was those IRA members and prisoners who had *opposed* the leadership's temporary ceasefires of the mid-1970s who were to become the strongest advocates of a permanent cessation of hostilities during the 1990s and beyond (Moloney 2002).

A small number of IRA's ordinary members did connect the events of 1969–72 with broader ideological and historical contexts from the outset. One IRA former prisoner from Andersonstown in West Belfast, who found that the fiftieth anniversary of the Easter Rising in 1916 stimulated some interest in republicanism, but did not feel sufficiently motivated to join the IRA until after Bloody Sunday, argued that it was 'a split call between ideology and a sequence of events giving me ideology'. For him, a 'united Ireland was Brits Out' and therefore the answer to the problems of perceived repression was the independent country demanded in republican orthodoxy. Less than one-quarter of other former prisoners claimed republican family lineage and generational transmission was a minor element of the rebirth of the IRA. The Provisional IRA was a 'new' IRA, but one also containing some members keen to reactivate a dormant family history of which they had hitherto been only vaguely conscious.

The reactive nature, defenderist attitudes and 'military' actions of the IRA produced charges – from a wide spectrum - of sectarian motivations (Walsh 1994). Imprecision in the deployment of the term 'sectarian' confuses the issue and the charge has sometimes been rejected even by those otherwise critical of the IRA campaign (English 2003). Some IRA members appeared sectarian in their stereotypical assessments of loyalists and loyalism, but these perceptions were not religious derivatives. As a female Belfast former IRA prisoner put it: 'It infuriates me that that the IRA were [claimed to be] in a sectarian war. It never felt like it was legitimate to kill someone simply because they were a Protestant. However, I felt it was completely legitimate to kill someone because they were in the UDR or the RUC.'

Nonetheless, some former prisoners concede sectarian impulses to the campaign, one such acknowledger declaring:

> the sectarianism was there ... Protestants were a target in the eyes of people ... I mean there was a stage in my life when I could have justified the IRA bombing bars and killing Protestants ... as far as I'm concerned it was a tactical military operation from the IRA that went in deliberately and bombed that bar to sort a problem out. Our people were getting slaughtered, the IRA then wiped out twelve or thirteen in the mini bus. I mean I argued that that was a military operation and they went down and solved the particular problem within the border triangle area (IRA male).

Few former prisoners cite the Catholic Church as a crucial element in their political formation at any stage during the conflict. Some display hostility to the Catholic Church for, as an IRA urban woman former prisoner claimed, 'letting our people down big time' with a lack of support (this prisoner was sharply critical of the Church's failure to condemn strp-searches) but indifference was a more common response.

Amid the mix of situationists and ideologues forming the IRA, one final category of member tends to be overlooked in the literature, Dooley's (2004) work providing a useful exception – those born outside Ireland and thus not normally directly affected by the situations supposed to have fuelled IRA membership. This republican 'tradition' has considerable historical lineage (e.g. James Connolly) and one of the Provisional IRA's founders, Sean MacStiofain, had not even visited Ireland until an adult. Several London bombings were ascribed to English-born IRA personnel, whilst a small number joined the IRA after becoming interested amid the echoes of the Northern Ireland problem evident in the West of Scotland. As one such joiner observed: 'you could be the same as most of the ones in Glasgow, sit in a bar and sing "Tiocfaidh ar la" [the republican slogan, 'Our day will come'] or do something positive or maybe give assistance and I just sort of made a decision.'

Given the importance of ideas of 'hitting back' at the enemy which fuelled republican and loyalist prisoners, it is evident that most ideological development occurred mainly after imprisonment. Ideological formation, which involved the deepening of the very thin republican set of ideas held at imprisonment, has been criticised by Alonso (2006) as the construction of a spurious justification of a cruel and pointless paramilitary campaign, which continued retrospectively even after release from prison. Within the gaols, there developed arguments in favour of local socialist politics amid a realisation that militarism was ultimately inadequate. Prisoners tended to view political work as having begun before electoral campaigning and vote-seeking. As a female West Belfast IRA former prisoner, gaoled several times, explained: 'The political started for me whilst the military [campaign] was still going on, by being involved in the likes of tenants' associations, when you knew that there was still nothing being done for your communities.' Such community activism raised problems. At one level the IRA was attempting to destroy the state, but at grassroots level, republicans were increasingly engaging the local state, attempting to shape it in their interests; a model eventually transferred upwards to the national level in respect of the government of Northern Ireland. The fusion of electoral politics and armed struggle as necessary dual components began in the gaols, but required the difficulty combination of maximising vote-seeking whilst supporting violence. The final stage of republican ideological development was the questioning of some aspects of traditional republican orthodoxy, demoting supposed principles to tactics and creating space for an embryonic peace process and marking a rapid retreat from the revolutionary leftism of the 1980s.

What characterised these phases of ideological and political development was their transience and many aspects of republican political development seen as central can be viewed properly as mere adjuncts. As an obvious example, the short-lived nature of the left-wing shift among the Provisionals leads to scepticism over its depth (Patterson 1997; Walsh 1994). Indeed the leftist posturing of the late 1970s and early 1980s was eventually displaced by a Sinn Fein political programme which, whilst left of centre, is bereft of revolutionary pretensions, ditched amid the prospect of entrance into government during the 1990s. Nonetheless, most former prisoners continue to eschew the label of nationalist, preferring to label themselves as republicans or socialist republicans. Republican former combatants usually define nationalism as the uniting of Ireland and socialism as the creation of an ideal political and economic system within a united Ireland, but there is little clarity on how either is to be attained. Given the explicit rejection of Marxism by Gerry Adams, who insisted in the late 1970s that 'there is no Marxist influence in Sinn Fein' (*Hibernia*, 25 October 1979), allied to the earlier hostility to the far-left of the Provisionals at formation, it appears that leftism was an ideological adjunct, rather than a central aspect, of Provisional Irish republicanism. Transient Marxism was more important in terms of the direction of the IRA and Sinn Fein. The temporary adoption of strongly left-wing rhetoric allowed the northern leadership of the movement to distance itself from the conservatism of the republican leadership of the 1970s, whilst the seeds of abandonment of strident leftism during the 1980s caused friction and the threat of a breakaway group among gaoled republicans.

Whilst ideological debates provided the main source of prison discussions, there were also internal differences among republicans over tactics within the gaols. Even the ultimate example of republican struggle, the ten hunger strike deaths of 1981, has been subject to revisionist criticism from a former prisoner (O'Rawe 2005). Although essentially an egalitarian environment, a hierarchy of prisoners existed. For example, those opting to wear prison uniform were described as 'squeaky-booters' (a reference to the noise made by their prison-issue boots) by other republican inmates maintaining 'no-wash protests' and other forms of non-compliance with the attempt to treat politically motivated offenders as ordinary criminals (Stevenson 1996). These divisions largely dissipated amid the more relaxed prison regime of the 1990s, under which much greater associational and recreational freedoms were permitted.

Loyalist paramilitarism was presented by its exponents as a continuation of historical assertions of the defence of Ulster; the changes wrought by the peace process were also presented as continuity rather than departure from previous principles. For loyalists, a cessation of violence required fewer accompanying political changes than those demanded of republicans. The UVF located itself within the tradition of the defence of Ulster by all means necessary; with the Union secured under the Good Friday Agreement, continued violence was unnecessary. As a more community-oriented organisation, reflecting its origins as an amalgamation of local 'defence units' (Harris 2008), the standing down of the UDA was more difficult and violence at sectarian interfaces continued beyond 'official' paramilitary ceasefires. For both organisations, however, violence was portrayed as reactive, part of a defence of Northern Ireland from a republican offensive to absorb the Protestant community into a united Ireland. As a male UDA respondent put it, ideological development was limited because the UDA 'didn't set out to do anything other really than defend'. The logical conclusion from such a reactive ideology was that when the IRA ceased violence, loyalists would be similarly obliged to discontinue.

The 'hitting back' which infused Provisional republicanism was evident within loyalist paramilitarism, a process of returning the serve to republicans (Taylor 2000). Yet given the frequent inability of loyalists to target republicans directly, there was also a proactive element of community deterrence involved in violence, a strategy of creating fear among Catholics to inhibit them from supporting the IRA.

As with republicans, loyalist former prisoners are anxious to claim that their activities were part of a campaign based upon attainment of a desired constitutional outcome, rather than the outworking of a sectarian ideology. Moreover, loyalists argued that shared prison experience had further dissipated the sectarian animosity. Thus a male UVF respondent insisted:

> I was never sectarian. There were about ten Catholic families in our village and I would never let anyone harm them. I had a lot of Catholic friends who were totally stunned by my arrest. But in another sense prison and education brought me into more deep contact with Catholics and with republicans in particular, so you'd get to understand their point of view, what drove them ... and their side of the story from prison. It probably opened my mind up a bit more.

An embryonic peace process required the transfer of the fusion of mutual respect but continuing ideological antipathy which characterised inter-communal relations among prisoners to the arena of conflict outside, to bring the war to a conclusion amid a claimed maintenance of principles.

The context of political compromise

By the mid-1980s, many republican combatants were sceptical of the possibility of outright military victory. The attrition of the Long War had been complemented, first by 'active abstentionism', involving engagement with community, but not institutional, politics, then by electoralism from the early 1980s. However, the electoral ceiling of the 'armalite and ballot box' strategy was evident by the end of that decade, given common Irish nationalist rejection of violence. Republicans sought further political advancement via a shift from violence. For loyalists, a combination of restructuring and collusion with the security forces led to their revival at the end of the 1980s and a belief that they could defeat the IRA. Nonetheless, this view was juxtaposed with a wider questioning of the functionality of armed conflict as a consequence of experiential reasoning. Prison, according to one loyalist prisoner, was an arena in which:

> everything is questioned, your cause is questioned, you question yourself, you question your society. Loyalist violence was looked upon as a necessity. I would say the purpose of Loyalist violence was to maintain the Union – simple, cut and dried. But then you began to question whether violence was the best way to go about it. (Quoted in Green 1998: 21)

Whilst it might seem logical to deduce from the shift from armed conflict that a mutually hurting stalemate had been reached – a common contributor to peace processes (e.g. Cochrane 2008; Darby and MacGinty 2003; Ramsbotham et al. 2005; Zartman 2003a) this was *not* the conclusion of those incarcerated in the Northern Ireland conflict. Loyalists believed that they were winning the war, whilst republican prisoners came to believe that greater transformative possibilities were possible through non-violence and that the advancement of 'their' community's interests could be furthered by peace. The republican perspective has been seen as a political fig-leaf, the so-called 'new phase of struggle' designed to cover retreat amid the stark failure to achieve the overarching goal of a united Ireland (McIntyre 1995). By the 1990s, the IRA was struggling to recruit new members; prisoners on temporary release became cognisant of the societal changes which were deghettoising nationalist communities (Bean 2007) and those prisoners became aware that many of those imprisoned were 'returnees rather than new recruits' (IRA male). Beyond the gaols, the IRA's campaign during the 1990s can be interpreted in two contrasting ways; the first perspective views the IRA's efforts as the last 'hurrah' of a largely spent organisation whose attempts to take the 'war' to the 'enemy' largely failed (McGladdery 2006; Moloney 2002); the second interpretation sees the IRA's tactics, notably the major bombings of economic targets in London and Manchester, as a strategic use of violence designed to force republican entry into political negotiations, the outcome of which, it was understood by all sides, would not yield a united Ireland, but would create some gains for republicans (Murray and Tonge 2005; Smith 2005).

Loyalist former prisoners tend to contextualise the onset of peace within a framework of a successful 'offensive' against the IRA during the late 1980s and early 1990s, with loyalist killings outstripping those committed by the IRA by 1992. The stepping-up of the loyalist paramilitary campaign in the late 1980s was nonetheless accompanied by increased discussion of political accommodation beyond the conflict. By the early 1990s, the PUP leadership, linked to the UVF, was convinced that the IRA was searching for a credible exit strategy from its war. Loyalists had already contemplated post-conflict Northern Ireland. The *Common Sense* document of 1987, produced by the New Ulster Political Research Group (NUPRG), linked to the UDA, offered proportionality in government for unionist and nationalist representatives, a power-sharing executive and a legislative assembly drawn from both communities, with safeguards for the minority community enhanced by a Bill of Rights (New Ulster Political Research Group 1987; Bruce 1992). *Common Sense* represented a strong rejection, by the representatives of those fighting the 'war', of any attempt to return to Unionist majoritarianism (still DUP and UUP policy at the time), from which the loyalist workingclass had failed to benefit. Many of its ideas of a politically shared (albeit not necessarily integrated) future appeared within the Good Friday Agreement. Politically, some loyalist former prisoners accepted that the Agreement was very similar to the agreement between moderate unionists and nationalists to share power reached at Sunningdale over two decades earlier. As UDA male conceded, the Good Friday Agreement was indeed: 'Sunningdale for slow learners ... maybe we [the UDA] should have let it [Sunningdale] go ahead.'

Despite the credible political contribution offered by the NUPRG, a large-scale loyalist political organisation failed to develop. This failure was a combination of strong distaste for association with violence; the essentially defensive reaction, rather than progressive vision of what loyalists were seen as articulating; the stridency of constitutional politics within the UUP and DUP and internal loyalist paramilitary division. Loyalist political structures outside the gaols reflected the long-standing UVF-UDA division. However, in formulating the ceasefire of the Combined Loyalist Military Command in 1994, the 'political' and 'military' wings of loyalism worked closely together. The PUP regularly met UVF prisoners inside the gaols, whilst the UDP did likewise in respect of UDA prisoners (Rowan 1995). Yet the PUP-UVF relationship was stronger than that of the UDP-UDA with the prisoners. Thus a PUP executive member, John Kyle, could legitimately claim that UVF prisoners were 'absolutely fundamental to developing the political philosophy of the PUP', whilst, in contrast, the UDP lacked authority within loyalist communities and within the UDA (Frankie Gallagher, Ulster Political Research Group executive, 5 April 2007). Although UDA prisoners voted in favour of reciprocating the IRA's ceasefire in 1994, some UDA prisoners were ambiguous over the peace process (Crawford 2003).

If the concept of a mutually hurting stalemate did not permeate the ranks of those imprisoned, neither, consciously at least, did the far-reaching global changes occurring during the peace process. Very few prisoner interviewees connected the advent of the peace process with geo-political changes and only a slightly larger number of republicans associated the Irish process with the growth of peace processes elsewhere, such as that in South Africa. Although the republican leadership may have made such connections, for most prisoners, endogenous, parochial and community-oriented explanations of the process were more important than exogenous factors, such perceptions perhaps an inevitable consequence of the impact of incarceration. What though, were the specific drivers for peace?

Republican drivers for change

Many republican prisoners accepted during the conflict that political organisation would eventually displace militarism. As a life-sentence male IRA prisoner from Andersonstown commented: 'The party had to dictate the activities of the army [IRA]. If our struggle is a political struggle then the military can't be dealing with it.' Yet the same former prisoner acknowledged that there was an interplay of the voluntary and the necessary in terms of the reordering of the leadership of the republican movement, suggesting that the 'military struggle was burning out in the 1980s and 1990s' and that it needed displacement by politics to protect that struggle. To provide impetus for this transition, five drivers for change – ideological, political, military, structural and personal – can be identified, yielding a multi-faceted rationale for republican prisoner support for the peace process. The interplay of these drivers, which were not equally weighted, ensured that those who had fought the war backed its ending.

Ideological change was perhaps easiest for many prisoners and embraced two dimensions. Few IRA members were wedded to the traditional republican shibboleth that their organisation represented a government-in-waiting. Significantly, strong support for the ending of abstention from Dail Eireann was received from prisoners, prior to the 1986 Army Council and Sinn Fein *ard fheis* decisions to drop the supposed principle. However, the claim to the 'six counties' held by the Irish Republic until the Agreement provided greater debate. Indeed, the constitution of the Irish Republic caused 'great big arguments in the Kesh' (IRA male) prior to the Agreement as prisoners argued over the significance of the constitutional claims to the 'occupied territory', enshrined in Articles 2 and 3. The prisoners decided they could accept changes to these arising from the Agreement, as the clauses had done so little to unite Ireland, providing mainly ideological fig leaves for Fianna Fail's claims to republicanism in the South.

The second dimension of ideological change was the removal of the left-wing stances developed during the late 1970s and early 1980s. For all the earnest studying of leftist political thought in the gaols, the republican movement within and beyond prison remained a loose and uneasy coalition of nationalist, republican and socialist elements. As Walsh (1994: 243–4) argues, the movement was 'anti-capitalist' rather than definitively socialist. This allowed republicans to offer at least a modicum of appeal to some highly differentiated constituencies: blue-collar Irish America, Irish small farmers and the Catholic working class in Northern Ireland. Within prison, as the former prisoner Tommy Gorman described, there were IRA members who were:

> traditionalists who were uncomfortable with Marxism and who would have branded you a Communist and remember according to army [IRA] regulations this was grounds for dismissal. Catholic republicans would have thought Communism anathema, they wouldn't have changed much during this period, so there were different level. There were others who took Marxism seriously and even formed the League of Communist Republicans. Others would just have been socialist. (Quoted in Bean and Hayes 2001: 70)

Left-wing politics were readily adopted in gaol by many prisoners concerned at the conservatism of the republican leadership and willing to try to move republican politics closer to the daily concerns of republican supporters. However, those trying to move IRA too far in this direction found themselves isolated within prison (and beyond) by a leadership keen to develop greater tactical flexibility during the embryonic peace process of the late 1980s. Outside the gaols, the development of pan-nationalist dialogue between Sinn Fein and the SDLP by 1988 indicated that revolutionary socialism might be displaced if the possibilities of common nationalist agendas were likely to be more fruitful in eliciting transformation.

The political driver for change was the need to end the isolation of republicans. Prisoners had been keen, despite a nervous leadership outside, for Bobby Sands to seek election in 1981. Electoralism became a permanent feature of the republican political strategy from hereon, assuming steadily increasing importance within the movement. Those who dared question the shift of resources to electoral campaigning, such as Ivor Bell (interned with Gerry Adams during the 1970s) were 'threatened' and 'forced' to quit the movement (Moloney 2002). The importance of electoral success – as part of a twin-track strategic approach and as a morale raiser for prisoners was considerable, a point reinforced when gains were reversed. Prisoners were 'devasted – absolutely devastated – and it was a big signal for us' (IRA male) when Gerry Adams lost his West Belfast seat at the 1992 Westminster election. The signal was not for a heightening of long-term armed conflict, but rather that the IRA's campaign was a barrier to support, preventing Sinn Fein from overtaking the SDLP. Electoral success was initially seen as bolstering of legitimacy. Although republicans continue to insist that the legitimacy of the IRA's campaign was a derivative of Britain's contested sovereign claim to a part of Ireland, election success was nonetheless a reinforcing agent of that legitimacy, something which 'smashed the British state's criminal conspiracy claims' regarding militant republicanism, as a South Armagh IRA respondent emphasised.

In terms of the military driver for change, former prisoners do not profess a detailed knowledge of the state of the IRA's armed campaign during the early 1990s (and much evidence has subsequently emerged of infiltration by the security services) but were aware that its roles by that point were predominantly as armed propaganda and as a means of vetoing an internal settlement in Northern Ireland, with a strong electoral mandate vital to complement either. Few former prisoners claim that they still believed in a military victory by the beginning of the 1990s and some began to make the distinction between partial 'physical withdrawal' via demilitarisation and administrative withdrawal, which would be a bigger task (IRA male).

Equally, a majority of prisoners interviewed over a decade after the event claimed they were aware a ceasefire was likely, although few were privy to details of its timing. Most prisoners remained uncertain over the permanence of their own organisation's ceasefire. This was perhaps unsurprising given the need for the leadership to continue to reassure its base and offer some form of credible threat of violence for a period of time after the IRA ceasefires, epitomised in the comments of the Sinn Fein *ard chomhairle* (executive) member, Francie Molloy, in Cullyhanna, South Armagh, in November 1997, that 'this phase of negotiations may fall apart, it may not succeed. And whenever that does happen then we simply go back to what we know best' (*Irish News*, 17 November 1997).

The onset of the peace process has been associated with the IRA's inability to sustain its Libyan weapons supply line after its interception in 1987 (Moloney 2002). Yet very few prisoners were aware of the precise state of military fortune, even senior prisoners being predominantly concerned with the internal organisation of their prison blocks. A majority claim to have recognised the need for political accommodation soon after their incarceration, but this was due to a general acceptance of the inability of their small guerrilla army to achieve outright victory, rather than an acute awareness of the ebb and flow of the armed campaign. What *was* apparent and disturbing for prisoners was an apparent shortage of recruits, with rearrests of existing IRA members, rather than new volunteers, being common. As one Belfast IRA prisoner put it: 'seeing the same faces coming into the gaols depressed me.' For those imprisoned from the mid-1970s onwards, the IRA's campaign was seen more as a means of movement towards goals rather than their full attainment. It is in this context that the 1990s English bombings of the IRA are perceived. In a typical argument, one female IRA former prisoner described the armed struggle as 'something which gave you leverage'. Its other purpose, cited by many former prisoners, was the positive effect on internal morale, even if some conceded that the human cost was too high.

Structural drivers for change arose from the growing recognition of prisoners released on temporary parole that the social conditions prevalent at the time of their imprisonment no longer prevailed. The deghettoisation of the Catholic working class was a slow process, but it was perceptible by the late 1980s amid a plethora of reformist measures, such as fair employment legislation, initiated under direct rule from Westminster. It is important to note the growth in the Catholic middle class in the past two decades, one of the most significant socio-economic changes in Northern Ireland since the inception of that state (Shirlow and Murtagh, 2006). Strong British security measures remained in place, which served to facilitate continuing nationalist communal bonding, but by the 1990s there were clear signs of relaxation of such repressive tools, indicated in new approaches such as the 'Derry experiment', a locally brokered agreement to reduce the British Army presence. As nationalists began to prosper, the structural imperative for conflict diminished. IRA actions were now seen as barriers to socio-economic progress, not as a means of its advancement. There was also a growing perception that community self-confidence and the local economy were being hurt by conflict, be it contemporary 'war' actions or even some aspects of commemoration. Former prisoners, for example, helped develop the West Belfast festival as an alternative to the internment commemoration bonfires which frequently led to confrontations in August each year.

The final driver for change, based upon an anxiety to avoid the personal sacrifices entailed in participation in an armed campaign, is difficult to quantify. Most former prisoners expressed relief that the conflict was over and gratitude that now they and their families could live more 'normal' lives. However, few expressed regret or remorse for what occurred and a sizeable minority declared that they would 'do the same again'. Such comments may not merely be dismissed as self-justification or false bravado, but reflect, first, the strength of support networks within and beyond prison, and, second, a belief among many prisoners that the circumstances they encountered made participation in a conflict inevitable. Nonetheless, a small, somewhat static, recruitment base for the continuing prosecution of the war and the changing domestic circumstances of volunteers did impact upon the prison experience, as outlined by an IRA urban male, who served three sentences:

> for most of my time in gaol I had a selfish way of looking at it. At first I was a single man and I wasn't exactly too concerned about how my brother and my sister and my da [sic] was doing. The last time I was in gaol I was married with kids. I had a totally different experience. The time when I was in gaol when I felt almost lost was last time.

The prospect of release via the Good Friday Agreement was acknowledged as an important factor in terms of support for the deal by some prisoners, 'at a very selfish personal level' (IRA male) with the same prisoner anxious that 'my kid might end up in the war. I never ever wanted that.'

Loyalist drivers for change

Loyalist prisoners recognised the inevitability of some form of deal with republicans as the only alternative to perpetual conflict. The UVF leader during the 1970s, Gusty Spence, had acknowledged this during the 1970s, as did his successor, Billy Hutchinson, but amid the stark polarisation and enduring conflict of the early 1980s, the influence of both was outweighed by militarist factions (Crawford 1999, 2003). Among loyalists, there were also military, political, structural and personal drivers for change, but of a different nature. The more relaxed prison regimes of the late 1980s and early 1990s afforded greater access to news coverage to inmates, which, combined with information from colleagues outside, bolstered the loyalist claim that they were enjoying success in targeting republicans. Collusion with elements of the security services assisted. As former prisoner Bobby Philpott once claimed: 'I had more information [from the security forces] than I knew what to do with' (BBC 1998). The stepping up of loyalist military action and the killing of IRA and

Sinn Fein personnel (although these killings were still a small minority of the victims of loyalist killings) was followed by the IRA ceasefire in August 1994. According to loyalists, the sequencing was not coincidental, instead reflecting a triumph for militant resistance to the IRA's campaign, which had ended in the non-realisation of republican goals. According to a UDA male:

> I do believe we did achieve our core objectives ... Not only that but it [the loyalist campaign] drove the IRA to talk, to doing the politics, because it was a war. I think in the latter stages, late 1980s, early 1990s, loyalist paramilitaries were killing more Catholics. Innocent Catholics it had to be said, but ... the way our thinking was, if the IRA killed one Prod, we're going to kill 5 to 10 Catholics ... I think that the Catholic community got up and got onto republicans and got onto the IRA and said we can't have this, this has to stop ... There's no army in the world that gives up its guns and says ah, but we didn't surrender. As soon as they decommissioned I seen [sic] that as an act of surrender.

Morever, a UDA male from Dromore argued similarly that the peace process was a consequence of loyalist military impact:

> I'll believe to the day I die that our strategy from the middle 1980s brought the republican movement to their knees. We were out-killing them, we were out-gunning them. We were hitting the right people, not matter what they cried we knew who we were hitting ... when I was in gaol I knew we were winning because I seen [sic] it on their people's faces. You just seen [sic] it when they come {sic} in. You knew they were a defeated people ... Militarily we won the war.

The belief among loyalists that they were winning made a ceasefire highly unlikely without a republican cessation. Nonetheless, the belief that republicans were heading in that direction prompted debate among loyalists by the early 1990s. According to a UDA rural male, the first vote within his gaol among UDA prisoners on whether to call a ceasefire was held in 'November/December 1993' and produced an '85 per cent majority' in favour of a continuation of the campaign until an IRA cessation. Given that the vote followed the IRA's October 1993 Shankill bombing and serious ensuing violence, a loyalist ceasefire at that time was unlikely. Some former prisoners, especially those from the UDA, whose political associates suffered several prominent losses from 1987 onwards, argued that 'going political' in the immediate pre-ceasefire years was too dangerous, hindering loyalist political development by raising the visibility of loyalists to republicans and leaving them vulnerable to assassination.

However, the IRA ceasefire during the following year radically altered the context and reopened the prospect. A UDA male claimed:

> I'd say for three days the whole wing, sorry two wings, debated it [a loyalist ceasefire] every night, debating should we call a ceasefire? And we managed to get down [convince] the whole wing bar one ... just through telling them, what are we

going to do? The Provies are on ceasefire. We always say we're only here to defend … We're not being attacked, we have to change mindsets.

Despite their claimed victory, not all loyalist former prisoners believed the IRA had entirely disappeared, an Armagh UVF former prisoner, for example, declaring himself 'very very wary' of continuing republican military activity. This was a minority view, although another longer term view offered was that 'history tells us no' in respect of the permanency of peace and the complete removal of the IRA.

However, the perception among loyalist politically motivated offenders of their 'military success' prompted concerns over new republican tactics in 'peacetime', seen as potentially more destabilising for the Union. Among a section of loyalist prisoners, continuing IRA activity beyond the ceasefire fuelled a belief that loyalist paramilitary activity should not be ended, a position exacerbated by an unwillingness or inability to cope with a post-conflict polity. Accordingly, the brief period of loyalist unity from 1994 until the completion of prisoner releases in 2000 soon dissipated amid the fracturing of ceasefires and inter- and intra-group rivalries. From thereon, loyalist former prisoners, in common with the broader unionist community, were divided on the merits of the Good Friday Agreement, UVF former prisoners being more united in support of the peace and political processes compared with the more divided UDA.

The political approach of loyalist former prisoners has been based upon a perception of agreement to differ. In common with republican opponents, loyalists do not perceive the Good Friday Agreement as the final outcome. A UVF member argued:

> The term transformation for me is more important than resolution, because I firmly believe that there are differences that I have with republicans and nationalists that are never going to be resolved. But my relationship with them has been transformed from one of demonisation and just wanting to destroy them, to trying to create a society in which we can live together and have those differences.

Another UVF former prisoner concurred, arguing that 'there is really no resolution of the conflict here, because you have two politically diametrically, unionism and republicanism and there is no resolution of that fact'.

Loyalist structural imperatives for peace were different from those of republicans. Whereas republicans acknowledged the improved economic fortunes of nationalists under direct rule, articulated the concerns of working-class Catholics and sought broader cross-class support, loyalists lamented the inability of a political vehicle to express adequately the concerns of the Protestant working class, which they felt was failing to progress. Whilst loyalist prisoners supportive of the political work of the PUP and UDP did not antici-pate an electoral peace divided similar to that accruing to Sinn Fein, there was an initial mistaken belief that peace would allow working-class loyalist political representatives to strengthen their position at the expense of the DUP. Whilst Sinn Fein attempted to achieve cross-class coalitional nationalist support, loyalist former prisoners continued to seek articulation of their working-class interests, seen as represented inadequately by mainstream unionism. An urban UVF respondent highlighted the distinction between unionist politics – 'all about the union' - and loyalist politics -'more about the people'. Another UVF member highlighted the problem of an ongoing struggle to establish loyalism as a credible and respectable political entity, arguing that as an ideology, 'it's like a dirty word for a unionist'.

Political incentives for loyalists to engage in conflict transformation were not as apparent as those for republicans. The broader unionist community was less receptive to new loyalism than was the nationalist community to Sinn Fein's new republicanism. The latter offered continued gains through an equality agenda, articulated in part from former IRA members whose efforts commanded sympathy within their community. New loyalism offered progressive, socialist politics of some interest to the loyalist working class, but of little import beyond a narrow structural base, with other unionists regarding with some disdain the 'ultras' who had purported to fight on their behalf. A former Red Hand Commando (RHC) respondent lamented defeat in the struggle for loyalist internal community legitimacy:

> The unionist community could never accept [loyalists] the way republicans were accepted into the political fold. And that's why the UVF and the RHC couldn't convert their physical and military strength into the political because the wider unionist community does not accept former prisoners or people involved in paramilitarism as a political representative … it is not in their psyche, because this is the first time that loyalists went outside the law.

This struggle for legitimacy underscores much of the discourse of loyalist former prisoners, frustrated that their own claimed role in defeating the IRA appears to have passed unrecognised beyond their own circles. In a common response, a UDA male insisted that loyalist paramilitaries should be regarded merely as 'counter-terrorists' and that their role was little more dirty than state counter-terrorist activities. The legitimacy problem was compounded by the inability of a working-class loyalist party to fully develop, with former prisoners struggling to find a political outlet and struggling for purpose and some declining to vote.

Personal incentives for an end to conflict were also evident among loyalists. For loyalist women prisoners, in particular, there was considerable isolation endured in the gaols. In Armagh gaol, for example, there was only one woman loyalist prisoner during the 1980s, compared with thirty-seven republican women inmates. Many former prisoners lamented the loss of family life, whilst accepting the choice they had made. A UVF respondent offered a typical response in claiming that the loss of 'my job, eighteen years of freedom, my marriage, the financial implications and whatever else' was nonetheless 'fair game' given the deliberate choice of joining the UVF. UDA former prisoners also had few regrets, whilst all declaring contentment that their offspring lived in a peaceful Northern Ireland.

Non-drivers of change

What is apparent is the lack of a *moral* driver for change, a perception that the war was unjust, or cruel. Instead, political and structural factors had far greater impact. The regular moral condemnation of IRA activity made by the Catholic Church made little impact upon recruits and few loyalists cited Protestantism as a significant political influence. McAllister's research (2004) suggests significantly more secular and non-church-going bases of Sinn Fein's support relative to the SDLP and the lack of religiosity among former prisoners is apparent.

There was a surprising lack of internal debate among prisoners over the impossibility of the Catholic Church ever operating as a cheerleader for a paramilitary campaign, with attitudes tending to be hostile to the Church. A female former IRA prisoner, a practising Catholic until the end of the 1970s, argued like many others that the final parting of the ways was the attitude of the Catholic Church to the prison protests of the early 1980s:

> I'm still angry at the Catholic Church about the hunger strikes. I don't know when that will abate. I'm angry with the Catholic Church over the way that women are viewed and treated. And I'm also angry at the way that people who had a lot of influence in our community walked away and let us down. Not them all, absolutely not them all, but as a structure, because the Catholic Church is a monolith, it's a structure.

The other driver conspicuously absent is the lack of exogenous referents. Few former prisoners (less than ten in total) made reference to external factors of globalisation, Europeanisation or international terrorism as an influence or motivation for political transformation. Occasionally, loyalists highlighted increased European integration as a factor which diminished the importance of Irish unification, but such claims did not register with republicans. Perhaps surprisingly, no republicans offered the growth of nationalism in Scotland and Wales as encouragement for their cause and this was rarely seen as a threat by loyalists, although one member of the UPRG which advises the UDA highlighted the constitutional restructuring of the UK as the most important threat to the Union, as devolution would 'compromise the unity of the state' (24 May 2007).

Some loyalists also claimed how the unacceptability of terrorist activity to the previously sympathetic Irish-American base had removed any prospect of an IRA return to violence, but such claims were not backed by republicans, who did not mention the impact of 9/11 in interviews. Localism dominated, which, whilst comprehensible given the incarceration endured by prisoners, did not seem diluted by a greater global awareness developed after release from prison.

Acceptance of political change among republican former prisoners

Had an elite-level consociation merely been imposed upon combatants it would have failed to endure. The acceptance of the limited utility of conflict, the belief in the possibility of political transformation through other means and the deal on prisoners within the Good Friday Agreement facilitated substantial support for a political settlement among those who had participated in the conflict. Changes in previously stated goals and renunciation of previous deeds were not required. The final Officer Commanding of the IRA in the Maze prison, Jim McVeigh, insisted at a H Block exhibition in Manchester (14 June 2006) that the ending of violence was 'not a moral decision; it was a practical one'.

A limited heterogeneity is evident among former prisoners. Three types of IRA former prisoner categories are evident. *Leadership adherents* constitute by far the largest group. These former prisoners tend to support the changes in the republican agenda advanced by Sinn Fein. The loyalty to the leadership evident during the IRA's campaign has been readily transferred to the political arena. A number of such former prisoners work for Sinn Fein, or have posts as community workers, or assist Coiste, the former prisoners' group. These former prisoners tend to be fully supportive of the peace and political processes, perceiving the evolution of republican strategy as a necessary response to the 'military', political and economic state of the nationalist community. Among these adherents there is a ready acceptance of the necessity of change and the absence of a credible alternative. A male Derry former prisoner summarised this approach to continuing republican activity, arguing: 'It's another phase and if you believe in that phase that you've moved into and you think, oh it'll work it's OK ... I can't see any other way anyway ... Stormont's only a name. If we're in there and it's changed, Stormont can become whatever we like.'

Yet some republican former prisoners, whilst strongly supportive of the political changes undertaken, root such transformation in the lack of community concern for a united Ireland. Despite spending twenty-two years in prison, a Belfast IRA former prisoner offered a realistic appraisal of the depth of nationalist and republican interest in the avowed end goal:

> I think that most people in this community would say they're republican, but they'd be very accepting of the British state. I think most people in this area, their main concern is getting a job, getting a better house, it's getting the hoods and the joyriders. That is their main concern. I don't think they're waking up in the morning saying let me read the *Republican News*, the republic will come some day.

Certainly people will go along to functions and sing the Soldier's Song and they'll cheer on certain songs. But I think that's as far as the republic will go. They will vote for Sinn Fein because Sinn Fein work on the streets. Sinn Fein will be out there trying to clean up these streets. They're trying to get better lighting in the area. We're seeing a lot of republicans in the area who are involved in CRJ, who are involved in the [West Belfast] festival, summer programmes for kids, trying to get graffiti off the wall. But that's the basis of support. I don't think people go out and vote Sinn Fein because Gerry Adams and the leaders of Sinn Fein will bring us into a greater Ireland and that reunification will come. Certainly it's an ideal, even for people who don't vote Sinn Fein, who vote for the SDLP and always have this sense of a united Ireland somewhere down the line. I don't think there'll be too many getting up in the morning and thinking the republic is near.

Leadership adherents acknowledge the difficulty of transition from military to political organisation, as the discipline required for the former does not automatically translate. One former prisoner summarised the problem:

If you're a member of the IRA you carried out your instructions, that was it. There was no debate about the operation so it was relatively simple ... Once you moved into the solely political sphere, be it social, economic, health, whatever it is, then ideology comes very much to the fore ... once the republican movement did make its change then that's when variation and opinion and views really comes to the fore and if the republican movement hadn't been expecting this it's pretty stupid. (IRA male)

Nonetheless, those who have failed to adapt to the changed political environment are treated with derision. Republican dissidents are eschewed as individuals whose focus 'tends to be anti-Sinn Fein, anti-IRA' (IRA female). Some leadership adherents see a distinction between electoral strength (attained) and political strength (some way from being fully realised). Nearly all accept that the Good Friday Agreement is, to cite three mantras, 'not a republican document', but instead should be viewed as a 'work in progress' and a 'stepping stone'. Such former prisoners tend towards vagueness over the means of transition towards a united Ireland from the document and there is considerable debate over whether equality within the northern state is, first, attainable, and second, transitional to an 'Ireland of Equals' in which the border is removed. There is recognition of the need for Sinn Fein to appeal beyond the republican core, but this is not seen as problematic: a West Belfast former IRA prisoner, who served seven years, in an example of the occasional elitism evident among those once imprisoned, claimed that 'the only real republican community that I've lived in was in the H Blocks'.

Insofar as leadership adherents offer any criticism, it is more of the sloganising used to reassure the base in the run-up to the political changes necessitated by the Good Friday Agreement. Thus one IRA male, in assessing the 'not one ounce, not one bullet' apparent rejection of IRA decommissioning in 1997 declared: 'It's mad to throw out political slogans if you have a strategy in front of you … it's like Freedom 74' (a reference to the era of the early 1970s when IRA sloganising declared that victory was imminent).

Mild sceptics are much smaller in number (less than 10 per cent of the republican prisoners interviewed). This category accepts that an alternative to 'armed struggle' needed to be developed and acknowledge the need for the growth of Sinn Fein. However, not all the changes are readily endorsed. Some registered reluctance regarding the decommissioning of weapons, but units such as the South Derry group of former IRA prisoners insisted that, as weapons could readily be replaced, disarmament was far less of an issue than political progress. Of much greater controversy, however, was Sinn Fein's support for policing. Although support for policing was viewed by many as an inevitable development following on from other policy changes, few perceived the Police Service of Northern Ireland (PSNI) as an entirely new beginning for policing and some still declined to accept the legitimacy of the new force. For mild sceptics, acceptance of policing owes more to an acknowledged need to control local criminals ('hoods'), some of whom appeared unrestrained by community-oriented restorative justice programmes, than any clear political transformation. Scepticism is sometimes more a product of personnel than policy changes, with an emergent 'careerist' wing of Sinn Fein viewed with some suspicion. An IRA rural male expressed his disquiet thus:

> I hate people saying Sinn Fein are all up at Stormont in Armani suits. But you do see wee things. People I've seen coming into the movement and you're saying where did they come from? Where were they when the war was on? It's not all of them. But are they coming from the same ideology that we had of republicanism? Are they coming in using the movement for their own aims? … I remember Gerry Adams turning around and saying just after the Good Friday Agreement he wanted the grassroots to stand behind him. He said we're going to bring people into the movement, in other words intellectuals. And I felt, and I know one or two other people did, that are we not good enough to be councillors or go into government?

A very small number of former prisoners can be classed as *neo-dissidents*. This grouping is critical of the political changes within Sinn Fein and sceptical over the need to stand down the IRA. Whilst not desirous of a return to armed struggle, their criticisms of the Continuity (CIRA) and Real IRAs mainly concern the perceived lack of 'military capabilities' of those groups. This perception was most graphically expressed in a group discussion by a former IRA prisoner from the Falls in West Belfast who asked 'when are these groups going to stiff a Brit?' (16 August 2006). The RIRA and CIRA are not seen as credible organisations even by neo-dissidents, even though such former IRA prisoners do not reject an armed campaign as a tactical option in the future, however improbable the prospect. This lack of credibility is heightened by the perception that dissident IRAs are heavily penetrated by the security services, although this was a problem from which IRA was hardly immune. Leadership adherents are much more critical of the CIRA and RIRA. One description, from another West Belfast female former IRA prisoner, was typical in highlighting the lack of backing for such groups: 'They're not a movement, they don't have the support … they have no right to prosecute a war on behalf of our people and our long-term goals.' Nonetheless, the majority of republican former prisoners across all categories believed that imprisoned members of dissident groups should be acknowledged as 'political prisoners'. Moreover, a sizeable number of former IRA prisoners believed the option of violence ought to be reserved, however untenable and unrealistic in the new political dispensation.

Former INLA prisoners

Non-IRA former republican prisoners tend to be highly sceptical of the peace process, which is dismissed as a 'pacification [of republicans] process'. Most INLA former prisoners concede that 'the British won – no sense in trying to deny the fact' and claim that former IRA prisoners are now 'running the northern state for the British' (INLA male). Two themes emerge among INLA former prisoners; a belief that Sinn Fein has 'accepted partition and … accepted the state' (INLA male) with no transformation possible via the Good Friday Agreement, given that, according to a former INLA prisoner from Strabane, the deal enshrines the 'unionist veto' over unification and represents a political 'cul-de-sac'. Second, there is a perception that the Agreement has failed to address inequality. However, despite continuing hostility to political institutions in Northern Ireland and rejection of the PSNI, INLA former prisoners reject a return to conflict as not viable and some are involved in conflict transformation initiatives. Despite their concerns over the direction of the peace process, INLA prisoners argued for a cessation of violence. They claim that the state of the 'armed struggle' was more apparent whilst within the gaols rather than outside, as a 'big picture' could be assembled from all parts of Northern Ireland, whereas outside the gaol, localism tended to dominate. Whilst not condemnatory of the CIRA and RIRA, they argue against the futility of a 'military campaign', given that 'even if the INLA, the Continuity IRA and the Real IRA amalgamated tomorrow we are still not strong enough to achieve the objectives of the armed struggle' (INLA male).

Bereft of a major political outlet, INLA former prisoners had much less of an electoral driver for change than IRA counterparts, preferring instead to mix 'revolutionary socialism' with elitism. All INLA prisoners argue that electoral mandates mean little, claiming that republicans would never have fought an armed campaign had they awaited such. As a male INLA former prisoner in Belfast graphically claimed: 'political power comes from the barrel of a gun', whilst another INLA member in Strabane dismissed electoralism as 'all about manipulation', highlighting the inadequacies of the Good Friday Agreement referendum as a means of Irish self-determination. Others dismissed election-eering and mandates as 'nice but not important', to cite one INLA male, whilst a Derry INLA former prisoner saw the pre-eminence of vote-chasing an as the means of dilution of goals, arguing that as a consequence 'the way Sinn Fein's going at the minute they're just going to be the new SDLP'.

Despite the apparent rejection of the need for mandates, lack of support for continuing violence *is* highlighted as a driver for change by INLA former prisoners, who 'accept that republican violence was one of the blocks on working-class unity' according to an INLA male from Belfast. A Derry-based INLA former prisoner insisted that 'social housing', 'better education' and 'jobs' were now of much greater concern to those who had once backed the struggle. Other drivers for reappraisal are similar to those experienced by IRA prisoners, with the exception that INLA former members downplay the struc-tural changes and supposed socio-economic ascendancy of republican commu-nities and, more generally, the working class in its entirety, who can never enjoy 'parity of esteem'. Despite their strong reservations over the Good Friday Agreement as a 'sectarian' and non-progressive deal', INLA ex-combatants made common cause with those from the IRA in drawing upon military 'stripes' to sell movement from conflict, an INLA male in Belfast arguing: 'I think the work of the prisoners has been key – it's been much easier for people who are involved in the INLA and stuff like that to argue for a peaceful strategy, coming from the situation that we've done it and that entails a certain amount of respect. The people listened.'

Moreover, INLA prisoners are supportive of conflict transformation involving dialogue with loyalists and the defusing of tension at sectarian inter-faces. Like IRA former prisoners, however, the ultimate motivation and defined endgame of such transformation is persuasion of Protestants that their better interests lie in a united Ireland, rather than an acceptance of the creden-tials of unionism. As an INLA male in Strabane explained:

> I think that we don't see the reunification of this country as a greater under-standing between republicanism and loyalism, unionism and nationalism, but eventually through dialogue the Protestant community will come round to accepting the best position that we could have in society is unification itself. But we won't do that through shooting and bombing, because that widens the gulf between us.

Yet there are doubts over whether the persuader role is achievable, regardless of which tactics are utilised, and INLA former prisoners are more explicit over the need to reserve violence as possible future direction. INLA former prisoners also tend to engage in historical determinism regarding armed conflict. Although IRA and INLA former prisoners share the view that abandonment of 'armed struggle' was tactical not moral, IRA former members do not (with a few exceptions) envisage circumstances in which violence could reignite. INLA former prisoners argue that 'the potential for armed struggle is still there sometime in the future' and even insist that 'the INLA at this present juncture should be preparing themselves further for their own involvement in armed struggle for the next generation' (INLA male). Moreover, the IRSP, as political associates of the INLA, criticise the manner in which 'political status was signed away under the Good Friday Agreement even though ten men gave their lives to attain it in 1981' and argued that 'dissident' 'prisoners of Magheraberry in 2003 are no different to the prisoners of Long Kesh in the seventies' (*Starry Plough*, August/September 2003: 1).

Loyalist former prisoners and acceptance of change

Whilst IRA members embraced many of the political changes wrought by the peace process without dissent, the movement from 'defending to mending' communities (UDA male) within loyalism was more problematic. Loyalist former prisoners faced a greater struggle for legitimacy within their own community and with few tangible immediate benefits on offer in terms of a peace dividend to end a war they felt they were winning/had won – with the very notable exception of early release from prison – movement towards conflict transformation was erratic.

For loyalist former prisoners, the absence of a large-scale political organisation and dual (UVF and UDA) leaderships exacerbated divisions over whether to support the peace and political processes. Loyalist former prisoners were instrumental in dissuading those inclined to return to violence amid the fracturing of the IRA's ceasefire in 1996–97. Although the IRA's renewed campaign mainly targeted English cities, the killing of two police officers in Lurgan and the bombing of Thiepval army barracks in 1997 strained the loyalist ceasefire; it held amid caution over the consequences of a return to violence. The centrality of prisoners to the maintenance of the peace was emphasised by the visit of the Secretary of State, Mo Mowlam, to the Maze, in January 1998, where she met five leaders of the 130 UFF and UVF prisoners remaining in the gaol, although the commitment to the process of some of those leaders later proved questionable.

Although the PUP and UDP were both elected to the 1996 'Peace Forum' and supported the Good Friday Agreement, the UDP's failure to secure the election of any representatives to the Northern Ireland Assembly in 1998 diminished support for the new political agenda among sections of the UDA. Intra-loyalist agreement was evident in support for the process, shown in the ceasefire pronouncement of the Combined Loyalist Military Command in 1994 and the seeming isolation of the DUP amid an unlikely (and loose) alliance of the pro-Agreement UUP-PUP-UDP in the 1998 Agreement referendum campaign. However, a combination of the electoral failure of the UDA's political associates, disinterest in politics in some sections of the

UDA/UFF, the emergence of a loyalist spoiler group, the Loyalist Volunteer Force, continuing small-scale IRA activity and growing disillusionment with the Agreement among the broader Protestant community ensured that an exclusively political route for loyalism was a 'hard sell' for those loyalist former prisoners who wished to achieve conflict transformation. Amid internal division within the UDA/UFF and some sympathy for the LVF, the outcome by 2000 was an intra-loyalist feud resulting in seven deaths during that year.

From 2003 onwards, following the eventual ousting of the renegades of the UDA's 'C Company', a grouping containing, according to a South Belfast UVF member, a 'bunch of moronic thugs' more interested in personal aggrandisement than the broader peace process, some stability returned to loyalist paramilitarism (Gallaher 2007; Spencer 2008). Criminality for personal gain proved divisive among loyalist former prisoners, who saw gangsterism and drug-dealing among some former colleagues further undermining an already difficult struggle for acceptance. A UDA urban male described the problem:

> I believe that paramilitaries did have local community support … But what came out of the paramilitary groups was, after the war, the paramilitaries, I don't know, gangs is probably not the right word, but the skills that they learned fighting was [sic] put to good use into drug dealing … They lost a big lot of support that way, so they did, in their community … They were running their own communities too. It has to be said. It was UDA men taking their money … People ruined their own communities.

By 2004, the UDA's publication, the *Loyalist* (April/May 2004: 2), claimed that 'all those within the Ulster Political Research Group, former prisoners' groups and the Protestant Interface Network are working extremely hard to ensure the interfaces and the all the loyalist communities with UPRG personnel are working towards peace and stability'. Nonetheless, scepticism over the 'wave of concessions towards republicans' continued, which contrasted with the manner in which 'many loyalist prisoners on licence have been returned to gaol with no appeal for the smallest of petty crime' (*Loyalist*, September 2005: 1). Whilst the UDA was triumphalist over having 'won the war', among UVF members there was more emphasis upon acceptance of the necessity of a credible ceasefire and recognition that 'for those who engaged republicanism with warfare the time is right for a change in tactics', although this call was accompanied by caution that 'the theatre has changed but the fundamental question of British existence within Ireland remains' (*Combat*, July 1999: 1).

Whilst recognising that the IRA has gone away and claiming the credit for its disappearance, loyalist former prisoners are wary of political developments in post-conflict Northern Ireland, fearing that military 'victory' may not be matched by peacetime success. The self-assurance of loyalist paramilitaries that they forced the IRA to seek alternative means of pursuing their goals dissipates when considering the risks created by new republican tactics, even though almost all loyalist former prisoners accept the necessity of inclusive power sharing. A UDA 'focus group' (22 May 2007) drawn from across Northern Ireland concurred with the claim of one group member that 'if you had five volunteers here from the IRA they'd leave us standing, because they've been brought up politically in the gaols, whereas we weren't'. The PUP leader, Dawn Purvis, conceded that 'the nationalist community as a whole is far more sophisticated politically' (24 May 2007).

The constitutional safeguards contained in the Good Friday Agreement do provide reassurance for loyalist former prisoners and the overarching principle of consent for change remains the basis for their support for the deal. However, a combination of lack of loyalist and unionist vigilance, the stigma attached to loyalism and the articulate approach of Sinn Fein are all offered as reasons why the Union may not be entirely secure, although loyalists are divided on whether it is seriously threatened. Continuing mistrust remains evident of a variety of actors, not merely republicans, epitomised in the clam of one UDA male that 'the British government is bringing the union to an end anyway' or the assertion of a former prisoner from the same organisation that: 'I honestly don't think Britain cares one or the other whether we're part of the UK or not.'

Moreover, the former prisoners are split in their political associations, between backing for the DUP, PUP or no political organisation, contrasting with the extensive support for Sinn Fein found among former IRA prisoners. Some newer UPRG executive members responded 'none at all' when asked which political party best represents loyalist interests, rather than highlighting the class-oriented politics of the PUP. Within the PUP, there is a belief that the party's community transformation initiatives and overtly class politics (on issues such as the 'eleven- plus' transfer test) are rebuffed not merely by that grouping's UVF associations, but by 'an innate conservatism' which means that working-class unionists can 'often be duped … we're the stupidest people on earth' (Colin Robertson, PUP executive).

Loyalists nonetheless believe that their initiatives have precipitated elite-level change whilst demonstrating that this need not mean fundamental political compromise. Davy Nicholl of the UPRG asserts:

> I met Bertie Ahern [then An Taoiseach] and took the UDA leadership with me; in terms of our discussions we've met on 3 or 4 occasions. And we did so that if we made the leap it would make it easier for Ian Paisley [then DUP leader] to make the leap and travel south as well … Paisley followed within 6 months. Bertie Ahern said to me 'it's my aspiration to unify Ireland, but I have to accept that in my lifetime I may not see it' and I said 'it's still my aspiration to resist you and my people will resist you'.

Some former prisoners also fear a pernicious chipping away at the border, whilst others argue that 'mutually beneficial' cross-border bodies are a good idea and that the Protestant community need not 'fear some sort of contamination by the merest contact', as a UVF former prisoner in South Belfast argued. The republican political 'machine' is afforded a status not apparent even to some republicans, a UVF urban male arguing that republicans are 'fighting a different war now, they're very astute and very good at it'. Others nonetheless distinguish between a 'very clever [republican] leadership' and 'the ordinary foot-soldier … probably just as lost as some loyalists are in some of the working-class communities' (UVF rural male). According to several loyalist former prisoners, republicans continue to engage in 'ethnic cleansing', with the claim that 'the Protestant, unionist, loyalist communities have lost out – they are still under siege' being common (UVF male).

Loyalists engaged in conflict transformation are divided over whether there has been mutual or asymmetrical community benefit, with some asserting that the size of Sinn Fein's mandate and the shrewdness of republican tactics have resulted in greater benefit for nationalist communities, at the expense of loyalists. UPRG executive member, John Nicholl, even claimed that 'nearly 70 per cent of all [EU] Peace I monies were invested in Irish republican communities and almost singularly in groups that were one religion or one political belief i.e. republicanism or associated with Sinn Fein'. Whatever the reservations, loyalist former prisoners have engaged in a substantial number of community initiatives, which have straddled the divide and contributed to a diminution of sectarian tensions. Interaction Belfast, for example, contains a large number of ex-combatants and attempts to reduce interface violence and 'move from sectarianism and bigotry', with former prisoners playing a significant role in, for example, ending the Holy Cross dispute in 2001, in which the route to school of Catholic schoolchildren was contested (Gerard Solinas, UPRG executive).

Conclusion: *'Je n'regrette rien, et plus ca change?'*

The limited studies thus far of what created a peace process and political change within republicanism and loyalism have tended to ground explanations within broad notions of an inter-communal mutually hurting stalemate, recognition of which created ripeness for a peace agreement (e.g. Cochrane 2008; Powell 2008; Zartman 2003b). Explanations grounded in theories of stalemate are, at best, partial, rooted in military considerations and insufficiently cognisant of the interplay of those military aspects with ideological, political, economic and personal factors which produce intra-group reappraisal. Moreover, the concept of stalemate assumes a military 'draw' or inability to win. Yet, in Northern Ireland, there were asymmetrical perceptions, not mutually agreed perspectives. Loyalist conclusions were not that their aims could be realised by giving up violence and using other methods, a perception central to 'stalemate' theories; conversely, loyalists were convinced of the utility of violence in having produced military victory which had bolstered the constitutional status quo. Republican perceptions, albeit with some dissent, were of the need for tactical adjustment to secure victory at an unspecified later date.

Most republican former prisoners continue to believe in the inevitability of a united Ireland and the legitimacy of the thirty-two county Republic is unquestioned; the end-of-history perspective remains intact. In a military sense, former prisoners continue to insist that the British Army, RUC and UDR were legitimate targets, whilst acknowledging that their targeting had ceased to have practical utility. In the ideological and political spheres, end-goals remain intact, with a new context based upon aggressive, but non-violent, assertions of Irish nationalist rights. The new dispensation merely ensured that 'identity politics were thus a continuation of war by other means, used to score points and politically undermine Unionism' (Bean 2007: 248) whilst juxtaposed with apparent 'outreach' to unionists.

As republicans continue to promote the ultimate inevitability of unification, loyalist historical determinism offers another perspective on inevitability; the resumption, at some unspecified date in the distant future, of republican hostilities. Given this, loyalist political change has not embraced recognition of the validity of republicanism, about which loyalists remain wary. Nor have the root causes of the problem been removed. Conflict transformation is a significant project, but one with limitations, a process of 'trying to transform it [the violent conflict] into a totally political conflict' (UVF male), but the term 'conflict' remains ubiquitous.

Intra-group developments among prisoners were thus crucial in movement away from violence; those who had fought the war were important in bringing about its ending. However, this tactical and pragmatic shift was nonetheless accompanied by avowed fidelity to traditional constitutional perspectives and retention of much of the inter-communal distrust which marked the conflict. Overwhelmingly, former prisoners support power-sharing and recognise an elite-level consociation embracing historic enemies as a necessary, albeit insufficient, feature of the post-conflict political process. However, former combatants lay greater emphasis upon local conflict and community transformation initiatives and the articulation of class politics. The aspiration of former prisoners is that the cumulative effect of local cross-community projects, progressive politics and an absence of violence permanently remove the actuality of conflict, amid continuing rhetoric and differences over constitutional ambitions. Meanwhile however, amid continuing zero-gum game inter-communal struggles for legitimacy, power and resources, ongoing inter-communal aggrandisement remains evident.

6 Conflict transformation and changing perceptions of the 'other'

> A peace process does not begin by some miraculous stroke of luck or genius. It requires conditions that need to be created and a series of steps are necessary to keep it alive and working towards a negotiated peace settlement. (Séan Lynch, 1996, former republican prisoner)

This chapter explores post-conflict attitudes and behaviour of those former non-state combatants who have engaged in broader formations of social and political reconciliation and transformation through various post-prison and community initiatives. In so doing it examines how the influx of former prisoners into organisations such as Sinn Féin, the PUP and the UPRG has reshaped the political thinking of those groups, and whether former prisoners have been able to maintain a distinct standpoint within such organisations or have been marginalised by leadership-driven change.

The chapter also considers contemporary reconstructions of 'the other' and whether, and to what extent, these have changed in the post-conflict era. At times, such considerations have also reflected flexibility in how individuals construct their sense of self-identity and the types of political processes with which they are prepared to engage. While the nature of the conflict may have changed, many still consider that its root causes and beliefs have not altered (Tonge 2005, 2006). Hence, despite visible efforts to build inter-community linkages it is also important to consider the ideological and discursive divisions that remain between loyalists and republicans.

Finally, therefore, the chapter also discusses whether ex-prisoners have recalibrated (or even abandoned) the ideological compass which permitted self and community justification of their actions and following the cessation of formal conflict the extent to which old ideological certainties continue to structure the Northern Irish polity. How, if at all, have views of the other and the enemy outlines in Chapter 4 changed and have such views been reshaped by the peace process and the transformation of conflict?

Most public attention in recent times has focused on the macro aspects of the peace process, the move towards party political accord through and following the Good Friday Agreement, decommissioning, the declining levels of non-state combatants' violence and the 'normalisation' of Northern Irish society. Much less attention has been given to what has happened at the localised level, where the accord and the provisions following political settlement 'has most immediate impact on the lives of ordinary citizens' (Manning 2003: 36). While attention to the macro level of post-conflict peace building is understandable, it is at least equally important to consider how and why the processes have been embedded at other levels of Northern Irish society.

The foundations of societal and political reconciliation in Northern Ireland rest at least as much at the everyday street level as they do in the public domain of politics; arguably more so, given that the lack of guidance and structures set in place by the Agreement. The top-down nature of the settlement (Acheson and Milofsky 2008) meant the need for the development of crucial leadership roles at the local level. These involved the formulation of 'everyday' strategies both within communities and for involvement with the other. Often these have been driven by who had been most directly involved in the conflict, including those who had been imprisoned because of non-state combatant roles.

Such localised interpretation of the high politics involved in peace accords is far from unusual. Bell and O'Rourke (2007) indicate how the 'legwork' in bedding down peace agreements often falls on those operating within civil society to develop a positive popular awareness. The input of former prisoners in civil society has been significant and their impact in translating and embedding political changes made at Stormont and inter-governmental levels in the everyday culture has been significant. Within this area former prisoners have demonstrated their capability to engage with the other, at both personal and structural levels, and there is clear evidence of former combatants working actively to minimise political tensions and hostility between communities, particularly along interface areas.

For some former prisoners this is a natural extension of the previous commitments to, and the development of, a process that facilitated the political accord in the first place (Von Tangen Page 2006). The positive input into the peace process was self-identified by many former non-state combatants prisoners. As one UDA former prisoner explained, 'I think former prisoners – they're absolutely instrumental and why we've got devolution today', and another suggested that 'mostly ex-prisoners would be more supportive of the peace process because they've seen it, been there, done it and spent time in prison for it and they've probably worked it out themselves' (UDA male).

Former IRA prisoners indicated that it was their political commitment both pre- and post-release which meant that they continued to occupy prominent positions within republican communities. As one explained 'at the end of the day, you know, people will go to ex-prisoners, a lot of ex-prisoners see the importance of their role within their community, the importance … that people do and may look towards them' (IRA male). For another, 'ex-prisoners … they played a big part of it at the end of the day. If I went up to people in my area and I said I'm going to Sinn Féin … I'm going to stand for election, I have no doubt that people would be behind me, and that would happen to a lot of ex-prisoners' (IRA male).

While republican and loyalist former prisoners occupy identifiable political ground and sometimes share common experiences, that is not to say that they are both on the same trajectory, or they have arrived at this point along the same path. While superficially it may seem that actions and dynamics amongst former non-state combatants in loyalist and republic areas has mirrored each other there are important differences in why each is taking the role they do and their objectives. There is no single route taken by former prisoners in promoting conflict and societal reconciliation. Partly this has been determined by some of the transitions undergone by individuals and groups as indicated in the previous chapter. Involvement in conflict transformation work is also framed by the direction and views of the organisations and movements with which they are affiliated.

Former prisoners and transformation

Former prisoners have been at the core in the formulation of the new politics within the republican movement. Their political development during imprisonment had important consequences for the construction of republican politics on the outside. Their strenuous campaign to present their prime identity as political actors rather than criminals resulted in the development of a different approach. This meshed electoral and non-state combatants dynamics, and was given momentum by the political mobilisation following the hunger strikes of the early 1980s. Thus, when republicans negotiated in the peace accord, prisoners were centered within it.

As a result former combatants were in reality treated as 'prisoners of war', and provided with the guarantee that they would be released within two years of any deal. This was made clear by Gerry Adams at the Sinn Fein *ard fheis* on 18 April 1998, where he saw the release of all political prisoners as a central expectation of the Good Friday Agreement, claiming that Sinn Féin would 'not rest until they are at home with their loved ones' (Adams 1998). More broadly, the peace process involved the recognition by Irish republicans that the goal of a united Ireland was unattainable, at least in the short to medium term and that such territorial demands were to softened to notions of the 'unity-of-peoples' and 'Ireland of Equals' (McAuley et al. 2008: 96). It also promoted an increased emphasis by Sinn Féin on an equality agenda emphasising human rights and parity of esteem, which were increasingly highlighting through community politics on a terrain where former prisoners were involved and effective in addressing such concerns.

Loyalist prisoners also saw themselves as politically motivated (Green, 1998) and the peace processes also saw a reconstruction of ideas within loyalist non-state combatants coalescing around the broad concept of conflict trans-formation. This notion had been in circulation within loyalism from around the mid-1980s (PUP 1985a, 1985b, 1986a; Rose 2008). Within the UVF/PUP grouping the role of former prisoners in seeking to transform the conflict was in currency for some time (Bloomer 2008; McAuley 2002, 2004, 2005), suggesting that while resolution between unionism and nationalism was impos-sible 'as they are diametrically opposed' the conflict could be transformed and 'out of this transformation can come a respect for diversity' (PUP 1986a). This became central to PUP policy, with as early as 1985 the leadership suggesting an 'agreeing to differ' programme for political progress and that Sinn Féin had the right to pursue its political goals by democratic means (PUP 1985a, 1985b, 1986b).

While the commitment to such notions took longer to build it has also become embedded within the largest of the loyalist non-state combatants organisations, the UDA. The reasons for the unevenness of commitment are far from insignificant. It took the UDA much longer to move to a position where the political was in ascendancy of over the military. Initially, at least, this was because many UDA members, including prisoners and former prisoners, believed the initial IRA ceasefire indicated weakness on the part of the republican movement, and that loyalist violence had unnerved the IRA and put them on the back foot. As one former UDA prisoner put it, the 'campaign we undertook did bring IRA/Sinn Fein to the talking tables' (UDA male). This view was expressed in terms of the surrender of republi-canism.

Even following the initial IRA ceasefire, many UDA members remained to be convinced that the Union was secure under the terms of the Agreement. The views of the following UDA former prisoner who was opposed to any ceasefire from loyalist groups (but who later came to support the peace process) is revealing of some of the tensions inherent within loyalist non-state combatant groups:

> I voted against it, I said no ceasefire now, because we were winning. Why would we stop when we were winning? I couldn't see the logic of it … It was said, if we get this sorted out youse'll be home at the year; but if you can't do the time, don't do the crime … and we argued and argued and argued and debated and debated. We didn't want to stop … Don't stop … See next week – hit them fucking harder. We wanted to hear them whinging. I could have done a hundred years in there when I heard them whinging. (UDA male)

These tensions within the UDA grouping intensified as the UDP found itself cut adrift from any serious level of public support, failing to secure any seats in the first Assembly election. Hence, the period witnessed the disbandment of the UDP and the increased marginalisation of those seeking to take the UDA in a more political direction. It was only following the IRA's announcement in July 2005 that its military campaign had ended, that there was some meaningful political movement around the notion of conflict transformation within the UDA community. This took shape following the publication of several discussion documents (see Hall 2006, 2007) and a widespread series of organised debates and discussions amongst the UDA's constituency.

Given that notions of transforming the conflict are now so deeply engrained across community-level politics in Northern Ireland it is worthwhile pausing to consider what is meant by the term. For Lederach (2003: 30) the approach 'centers its attention on the *context* of relationship patterns' allowing an approach that gives the opportunity 'to explore and understand the system of relationships and patterns that gave birth to the crisis'. At its core is an approach that targets the building of long-term relationships through mid-level groups and enabling them to develop tactics and processes of reconciliation (Lederach 1997; Rupesinghe 1995). It is anticipated that these 'peace constituencies' will be able to exert direct influence upwards to the macro level and downwards through leadership at grassroots level through supporting local actors and developing contacts with external providers. One former UDA prisoner put it rather more directly when he said:

> The term conflict transformation is about people who have been actively and physically involved in a conflict, that have come to a realisation that it's over, it has to stop, it's madness or whatever you want to say. You know, killing is futile, murdering people is futile, or we've had enough. Whatever, there's a realisation people come to and they say no we've got to move on, we can't stick here, we can't stay here. Like the Balkans or somewhere like that. We never went to that degree but we could have and thankfully we've got to a stage now where we realise we want to move on. So transformation is about that new reality and that new thought in your head saying I want to move on. (UDA male)

Across both loyalism and republicanism, various community-based initiatives testify to the central role former combatants hold within respective place-centered communities. A prime example are the restorative justice programmes which have developed as direct responses to informal policing and physical punishments undertaken by non-state combatants in Northern Ireland (Gormally et al. 1993). Restorative justice is by no means a new notion and remains far from unitary in its conceptualisation or implementation (Crawford and Newburn 2003; Maxwell and Morris 1995). Broadly, however, restorative justice focuses on a community response to law breaking

(White and Haines 2004: 183–4) through which offenders are obliged to take responsibility for their actions, and the victim and wider community are involved in defining the obligations placed on the offender with the over-arching aim of reintegrating the offender back into the community (Johnstone 2002).

The resulting engagement often includes making amends to their victim, community reparation, and developing strategies for self-improvement around social problems affecting a specific local community (BBC 2005; Neumann 2002). Since the late 1990s both republican and loyalist working-class commu-nities have been involved in operating restorative justice schemes whereby community leaders, including ex-combatants, have sought to instigate processes to develop non-violent alternatives to punishment beatings through schemes of restorative justice operating at a community level and focusing on anti-social behaviour. There are, however, different dynamics at play within loyalist and republican communities.

Those restorative justice schemes which have emerged in republican districts have been run as independently as possible from the formal state system, and in particular, the police service, albeit it now in the shape of the reformed PSNI. Those involved have often claimed, with some justification, that to engage fully with the PSNI would mean the loss of much creditability in the communities within which they operate. Although this is likely to change following the decision from Sinn Féin to sit on policing boards, remaining tensions were revealed when, following the move by Sinn Féin, threats were made by dissident republicans to those involved in restorative justice schemes (BBC November 2008). While there has always been a degree of alienation between the police and working-class loyalists, restorative justice programmes have developed in a context of working within the rule of the law as opposed to presenting any direct competition to the statutory law enforce-ment authorities. As McEvoy and Mika (2001a: 282) suggest, while loyalist community justice groups are often projected as an alternative to the state in their communities they are rarely seen as competing with it.

Despite fundamental differences in their ideological starting points, restorative justice projects in across both loyalism and republicanism present clear examples of the positive involvement of former non-state combatants in their respective communities. The membership of former prisoners in such groups has been one of their a defining features (McEvoy and Mika 2001a, 2001b; Winston 1997) and former prisoners, who often hold positions of credibility within identifiable working-class communities, are active in a wide range of non-pay-based groups and engaged in a broad spectrum of community work designed to move away from violent conflict (Gribben et al. 2005).

The perceived integrity and trustworthiness and community standing of those involved were recognised by one former IRA prisoner who explained 'you would have people who would look up to them [former prisoners] and who would follow you' (IRA male). One loyalist summarised the position of former prisoners in relation to their respective communities as follows:

> They've had the experience. I think they're absolutely instrumental and why we've got devolution today. I mean these groups who work around interfaces and stuff like that, whether they be INLA, Provisional IRA, Stickies, UVF, UDA. These guys will all be meeting each other and they'd be instrumental in community relations and starting cross-community dialogue and start getting us to a point where we can actually get a bit of peace in interface areas and start to move away from sectarianism and bigotry. (UDA male)

Community transformation and legitimacy

So how can we understand the relationships between former prisoners and the broader community? Upon release former prisoners face several issues. Some of these are problems common to all, whether having served time for politically motivated or 'ordinary' offences. These include how to negotiate access to emotional and economic resources, including for example, shelter, food and employment. There are broader concerns surrounding access to welfare support and social networks, either old or new, and how to make or reconnect social relationships (Wolff and Draine 2004).

For politically motivated prisoners in Northern Ireland there are other levels of transition and negotiation, including 'negative and discriminatory attitudes' as well as 'legal restrictions with regard to travel, parental rights, and retirement benefits' (Féron 2007: 450). Further, former politically motivated prisoners must negotiate other relationships with their non-state combatant organisations and their 'host' communities. Put starkly the initial decision facing former prisoners rests on a continuum between walking away from further involvement to continued commitment to the cause. Those former prisoners who remain engaged have sought to exert direct influence in two main realms: first, through party political organisation, and second, through a range of community-based organisations within which former prisoners formed a key dynamic. Here in particular former prisoners have undertaken key roles to prevent a return to conflict and to inhibit the influence of any potential spoilers of peace.

Personal and group transitions involving former prisoners have been crucial to the peace process and the embedding of changes to social and political relationships at the community level. Republican and loyalist prisoners who have continued to seek change under the broad banner of conflict transformation have developed a sophisticated range of tactics to support the transition from overt conflict. For politically motivated former prisoners conflict transformation operates at different levels: internally it is 'concerned with the cultural, social and economic dimensions to community development', while externally 'conflict transformation can involve dialogue between former combatants; attempts at understanding each other's perceptions and histories' (Shirlow et al. 2005: 18). What follows highlights some of the major activities of former non-state combatants following their release, while identifying patterns of difference that emerge in experiences between former loyalist and republican prisoners.

For some, particularly many from a unionist background, the idea that former non-state combatants can provide strong political (perhaps at times even moral) leadership is difficult to even contemplate, let alone support. This is particularly so when it comes from those who can directly be associated with performed violent acts (Shirlow and McEvoy 2008: 130–2). There can be little doubt, however, that many former prisoners actively performed in reducing conflict and confrontation. One former UDA prisoner suggested that it was former prisoners who:

> laid the ground for devolved government ... enabled through their community leadership at grassroots level, stopping trouble at interfaces, promoting the community to do community development, working in community relations. They've had the experience. I think they're absolutely instrumental and why we've got devolution today, they've shown great leadership. (UDA male)

Former prisoners see areas such as conflict-management education, restorative justice, campaigning around social and economic issues, and the facilitation of cross-community contacts as legitimate arenas in which to work. Much of this involves representing their communities to statutory bodies, and means that loyalist and republican community activists often work side by side through cross-community projects and issues of joint concern.

The negotiation and direction of involvement in these issues is for a large part determined by the status and legitimacy that former prisoners have in their community. The existence of strong links between those imprisoned for non-state combatant offences is undeniable. It is also important to consider how these relationships have been mobilised to seek to achieve wider community goals. Such concerns have resonance with recent debates around the notion of social capital, which has been placed centrally in research agendas, by the works of Putnam (1993, 1995) and Coleman (1988, 1998) the response to which has spawned an extensive literature (Portes 1998).

While the concept is used diversely (Anheier and Kendall 2002; Harper 2001) uniting aspects of its conceptualisation are membership of social networks, and the emergence of relationships of trust and other meaningful social relationships through the development of these networks (Pretty and Ward 2001). Perhaps most important in our context is Putnam's claim that the production of social capital can bring about shared social values and social bonds that enhance civil society and enable levels of trust to be built that ensure working civic institutions may be formed. This is enabled through the development of bonding capital. Other forms of social capital, most notably bridging capital, help generate broader identities which connect the local to other groups in society up to the macro level (Beem 1999: 22–3).

The contemporary construction of politics for republican and loyalist former prisoners draws on intense senses of internal social solidarity and the strength of the social networks that reinforce these bonds. It focuses on the areas of social life where civil society and politics meet, and at times are overlaid. One does not need to go far in Northern Ireland to find evidence of the strength of continuing reproduction of social relationships and social bonding that rest on a strong sense of community identity (Shirlow and Murtagh 2006). Within what remains of working-class communities in particular, social bonds remain strong (Hall 2002); indeed the development and growth of non-state combatants groupings can only be understood in the context of closely bonded and often geographically demarcated working-class communities.

Former republican prisoners and community

There are important similarities and differences between loyalist and republican communities. Republican former prisoners faced some advantages upon release, compared with their loyalist counterparts. Not least were the structural opportunities for reintegration that existed through political roles within Sinn Fein and the various republican prisoner support groups. As Féron (2006: 451) suggests, for former republican non-state combatants 'there are many possibilities for reconversion: either as activists in … Sinn Féin, or through the dense networks of community activity in the Catholic community'. Moreover, as Bruce (2004: 505) points out, for republican former prisoners, involvement in the community politics structured around Sinn Fein allowed them to remain true 'to some part of their self image as rebels'.

Indeed, it has been argued that widespread support for Sinn Fein within nationalist communities and perception of the armed struggle as having once been necessary means that former republican prisoners operate within what can be seen as broadly positive local environment (Shirlow 2001: 24). Most republican former prisoners interviewed claimed that it was 'the IRA's armed struggle [that] brought the Brits to the negotiating table' (IRA male) or 'brought the Brits to a position where they knew they had to negotiate' (IRA female) and that 'the armed struggle was necessary … to bring us to this point' (IRA female).

These views were commonplace amongst former republican prisoners. Certainly the end of IRA activity did not precipitate deep questioning amongst activists regarding the justification for the IRA's military campaign. Upon release, the final Officer Commanding of republican prisoners in the Maze prison insisted that prisoners were 'unbowed and unbroken' and 'determined to pursue and achieve the goals for which so many gave their lives, that is the establishment of a united democratic socialist republic' (BBC 2000). The claims of past and continuing legitimacy are vital to the republican senses of image, self-worth and justification across the broader nationalist/republican community. As this former IRA prisoner argued:

> in reality it was only a small amount of people who took up arms and fought in the armed campaign. Well now, we've come out and we have a certain legitimacy among communities and people are beginning to say to you, sorry I never joined. We took our own decisions and lives, but we haven't anything against you, but people are beginning to say there's no way we'd be here today without the IRA. My own view is the same, it was the foundation – like the hunger strike-at the end of the hunger strike period. When I seen [sic] outside the huge support and the huge number of people who came out in against H blocks and hundreds of thousands of people all over the island. Some people would argue that if hadn't done the armed stuff you'd be further on. I don't know. My view is, no, we had to. (IRA male)

While the new republican politics, partly formulated by prisoners, involves the disavowal of armed struggle and the promotion of electoral politics, involving support for the police service and entry into a government of Northern Ireland this has not eroded communalism, which remains stark within the Northern Ireland polity. As one former IRA prisoner put it: 'many ex-prisoners have actually been involved in developing Sinn Fein, have been involved in community work, etc. I mean they're everywhere … ex-prisoners are part and parcel of the community … in lots of ways the ex-prisoners are actually the backbone of an awful lot of things that go on within communities now and always have been' (IRA male).

Within the grouping of former prisoners (and republicanism generally) this sense of communalism is maintained through the belief in the legitimacy of what they had done and that recent changes in political direction and method-ology will still realise their ultimate political goal. A republican former prisoner contended:

> The IRA had a job to do. It was to put the British under pressure in a military sense to force them to sit and talk. Get Sinn Féin involved and talk. And then through that there – they achieved it … Us, the IRA, we're still here. And as long as we're here we'll do the damage. Their politics didn't change – their [the IRA's] policy changed. What they were doing they were doing for Sinn Féin … always had a sort of plan laid down. Gerry Adams shifted, the whole leadership and the movement in general. I don't think their core ideology has changed. … I think it's all tactical. It's they way they use and the way they do things – going from A to B. They have to get ways round those obstacles. Those were the stepping-stones. (IRA male)

Thus the decision to abandon violence is regarded as purely tactical rather than any weakening of republican principles. These themes were clearly reflected in the following:

> Well the terminology used by the republican leadership at the minute would suggest that maybe, maybe it has tempered what it wants to achieve … you no longer hear terms of the IRA, or you know, cutting edge of the armed struggle. Now it's an Ireland of equals and the peace process and so on. I don't think … that the optimum objective has changed, but if you were to say to us ten years ago this is how we're going to go about it, you'd, you'd have been laughed at. I think that that's one of the biggest reasons why unionists are so fearful of republicans sharing power; because they know republicans are motivated, they know republicans will work the institutions … realistically Unionists know that they're on the back-foot and they're trying to delay change. (IRA male)

As this former IRA volunteer recognised, however, the new approach was not straightforward in its application:

> I think the armed struggle did keep people together. You can get very weary of it and that might sound a bit maybe cruel given the human cost, you know, people kept their spirits high and people knew where they belonged and it was easy to see, you know, it was easy to do what you did in certain ways. It was clear what you were doing. The political route is much more cloudy, you know. It's hard to see the effects of your actions and that sort of thing, it's hard to see success. It's a much longer, more tortuous route but the armed struggle, which I've no doubt brought us to the position where we're at. (IRA female)

This view was also reflected by the comment of a male IRA former prisoner who acknowledged: 'Unarmed struggle? I am finding it hard to get my head round concepts of it because I don't think there's as much urgency about what is happening now as opposed to what is happening ten years ago and I think whereas you always had a clearly defined role in the movement … now it's not so clearly defined.'

Given these concerns a crucial part of the roles of former prisoners has been in building bonding social capital within the republican community. For many republican former prisoners the move from armed conflict to community work is seen as 'seamless' (Mike Ritchie, cited in McKeever 2007: 429). Thus, for example, the prison experience is regularly recounted through a seemingly ever-expanding calendar of commemoration events and celebrations, all of which are used to link previous armed struggle with its contemporary unarmed phase. The overall result for Mulholland (2007: 414) is that while the armed struggle may not have brought about a break with the *de facto* legitimacy of the Northern Irish state, working-class nationalist and republican enclaves nonetheless 'developed in the course of the conflict a resilient local public sphere structured by heavily nationalist republican discourse – encoded in festivals, commemorative ritual, non-government al community services, murals, memorials, posters and so on'.

Former loyalist prisoners and community

It is now fairly widely accepted that 'more often than not Protestant paramilitaries enjoy less prestige in their community than their Republican counterparts, who managed to preserve their image as defenders of the people' (Féron
2006: 451). That is not to say that loyalist non-state combatants do not also
have a community focus and are not embedded in some sections of Protestant
working-class social structure. From their emergence, defence of community
was central to their ideology, and many who took an active role in non-state
combative organisations were also involved in community development,
housing issues and local politics (Winston 1997: 122–8). Indeed, at one point
in the 1970s the UDA oversaw the formation of the Ulster Community Action
Group (UCAG) to co-ordinate community development initiatives in loyalist
areas. As this former UDA prisoner saw it:

> I would say that the ex-prisoners probably, had there been no Troubles, would have
> been activists in their own community anyway. They have that in them, they have
> that sort of burning in their stomach, that drive in them. They say here this is
> wrong what's happening in our community, so if there hadn't have been the
> Troubles, they would have been activists in their community anyway, in the labour
> movement, or trade union movement. You know, they're leaders in their own way,
> in their own communities even before they'd go into prison. (UDA male)

The levels of interest displayed in community-level politics by loyalist non-
state combatants has fluctuated throughout the conflict, but in the contemporary period as prisoners were increasing released under the terms of the
Agreement there was a growth in self-help organisations and projects for, and
organised by, former prisoners (Bacon 2001; Gribbin et al. 2005; Hall 2002).

Loyalist combatants, however, never enjoyed the breath or depth of
support given to their republican counterparts. The loyalist perspective on
differences in the relationships between former non-state combatants and their
respective communities is neatly encapsulated in the following statement from
David Rose, an executive member of the PUP:

> Catholics tended to see the prisoners and the paramilitary groups (Provisional Irish
> Republican Army/Irish National Liberation Army) as politically motivated
> defenders of their community and thus were solid in their support for the release
> of detainees. Most Protestants saw the 'security forces' as defenders of their
> community and consequently viewed the prisoners as 'illegitimate' or 'criminal.'
> (Rose, 2008)

The perceived differences in the relationships between loyalism, republicanism
and their respective communities reflect other consistent voices heard from
within loyalism expressing broader mistrust of the established unionist political
leadership. First, the representatives of loyalism have decried the traditional
unionist leadership, by which they mean both the UUP and the DUP, as

distant from the needs and everyday concerns of ordinary Protestants. The PUP has consistently claimed that traditional unionism is driven by a middle-class leadership unconcerned for working-class issues and values. Indeed, the PUP has consistently argued that the intransigence of DUP and the UUP throughout the peace process has been highly detrimental to the broad aspirations of unionism, and specifically working-class loyalism. The antipathy between the political representatives of loyalism was so strong that David Ervine of the PUP was once led to claim that many unionists hated him more than they hated Gerry Adams, because 'We were alien in so much as we were "breaking the line". Wee working-class boys, such as us, are not expected to have opinions' (cited in Sinnerton 2002: 218).

Second, there has been a constant discourse from within loyalist non-state combatants suggesting that many young working-class men who joined organisations felt they were responding directly to the demands of the unionist political leadership, which in turn then overtly criticised their actions and left them unsupported them in prison (Coulter 1999; McAuley 1991, 1994, 1995). This former UDA prisoner made this position clear when he claimed:

> I think we were used and abused by the wider unionist community, there's a lot of hypocrisy within middle unionism. I think they used paramilitaries in order to strengthen their negotiating position. You know the type of thing 'if you don't deal with us then there's these sort of bogymen behind the door ready to come out'. There is a traditional hypocrisy in Protestantism, while they would possibly give their tacit support to paramilitary actions in the past then they don't like to be seen up front supporting people who would have tenuous links with these paramilitary groupings so they won't give it their support. (UDA male)

This social and political distance is understood to still exist within unionism. One UDA leader recently expressed his concern that 'the loyalist community will become the forgotten people of the peace process' (cited in Rowan, 2008: 157). A male UVF respondent outlined what he saw as the current situation of former prisoners within the Unionist community, arguing that: 'It wouldn't matter that you would argue how well you're educated or how well you have done since you have come out of prison, you've been in work all that time and you have got on with your life etc, etc, they will still say this thing 'aye but thirty years ago you did A, B and C'.

It is now commonplace to hear loyalists express concerns that they are marginalised economically, socially and politically and have been abandoned by the unionist politicians and fared badly from the peace process. One male UVF former prisoner, discussing the legacy of paramilitary involvement, claimed: 'I don't think they [loyalist paramilitaries] ever had the support republicans had, and even now I think that is even worse now in unionist communities. I think it is because former paramilitaries particularly prisoners are seen as blacklisted and all that there. It is almost like you can't escape that past.'

Despite different patterns in the levels of political mobilisation between the UVF and the UDA (McAuley, 2004; Wood, 2006) and while it has taken more time to establish amongst the UDA grouping, it is now clear that the political leadership of the all loyalist non-state combatant groups are committed to the concept of conflict transformation (Bloomer 2008; Hall 2007). For some former prisoners, however, there remains a view that the contemporary changes within the republican movement has merely resulted in a differing form of conflict. Thus one suggested 'I think their military war is over but they're fighting on a different battlefield now. So I don't think it's really over' (UDA male), while another argued while 'Physically their armed struggle is over ... the political war still goes on' (UDA male). One member summarised his perception of the political position of contemporary republicanism as follows:

> I believe they've reached another strategic decision in their long history of mutiny, of trying to get British people and systems out of Ireland and part of that has always been to evolve politically. And we've seen that with Michael Collins 1916-21 and we see De Valera after that when he split the movement and went into opposition in Dail Eireann and basically the same thing happened in '75 when the Official IRA split ... Sinn Féin has split, some of its members have left other have formed armed splinter groups and taken arms from the main movement with them and formed the Real IRA and there are others who are still there like the INLA, who have never went away, who have their arms and the right to use them as well. So in terms of that they will strategise ... So all the while there will be acts of war brought on by political means within the new institutions of the state with the police attacking unionist culture and downsizing our identity and more investment being deployed to promote the Irish culture and identity. (UDA male)

So what forms have the leadership taken by former prisoners taken? It is apparent that 'on-the-ground' action by former non-state combatants has offered political direction and everyday guidance that has directly challenged a return to conflict on the streets. Moreover, they have sought to change cultures of violence in Northern Ireland, for example, as Gribbin et al. (2005: 60) point out, within loyalist communities, practitioners involved in conflict transformation 'are often, but not always, former paramilitaries' and the efforts of former prisoners to reduce tension at interface areas and during contentious marches have been widely viewed as a key element in the comparatively peaceful marching seasons in recent years (Jarman, 2004). For some the role for former prisoners is clear: to

> start to break down the barriers and the dehumanisation and stuff like that. People will say 'why meet them? They're the other side. I'll get killed by my own community if I meet them ones.' But if you see a leading loyalist, an ex-prisoner, coming out to meet them, they're like that 'fuck me, he's gone away and met the other side. I'll go and meet them.' You know what I mean? It's all right if he's doing it. So I think [former prisoners have] shown great leadership. (UDA male)

Loyalist former prisoners operate within a particular context, however, and much of the role of community politics remains contested within unionism. Throughout the past decade the term 'weak community infrastructure' has increasingly been used by and in relation to loyalist communities, where civil society is seen as less developed than it is in Catholic districts, and where it is also seen that there is a continuing reluctance to engage in the politics of community development or to organise any collective community or political actions (Cairns et al. 2003; Community Convention and Development Company 2006; Langhammer 2003; McCarron 2006). That said, former loyalist prisoners are integrated into processes of change within their working-class communities, revealing the capacity and ability to exhibit positive community roles around, for example, restorative justice, campaigns supporting the development of local resources, against anti-social behaviour and other positive inter- and intra-community approaches.

Civil society and social bonds

Central to the processes of conflict transformation are the effects of social cohesion on the broader civil society. It is possible to understand social capital as a 'web of cooperative relationships between citizens that facilitate resolution of collective action problems' (Brehm and Rahn 1997: 999) seeking to create 'a culture of trust and tolerance, in which extensive networks of voluntary associations emerge' (Inglehart 1997: 188). So how successful have these strategies been in altering cross-community views and building social bonds and norms?

If we refer back to the centrality of the deionisation of the other highlighted in Chapter 3, Fitzduff and Gormley (2000: 62 – 63) suggest that the deconstruction of the negative other involves a three-stage process. The first is the recognition that perceptions of the 'other' actually exist. The second is the realisation that processes of alienation and ghettoisation perpetuate negative perceptions of the other. Finally, the third stage is to seek to deal with the attitudinal and behavioural results of ghettoisation. This is to be done by bringing the communities together by implementing social and political processes, which challenge the myth that the others are different and that this brings negative consequences.

Despite some of the important transformations indicated throughout this book, it would be wrong to suggest that there is linear progress towards societal reconciliation in Northern Ireland. Any long-term conflict, such as that experienced in Northern Ireland, involves the social construction of opposi-tional groups based on the delegitimisation, demonisation and depersonalisa-tion of the other. As Lederach puts it, conflict 'transforms perceptions, of self, others, and the issues in question, usually with the consequence of less accurate understanding of the other's intention and decreased ability to clearly articu-late one's own intentions' (Lederach 1995: 18).

The crucial roles of former prisoners in developing and building organic relationship between individuals and the communities have increasingly been recognised (Cassidy 2005, 2008; Shirlow and McEvoy 2008). Elsewhere, McKeever (2007) has provided clear evidence of the willingness and ability of former prisoners to be 'good citizens' and engage positively in political and social transition, albeit from very differing perspectives.

Former prisoners have begun to offer new possibilities through processes of personalising members of the oppositional group and accepting that the needs and goals of the other may be legitimate. Here, undoubtedly there has been movement; particularly recognition by former prisoner groups that that they inhabit similar social worlds of economic marginalisation and social exclusion. Community activism is seen as a crucial way to challenge this social position and a key means of delivering the peace process. The role of former prisoners as organic intellectuals has been used in ways to promote and reinforce existing group identities and political structures. This allows groups, including former prisoners, to promote their legitimacy and broader beliefs, albeit in a structured and non-violent manner. Given this one set of relationships to be considered are the perceptions and understandings across the two communities. Indeed, a crucial change in transforming any conflict situation is a shift in views concerning perceptions regarding the rival group.

In terms of the relationship of former prisoners to civil society, it is useful to refer to Woolcock, who distinguishes between different forms of social capital that can be created. For him, bonding social capital identifies those relationships 'between people in similar situations, such as immediate family, close friends and neighbours' (2001: 13). Taking this definition the level of bonding within working class communities, both republican and loyalist, is high. Woolcock further identifies bridging capital which 'encompasses more distant ties of like persons, such as loose friendships and networks' and linking social capital 'which, reaches out to unlike people in dissimilar situations, such as those who are entirely outside of the community' (2001: 13–14).

Former prisoners possess and utilise various forms social capital. While those who successfully build and draw upon bridging and linking capital may provide evidence for those who argue that contact is important in reducing conflict (Hewstone and Brown 1986; Niens et al. 2003), processes of ideological transformation and reconciliation remain limited. Although perhaps not as strongly demonised as they once were, strong beliefs regarding the 'other' are sustained despite the development of inter-group activity. Much social capital remains inwardly focused, and to ensure legitimacy primacy continues to be given to bonding rather than bridging social and political relations. Intra-community cohesion remains high. Equally observable, however, is the level of social division between communities, where lack of meaningful levels of social trust constantly reinforce social distance from the other (Bacon 2001; Gribbin et al., 2005).

Limits to change: loyalist perceptions of the 'other'

None of the loyalist former prisoners interviewed claimed to have lessened in their commitment to the Union or professed to be feeling any weaker in 'loyalist' identity. Political change was preceded by cognisance of the limited utility of violence as a tactical tool. This recognition, however, lies a considerable distance from repudiation of the past, or acceptance of the contemporary legitimacy of opposing ideology. Unease over the baldness of previously stated views, as discovered among republicans by English (2003), does not equate to endorsement of counter-views. The breadth and depth of support for the peace process among prisoners does not necessarily equate to substantial ideological change. Instead, the movement away from conflict can be seen predominantly as political expediency, which allows stated goals to remain intact and permits continuing denial of the legitimacy of rival ideologies. The Good Friday Agreement shifted inter-communal struggle into political institutions, but this only ameliorated, rather than removed, the territorial aspects of conflict causation and arguably enshrined communal differences. Intra-group deliberations over the conduct of that struggle have not required disorienting movement from earlier negative perceptions of opponents. What has been sought has been accommodation, not integration, or even fundamental reappraisal. Cordial personal relations among former prisoners across the divide have been accompanied by limited political thawing and social trust and bonding relationships are not widespread. Perceptions of the 'other' community in general, and Sinn Fein in particular, remain highly negative. In particular, hostility is expressed towards the 'Sinn Fein machine', and an unquestioning following of the republican leadership. One UVF member offered a typical view of Sinn Féin senior members as 'all control freaks', who shunned 'anyone who disagrees ... even ex-republican prisoners' (UVF male).

Most loyalist former prisoners regard republican conversion from physical force to politics as enforced by loyalist actions and bereft of meaning among republicans, who are still attempting to win a war by other means. Loyalists argue that they helped defeat the IRA, but tend to covet what they commonly regard as the political machine of Sinn Fein. Some fear losing the peace as a consequence, but others are more confident, a UDA former prisoner saying: 'they [Sinn Fein] tell their people about a united Ireland. In their dreams ... it's never going to happen' (UDA male). Loyalist antipathy towards republicans is maintained through a residual bitterness towards the perceived sectarian nature of the republican war and the 'Roman Catholic nationalist' outlook of Sinn Fein (UVF male); irritation at the supposedly more favourable perceptions of republicanism as a coherent and progressive ideology and frustration at the continuing rejection of the British identity of loyalists. An urban male former UVF prisoner articulated these concerns as follows:

in many ways it was a sectarian war, not about religion as such but more about
identities … I think republicans have this myth around them that they were
fighting this ideological war, it's a nonsense. I think through conversations that
we've had with republicans that they are under the impression that we are all going
to wake up one day and realise that we are Irish. I think that's a nonsense.

Sectarian attitudes remain evident within loyalism, encapsulated in the
assertion of a UDA former prisoner: 'I don't see anything positive about the
Irish at all, because of their religion and I'm not anti-Catholic, I'm just anti
Roman Catholic.' Loyalists deny the emergence of new republicanism, arguing
that their views are 'entrenched' (UDA Belfast former prisoner) whilst as a
collective republicans are 'brainwashed' (UDA male) with the only positive
aspect about them, according to another UDA male former prisoner, being
that 'they've stopped bombing and killing for the time being'. Moreover, there
remains considerable scepticism among loyalists over whether the conflict has
been transformed. Thus a UVF rural male was scathing:

Sometimes I think some of these terms that they use are a lot of crap. I honestly
do. I mean conflict transformation, what do they mean? The conflict basically is
over, but as far as I'm concerned there still is a war going on in other ways politically and even on the ground territorially that war is still going on.

A now leading member of the PUP and former prisoner suggested 'a different
type of conflict is going on now' (UVF male) while another loyalist argued
'politically … there's still a war going on' (UDA male).

Many loyalist prisoner groups work between and across culturally and
politically polarised communities. The primary goal for much of the developmental work undertaken, however, is to bring benefit to their community and
indeed this is how such actions are often justified to the wider loyalist
community. Although accepting the broad framework of conflict transformation that has been created, many former loyalist prisoners remain more
concerned with conditions in their own communities and the creation of
bonding social capital, rather than with that which bridges the sectarian
divide.

Many loyalists expressed frustration at their inability to mobilise the
loyalist community: 'getting involved in street politics and community politics
and eyeballing the enemy and putting your point of view across is the positive
way forward and unfortunately there's not enough of us doing it', was how one
UVF male articulated what needs to be done. Others, while stressing the lack
of trust, argue that republicans 'believe in something and they stick to it'
(UDA male) and that Sinn Fein had done a good job for 'their' community
and they were far ahead of loyalists in community organisation. One former
UDA prisoner wished for loyalist community involvement 'going along the
same lines that the Shinners [Sinn Fein] went; working from grassroots, getting
people identified in communities that work for people and then stand them for

local council elections. Get a big enough profile by doing work for people and then get MLAs [Assembly members]' (UDA male).

Another loyalist former prisoner recognised the political ability of Sinn Féin, even claiming that if he were Catholic he would be a Sinn Fein voter. He continued as follows:

> I know we hear all the time about this machine but I think their electoral people that have been as successful as they have done, have come from that working-class background that they engage with their community. Whereas I don't see that in unionism because they have been elected from the middle-class business type community and in my opinion they don't share our communities interests (UVF male).

More limits to change: republican perceptions of the 'other'

Despite dramatic u-turns in terms of IRA military and Sinn Fein political tactics, including weapons decommissioning and disbandment, the end of abstention from political institutions and support for policing, republican former prisoners tend to claim fidelity to some traditional positions. Few accept the principle of consent for constitutional change and most continue to question whether nationalists can ever enjoy full parity of esteem within the northern state.

Republicans do not accept the claims of loyalists to have 'won the war', but acknowledge that loyalist agreement to political change would at least be useful. Republicans are scathing over the lack of political development among former loyalist paramilitaries and condemnatory over the nature of their 'military' campaign, whilst acknowledging the effectiveness of pro-state terror. Thus a former member of the Belfast IRA, Tommy Gorman, claimed that:

> The Loyalist campaign of violence was pure British logic. Counter-gangs happened in Aden, in Egypt, Kenya and elsewhere. Even with the 'Shankill Butchers', who mutilated people because just killing wasn't enough, it was designed to terrorise Catholics into rejecting the IRA. It was indiscriminate and, to a degree, it worked. People were very scared. (Quoted in Bean and Hayes 2001: 99)

What to 'do' about loyalists has often rendered republicans uncomfortable, the British presence on the island of Ireland complicating the presentation of the political problem as merely one of Britain's sovereign claims. During the conflict, republican 'thinking' on loyalism underwent several unsatisfactory developments. Throughout the 1970s, loyalists, viewed naively as merely deluded Irish people suffering some form of British false consciousness, were to be accommodated within a new, federal Ireland, Eire Nua. During the following decade, republican policy was one of no concessions to loyalism, an illegitimate entity which was to be defeated in the formation of a unitary state.

By the 1990s, amid the launch of Sinn Fein's (1992) document *Towards a Lasting Peace in Ireland*, there was greater cognisance of the identity of loyalists and acknowledgement that they needed to be persuaded of the merits of a united Ireland. Unlike other aspects of republican activity, such as the move into electioneering, little of the limited intellectual development on what constituted loyalism – or how to deal with loyalists – during the 1970s and 1980s came from republican prisoners, policy in this respect being formulated 'on the outside'. The gentler, more conciliatory tone of republican policy since the 1990s has been derived partly from the recognition of the need for mutual co-existence developed within the prisons. According to Gerry Adams, loyalist paramilitaries were 'used and abused' by unionist politicians and it was thus necessary for republicans initially to seek political partnerships among an emergent pragmatic wing of loyalist paramilitarism, movement reciprocated among loyalist former prisoners such as David Ervine and Billy Hutchinson of the PUP (BBC September 2008).

Shirlow and McEvoy (2008) demonstrate the willingness of former non-state combatants to display political generosity to rivals from the other ethnic bloc. Although there are dissenters who reject either the 'deceptions' or 'sell-outs' of the Sinn Fein leadership, the new politics and tactics of Sinn Fein have been recognised and embraced by most former republican prisoners. These new tactics require pragmatic, not ideological, accommodation with opponents. Some former prisoners 'have absolutely no problem working with loyalists or unionists' (IRA male) while others recognise 'it's the same with any grouping or community; there's – you would say good ones and bad ones' (IRA male). Another identified the relationships built up as follows: 'We do know a number of them that you can work with that you'll be able to work with in the future' (IRA male). Thus, some forms of reconciliation are evident through working personal relationships that exist between many former combatants. One former IRA prisoner put this directly when he said 'I can see a small group of them that really are politically motivated, have good intentions, do not have bad intentions against Catholics anymore, who aren't sectarian in the way they used to be' (IRA male).

Such views were not widely held, however, and there is no evidence to suggest that relationships extend to accepting core political or ideological perspectives of 'the other'. As one former combatant suggested: 'there are some people within loyalism who I actually trust and there's more that I wouldn't' (IRA male). The shifts in political relationships have not in general been accompanied by ideological reappraisals of unionism or psychological shifts in attitudes towards unionists. Loyalism is still understood as an ideology that is illegitimate and irrational, certainly in comparison with what is perceived as the coherence of republicanism. The view of one former IRA prisoner that his attitude 'towards loyalism and unionism as ideologies is – more pity than sympathy' (IRA male) is typical.

Others believe that loyalism and its ideological base are best understood as an expression of supremacist politics. As one former IRA prisoner sought to explain:

> I think that all they're sort of fighting for is … we were the masters, we had everything we want; we could do what we want. Now they're scared of losing that. Now they're seeing the nationalist community are educated and they're not going to back down, we've been oppressed for so long. And they're looking at us, saying look at the difference. Them Taigs had nothing, now look at them, their areas – they're getting all this funding, apart from a few things. (IRA male)

Moreover, the existence of loyalism as an autonomous social and political force outside its British connection is denied. Reflecting ideological positions laid down in the 1970s and 80s (Bell 1976; De Paor 1970; Farrell 1976; McCann 1972), working-class Protestant workers are seen as a grouping, which at partition surrendered any notion of independence and tied itself directly to the British presence. Loyalists are still essentially seen as part of the British 'opposition', associated directed 'with the British state' (IRA female), and as a grouping 'largely based in sectarianism' (IRA male) and 'used by the state' (IRA Female). One former prisoner summarised this position as follows:

> Broadly, for me, loyalism has only been a front for the Brits. It's always been the patsy, it's this normalisation, Ulsterisation thing, that the Brits were able to step back, become the honest brokers. I mean, you see it in unionism now, and the sort of process they're involved in now. The Brits want to always step back now and say 'It's these ones'. It's more – loyalism – the development in loyalism now has more to do with British strategy rather than internal development. (IRA male)

Despite the good working relationships between different former prisoners and in some cases the strength of personal bonds created across the communities, the level of social trust remains restricted. Some former republican prisoners expressed this directly stating about loyalists: 'I don't trust them. I'm just being honest about that' (IRA female) or 'I don't trust them. The same way I don't trust the British' (IRA female). Contact with loyalists did not always strengthen individual or social bonds: 'Loyalists today, I have been at workshops with them, I have been at planning days with them. They would be very hard to trust. I don't think they know where they're going. They take the jail experience with them … you could never trust them. I don't think they knew where they were going' (IRA male).

Since the conflict, republicans have developed a programme of unionist outreach. This does not require any ideological conversion or adaptation, but does demand local conciliation and accommodation with the 'rival' community. There are six core elements to the outreach programme: working with unionists to reduce inter-community tension, particularly in sectarian interface areas; joint challenges to inequality and social tension; joint initiatives to build mutual trust and respect; the development of social capital and facilitation of sustainable relationships; contributions towards a shared future and the prevention of 'negative elements', such as 'dissidents', from fostering division (Martina Anderson, former IRA prisoner, now Sinn Fein Assembly member).

Set against outreach are the communal instincts which characterised aspects of northern provisional republicanism. Communal exclusivism is nonetheless blamed on the other side. Thus a Belfast republican former prisoner argued of loyalists that 'because they are interested in their community, they are interested in basic rights for their people. Their problem is that they don't really want them for other people ... so they'll be reactionary whether it be immigrants, blacks, nationalists, republicans'.

Another Belfast republican former prisoner was explicit in his view that peace was to be won in a similar manner to war and that unionists were to be defeated:

> If I was a unionist I'd be terrified and to be honest I'm proud that unionists are terrified. I'm not going to be the advocate of unionism here. I am delighted to see disarray, lack of leadership, lack of policy, lack of practically anything regarding politics because I am anti-unionist. I'm pure anti-unionist. And I'm going to see unionism fail as a political entity. (IRA male)

Negative republican former prisoner perceptions of loyalists thus contain four aspects. First, loyalists are seen as non-autonomous, frequently described in group discussions as 'agents of the British state'. Second, they are seen as sectarian, a view typified in the pithy comment of one male former IRA prisoner that 'Protestants in the Six Counties hate Catholics'. Third, the progressive aspects of loyalism are denied, those who have 'strayed on the path of equality or socialism' having been 'slapped down' according to one urban woman former IRA prisoner. Fourth, as another woman former IRA prisoner argued, 'loyalism embraces everything that's wrong with British society instead of grasping what's good about British society, i.e. ordinary working-class British politics, socialist politics maybe'.

Some republicans even believed it possible that the loyalist groups might return to conflict, another male IRA former prisoner insisting: 'I think that they talk the talk when it comes to building peace and, and they pretend that they want peace but I would think that the first indication that there's gonna be a majority of people here voting for a united Ireland maybe they'll start killing again.'

While recognising the depth of social bonding between former prisoners and their respective communities there remain identifiable social and political barriers to the development of social trust and bridging networks. In spite of the valuable contribution that many former prisoners have made, and continue to make, in the sphere of conflict transformation and community development, the ideological and political distance between loyalist and republican former prisoners remains apparent.

Conclusion: working together; staying apart

Clear working parameters and even strong personal relationships have been developed between many republican and loyalist former prisoners operating leadership roles at community levels. Loyalist perceptions of republicans, and republican perceptions of loyalists, have not altered markedly in ideological terms. Former prisoners have played important roles in preventing a drift back towards conflict and in developing confidence in political futures, both within their ethnic bloc and in formulating the new relations between unionism and nationalism. At times, this has reflected flexibility in self-identity, and provided the legitimacy to build inter-community linkages. Despite the success of such strategies, however, it is also important to state that ideological and discursive divisions between loyalists and republicans remain deeply embedded. The valuable contribution that many former prisoners have made (and continue to make) in the sphere of conflict transformation and community development should not be allowed to mask the continued ideological and political distance between loyalist and republican former prisoners.

7 Former prisoners and societal reconstruction

The 1998 Good Friday Agreement laid down procedures for the accelerated release of prisoners affiliated to groups that had committed to a 'complete and unequivocal ceasefire' and acknowledged the need to 'facilitate the reintegration of prisoners into the community by providing support both prior to and after release, including assistance directed towards availing of employment opportunities, re-training and/or re-skilling and further education' (HM Government 1998: 30). McKeever (2007: 423) contends that 'the reintegration commitment within the Agreement implicitly (and positively) recognises the particular role of ex-prisoners as protagonists, not only of the conflict, but of the developing post-conflict society, and of the social value in ensuring their inclusion as central stakeholders in this developing society'. Other government documents have echoed this; for example, nine years after the Agreement, advice to businesses on employing former prisoners contained the following assertion: 'Many ex-prisoners, since release, have played an active and positive role in conflict transformation processes within republicanism and loyalism. The importance of these processes has been well documented by a number of international studies' (ofmdfm.gov.uk 2007). In addition, former prisoners and their organisations have been keen to stress that they have proved a positive social and political force.

Mitchell (2008) points out that prisoner releases were an unpopular and controversial element of the Agreement and survey data shows that the policy was supported by 31 per cent of Catholics and only 3 per cent of Protestants (Northern Ireland Life and Times Survey 2000). Negative views of former prisoners and paramilitaries in general have persisted in media, political and popular circles and Mitchell argues that establishing legitimacy has been a particular problem for loyalists. She believes that 'until politicians, employers and other actors in civil society address the issue of legitimacy, serious barriers to former combatants' organisations fulfilling their potential and so inclusive re-integration will remain' (Mitchell 2008: 16).

This chapter explores the extent to which prisoners have managed to leave behind inter-community mistrust to attempt societal reconstruction from below, within a context of hostility towards them beyond their immediate community of support and personal difficulty in achieving reintegration into mainstream society. The peace process and the resulting Agreement involved the British and Irish governments, political parties and representatives of non-state combatant groups, including former prisoners and those still in prison during negotiations. However, former prisoners have also stressed the importance of activism at the grassroots level as a means of fostering social and political change from below and buttressing support for the new political dispensation. They present themselves as a unique cohort, who are able to cross not just sectarian boundaries, but who can act as a bridge between communities and government and other agencies. However, as well as proclaiming that that they have promoted stability and lessened the potential for violent conflict they have also used community work as means of demonstrating that turning swords into ploughshares does not mean denying the legitimacy of earlier actions:

> When we were in the struggle we were very clever. We were fighting a massive enemy and that talent that we had then, we haven't lost it. They [prisoners] should be put to use for communities. I'm glad to say and I do say it, they're not just there as a group to march up and down at commemorations. They're there to take any everyday active part in the communities. The communities that they defended, that some lost their lives for. (IRA male)

This chapter will critically evaluate the role of prisoners in Northern Irish civil society and look at their role as leaders of their community and negotiators with other communities and agencies. This inevitably involves considering issues of both leadership and legitimacy, not just for former prisoners as a whole but in the context of differences between loyalism and republicanism and within loyalism. It is also necessary to considering the dilemmas inherent in demilitarisation, demobilisation and reintegration programmes across the globe; that is whether reintegration is promoted or diminished by treating former combatants as a separate group and maintaining their military identity (see Kingma 1997; Özerdem 2002). However, before these issues are explored, context will be provided with an overview of the civil society in which these activities and dilemmas are pursued (Shirlow and McEvoy 2008).

Northern Irish civil society

According to Walzer 'the words "civil society" name the space of un-coerced human association and also the set of relational networks – formed for the sake of family, faith, interest and ideology – that fill that space' (1992: 105). Pierson points out that that civil society 'has often been used to define a realm outside of, often contrasting with or indeed counter-balancing the jurisdiction of the state' (1996: 67). However, Walzer believes that the state 'frames civil society and occupies space within it' (1992: 103). Civil society has usually been perceived as a positive phenomenon in academic debate and one of the reasons for this is that 'a good society is conceivable only if there are good citizens' (Porter 1996: 177). Therefore, action in the civil sphere elevates citizenship beyond the passive enjoyment of rights and minimal discharging of obligations, promoting a healthy and vibrant democratic polity (see Alexander 2006; Keane 1998). Others have pointed out that the assertion that civil society breeds civic virtue 'is an empirical claim, for which there is no hard evidence one way or the other. It is an old and venerable view, but it is not obviously true' (Kymlicka and Norman 1994: 362).

In Northern Ireland, where a significant number of the population have contested the legitimacy of the state and where relational networks have developed in a polity beset by sectarianism, the existence of a distinctive Northern Irish civil society has been thrown into question. Some opponents of top-down consociational settlements have argued that elite accommodation should be supplanted by a bottom-up civil society model of social transformation (see Dixon 1997; Taylor 2001). McGarry and O'Leary (1995) have questioned this faith in the civil society model, pointing out that the largest groups operating in what could be termed Northern Irish civil society are the Gaelic Athletic Association, the Orange Order and the various Christian churches. Yet, earlier assessments of the suitability of consociational democracy for the creation of a peace settlement considered that Northern Irish society was not segmented enough. For example, Lorwin (1971) believed that European states with successful consociations rested on much more segmented civil societies than Northern Ireland, citing stratification in crucial areas such as the trade union movement as a key element for supporting the elite negotiation and compromise on which consociational democracy depends.

The segmentation and segregation that does exist has a clear socio-economic dimension in Northern Ireland. Residential separation and segmented and segregated internal labour markets based on informal local networks have a particularly strong impact on the ability of working-class people to move between areas in search of work (Cebulla and Smyth 1997; Teague 1997) and many areas of working-class housing have become increasingly segregated, something that has been accompanied by an increase in 'chill factors' such as graffiti, flags and kerb painting, which serve to demarcate territory (Hughes and Donnelly 1999). However, whilst poorer areas may exhibit a greater manifestation of symbols and activities that would deter relational networks forming between republican and loyalist communities, compared with other communities of a similar socio-economic profile, they 'often also have high levels of engagement in local, civic, church and other 'community' related activities' (McEvoy and Mika 2002: 549). So whilst opportunities to work together on issues that could cut across a sectarian cleavage can be limited, this does not mean that either sectarianism or deprivation has wiped out the virtues of collaboration and working for others associated with a healthy civil society.

The activism and negotiation associated with civil society is evident in the vast array of non-governmental organisations operating in Northern Ireland, with approximately five-thousand organisations serving a population of one-and-a-half million (O'Brien 2007). A study of the impact of the voluntary sector on conflict resolution concluded that 'the argument of many groups is governed by a desire to see the broadening of political dialogue and an inclusion of civil society within the debate', but that many of these groups are themselves single identity, concerned with working within one community only (Cochrane and Dunn 2002: 83).

So Northern Irish civil society at once demonstrates the key virtues of the civil sphere, namely there is evidence of a lot of activity and a healthy level of engagement with others for the pursuit of social and political goods, and this applies not just to those with wealth and education but also covers groups from communities more likely to be depicted as disengaged and marginalised elsewhere in the UK. However, these networks and activities also reflect the divisions within Northern Ireland that have become increasingly apparent in physical segregation for working-class citizens on sectarian lines and it would be naïve to present civil society as a discrete alternative to top-down political processes in the search for accommodation and reconciliation in Northern Ireland. These factors must be borne in mind when considering the community role of former prisoners. In the interviews conducted for the project, former prisoners were keen to stress that their experiences had allowed them to breach sectarian boundaries in a way other individuals or agencies could not:

> [Prisoners' groups] could do things that other people didn't want to do. They would say oh, I'll go and meet such-and-such, I don't mind, I'll do it on behalf of the prisoners' group, where they might be sworn enemies. So it allowed for that middle ground stuff. So they would be an important part of the work. (INLA male)

These factors are also important because when it comes to investigating these claims and assessing the ability of prisoners' groups to foster transformation and reconciliation at the grassroots level, their efforts should not be measured against the perception of an integrated and cross-cutting voluntary sector that is not actually operational in the province.

Restorative justice

Former prisoners' community work covers many areas. The first prisoners' groups, such as Tar Anall, were formed specifically to help prisoners and this is still an important element of their work. However, these groups and individual former prisoners have sought to offer the communities to which they have returned leadership and support. For example, the PUP has, since its inception, been a forum for former prisoners to offer political leadership to working-class loyalism and the party has been keen to stress in party literature how the party and the community are one:

> When we want to know what the people want we ask ourselves. When we want to know the people's priorities we just look at our own hearts. When we want to know of hardship we just look at our own plight. Because whatever adversity faces us too since we live and move and have our being in the working class districts of Northern Ireland. (PUP 1998)

Whilst former prisoners present themselves as offering their authority and leadership to communities, it could be argued that this is a reflexive action, in that they believe community activism will give them authority and make them leaders. Community activism is more than the disinterested pursuit of good works. These activities are bound up with consolidating the legitimacy of these individuals and their organisations as it shows how former prisoners have always had the best interests of the community at the heart and have always acted as advocates for the rights of others, whether through violent action or charitable work. However, it must be noted that community work does not necessarily confer legitimacy or authority upon those who are engaged in these practices and it can in fact contradict people's expectations of paramilitaries in a way that has not been anticipated.

Restorative justice is an excellent area for analysing the activities of former prisoners within their communities and looking at the problems that can arise. It is one of the areas that former prisoners have proclaimed an effective improvement of community life as a result of their activities and something that demonstrates their commitment to relinquishing claims to authority through physical force. Most importantly, the creation and development of such projects originated in the research of the loyalist former prisoner, Tom Winston, who was convinced that 'non-state combatants groupings are anxious to find a viable alternative to the present method' of informal justice, namely punishment of suspected offenders by issuing fiats for beatings, shootings or exile (Winston 1997: 125). Winston's research was the basis of the development of the UVF-backed Greater Shankill Alternatives project, which engaged with young offenders and brought them face-to-face with their victims in order to elicit an apology and/or restitution. Similar projects sprang up in other loyalist areas, but also in republican ones. Backed by the Northern Ireland Association for the Care and Resettlement of Offenders (NIACRO) and private sources of funding, the Community Restorative Justice (CRJ) initiatives in republican areas widened the scope of such schemes by creating a system of referral to other agencies, such as addiction charities, and involving families and the wider communities in the mediation process.

The success of these schemes in reducing recidivism or consigning punishment beatings to the past is difficult to measure and the persistence of punishment attacks has encouraged cynicism about the worth of these projects. Monaghan (2008) argues that the figures on punishment beatings kept by the PSNI are not detailed or localised enough to allow for a comparison between areas with a restorative justice scheme in operation and those without and so the schemes cannot be subjected to a statistical analysis. Her own view is that restorative justice has become a respected method of community management for minor offences but that punishment beatings still prevail when crimes are judged to be more serious. A former UDA prisoner involved in such a scheme admits that the new system has not yet completely transcended the old:

> I was involved in a restorative justice scheme, in which victim and perpetrator were brought together and restitution was made. Now sometimes that doesn't work because they keep going back and doing things and there have been exiles. The reason why they're exiled is because we're not going to shoot them. Exile is just displacing the problem. There has to be a whole new way of thinking and dealing with it. The UDA has started doing that. The UVF is just the same. We all belong to society. (UDA male)

That punishment beatings have not been pushed out entirely in favour of restorative justice has been problematic for paramilitary authority and legitimacy, especially for loyalists. Monaghan points out that loyalists could not rely on the republican explanation of non-acceptance of the law and order of a state whose authority they rejected. She argues that loyalists were under greater pressure from their own communities to turn away from this path because 'beating and shootings were used to maintain internal discipline within and between the more heterogeneous loyalist factional groups' as much as to exact justice on behalf of the community (2008: 91).

However, the attempts by former prisoners and other non-state combatants' group members to establish restorative justice projects have highlighted issues of legitimacy in another way. Winston (1997) interviewed local community members as a part of his research and found that punishment beatings were popular, not just because they delivered tangible and effective retribution, but for the simple reason that victims were far more likely to recover stolen goods. McEvoy and Mika (2002: 536) back this assessment, stating that 'an unpalatable but indisputable fact often missed in some of the less subtle accounts on the issue, is that punishment violence is often actually quite popular in the communities where it occurs as a swift and visible dispensation of justice'. They argue that dissident republicans have decried CRJ as a prime example of an IRA sell-out, because it requires a high level of co-operation with state agencies. Persisting with punishment attacks has made paramilitaries unpopular, but so has desisting from them. Former prisoners have been involved from the beginning in formulating alternatives to punishment attacks, but whether their authority rests on their status as people who have demonstrated their commitment to their community by years of incarceration or because local people are still aware that paramilitaries are capable of demonstrations of physical force within those communities is open to question.

Community activism

Prisoners and prisoners' groups have been highly visible in a number of grassroots projects that address the needs of their community. This work has served to effectively accommodate prisoners within their local neighbourhood and allowed them work for their neighbours. The chair of the republican ex-prisoners' group Tar Isteach, Paul O'Neill, argues that 'Tar Isteach's unique services offer a genuine alternative approach to the mainstream in encouraging those most marginalised and disadvantaged to participate in self-improvement and community activism' (O'Neill 2007: 4). His Chairperson's Report makes it clear that this applies both to the ex-prisoners of the group and the residents of North Belfast who they serve.

Community leadership has become an important source of affirmation for former prisoners, but the choice of community activism as a career path also has solid pragmatic roots. Gormally argues that the community sector is 'an area where the main qualification is the ability to lead and motivate the community' (2000: 14). Thus, former prisoners do not have to supply a CV filled with the qualifications and experience that are usually acquired outside prison walls. Training and employment have been crucial issues for all ex-prisoner groups. The difficulties previously discussed of trying to move between areas to pursue jobs is arguably even more difficult for former prisoners, who employers fear may be targets for violence and even assassination (Jamieson and Grounds 2002). Working within the community sidesteps many of these problems and prisoners would argue that they are integrated and respected members of the community (Gormally 2000) and therefore not subject to the same mistrust and fear they would face seeking employment elsewhere.

Throughout the conflict, republicans and loyalists formed groups such as the Orange or Green Cross in order to provide support and welfare to prisoners and their families. However, from the early nineties, groups were formed with the more specific purpose of integrating ex-prisoners back into their communities. EPIC (the Ex-Prisoners' Interpretive Centre) served the UVF and RHC, whilst Loyalist Prisoners' Aid worked on behalf of UDA prisoners. Gormally (2000) notes that the first of these groups, the IRA's Tar Anall, was founded by female ex-prisoners, but argues that since this time women have become less visible.

In interviews, former prisoners outlined how these groups had provided them with vital assistance:

I think it's sort of co-ordination of Coiste, especially the campaigning on prisoners' issues. If the Coiste wasn't there, raising those issues - like now, they're able to influence government departments on issues that they would just not take up whatsoever. It wouldn't have been anybody else who would have brought them up. Even Sinn Fein at the time would consider it a low priority, prisoners' issues, because they're in the main the same as what ordinary working people need addressed. But there are actually complications - unemployment, travel. The things that for a relatively small group of people, people aren't going to get that exercised about. And I think that with Coiste it's a role that nobody else will take on. There's nobody else raising the issue of criminal records and the effects they have on prisoners and their families. (IRA male)

Prisoners' groups sought to reintegrate prisoners, not just by supporting them through training schemes and acting as advocate for prisoners who were dealing with housing and benefit issues, but by resisting what they saw as attempts to impose criminalisation after release. At a Coiste residential in South Armagh in 1999, one of the founder members of the IRA prisoners' magazine, *The Captive Voice*, Laurence McKeown told the assembled company the one of the key roles of the new prisoners' reintegration group Coiste would be to tackle any legislation that put its members on the same footing as 'Ordinary Decent Criminals'. He wanted to his audience to know that 'they were engaged in a struggle, a struggle that goes back to the attempts to criminalise republican prisoners' (*The Captive Voice*, Summer 1999). This discrimination covered a range of problems for former prisoners, from difficulties in getting insurance, to receiving a diminished state pension, to facing bars from employment in the civil service.

Reintegration also involved training former prisoners for community work. The EPIC website proclaimed:

> It is a reality in our society that political ex-prisoners carry with them a mantle of local influence. With this harnessed and directed towards community development ex-prisoners can not only reintegrate more fully within their community but can also be a resource for their community of origin and beyond. (EPIC 1999)

In addition to restorative justice initiatives, former prisoners and ex-prisoners' groups have been involved in a number of community and political initiatives. For example, Coiste runs regular youth events such as summer camps and the INLA ex-prisoners' group Teach Na Failte has been active in the campaign for a bill of rights in Northern Ireland. The Tar Isteach Centre in North Belfast, run by IRA ex-prisoners, offers a free welfare advice service for their local community.

Charitable work and community activism has been the focus of much government and NGO attention since the outbreak of conflict in Northern Ireland in the late 1960s. It was often viewed as an area that could provide an alternative to paramilitary domination in loyalist and republican communities, but it was also seen as a way of controlling and taming non-state combatant groups themselves. The British government and the Rowntree Trust provided funding for the Ulster Community Action Group, which was formed out of various UDA-sponsored initiatives in 1976. Since 1972 the UDA had been involved in local protests against housing provision and had managed a squatting campaign in Belfast. They then branched out into providing advice on housing and jobs, as well as providing opportunities for local people to engage in handicrafts and music, which caused the *Sunday Times* to marvel at the idea of 'the tough UDA' engaged in 'nursery groups and sewing classes' (16 March 1975). UCAG reflected the desire of the UDA leadership to maintain and adapt to a grassroots community base (McCready 2001), but the provision of government funding suggests a belief that such activity could steer the organisation away from violent conflict altogether. UCAG was virtually defunct by 1981. Poor leadership and an inability to forge links with other groups for lobbying purposes had rendered it ineffective. From the UDA's point of view the group had not consolidated the desired role of community leader and for individuals from the organisation who did whole-heartedly involve themselves in such projects 'the effect was often that they left the UDA' (Nelson 1984: 195).

In 1985 political vetting (known as the Hurd Criteria) was imposed on community funding provided by government sources. The aim of the vetting was to prevent non-state combatants using community initiatives as a front for channelling government funds and ensuring that community activism was clearly separated from paramilitary causes. The Hurd Criteria hit early ex-prisoner projects, such as the partnership between republicans, NIACRO and the Open Door Housing Association which allowed ex-prisoners to get involved in building their own new home. However, by the early 1990s the Hurd Criteria had been quietly dropped (Gormally 2000), an action that has been attributed to the need 'to lay the ground for a political accommodation that would bring about ceasefires and an end to political violence' (Birrell and Williamson 2001: 207).

The belief in the power of civil society activity, directed by the third (voluntary) sector, to ensure reconciliation and peace in Northern Ireland has translated into funding from UK government sources, but also from the European Union through the Special Support Programme for Peace and Reconciliation. However, the involvement of former prisoners and other paramilitaries within these grassroots initiatives has not been completely unproblematic. The row prompted by the Social Development Minister, Margaret Ritchie, over her decision to freeze a funding package worth more than a million pounds demonstrates this. The money was intended to support the Ulster Political Research Group, on behalf of the UDA, and the foundation of a Conflict Transformation Initiative (CTI), which would propel the UDA towards a new existence, separate from any paramilitary past. The CTI was intended to fund a series of projects that would put the UDA at the forefront of cross-community dialogue and intra-community support, which would foster social change. Former prisoners were intended to be central to this work:

> It's about teaching people; it's about educating people that this is the only way open. That this is the way we have to go. So I mean, unionists have got to respect that all our politics and all our energy in the past was defending our people and we are now in the process of mending our people. Our motto in the CTI is from defending to mending, so that would be our philosophy. (UDA male)

The decision to withdraw funding was justified on the grounds that the UDA had not demonstrated it was ready to carry out this work, because it had not committed to a decommissioning timetable and because sporadic violence in places such as Carrickfergus suggested that the official leadership had not successfully addressed the problems inherent in its loose and haphazard structure. Ritchie said she needed to 'see evidence that the UDA has moved irreversibly away from criminality and violence to positive and lawful community transformation' before she could feel comfortable about authorising funding for the CTI (dsdni.gov.uk 2007).

Former prisoners have been lauded for their community work, but this can still provoke controversy. For loyalists, problems such as the row over CTI funding have revealed the gap between the aspiration of former prisoners to offer leadership through community work and the perception that those associated with paramilitaries are anything but a resource for loyalist communities. This has been particularly acute for the UDA. The amorphous nature of the organisation means that the problems of engaging in grassroots campaigns for social and economic change remain the same as those of the initiatives of the 1970s: there are no mechanisms for corralling the majority of members into societal reconstruction. This has been identified as an ongoing problem for the UDA as a voluntary sector director acknowledges:

> The UDA have grabbed the terminology ... it doesn't go much beyond that to be honest with you, it's a wee bit like the terminology around community development. That's not to say that there aren't individuals that are very genuine, but they don't think things through, they sort of react on a sporadic basis, which is always a problem to be honest in terms of that they can't deliver because they don't do the groundwork so they don't know the people with them and then if one of them is knocked off or say pulls off in a completely different direction, so there is a real problem there and they are looking for results too quickly. (Shirlow and Monaghan 2006)

For republicans, the fact that government agencies hope to influence what happens at the local level through funding strategies means that engagement with community activism could lead to accusations of collusion or selling out.

Republican prisoners in the early years of the conflict were suspicious of accepting any state help. There was a palpable fear that accepting Northern Ireland Office (NIO) funding would be a tacit admission that the conflict was between two groups in Northern Ireland rather than a war between Irish republicans and the British (Shirlow et al 2005).

However, Mac Ginty points out that, given Sinn Fein had to embark on an 'enormous volte face' over accepting the constitutional status of Northern Ireland, even if just as an interim measure, 'the real story here was the lack of splits within republicanism' (Mac Ginty 2006: 160). The adroit management of the mental accommodations and compromises made during the peace process by the Sinn Fein leadership has dimmed the power to any intellectual challenge to the worth of community work, allowing those involved to embrace the idea that such activities represent the transformation of the conflict, not its abandonment:

> This is a political battle now and has been for many years. And I think that the reason why it is a political struggle is now obviously because of the impact of the armed struggle. You can't divorce from one another … There's always going to be a battle of some description. And that has been part of the experience and that has been part of the process and it will continue to be. (IRA female)

This ability to embrace non-military activity as the latest phase of a conflict has allowed the role of former prisoners in community activism to develop a sense of authenticity and legitimacy, which has boosted the confidence of those involved in such projects: A male former IRA prisoner argued in respect of republican former prisoners:

> I think they've had a massive influence on ordinary social and economic development within these areas. I think participating in commemoration and republican events. The way they have been organised to steward events like the marches, but even in our own wee areas like this, for the likes of our fun day, we can muster thirty or forty people who we can go to because they're ex-prisoners and ask them to take part in it and they will and they'll do it because they have that sort of allegiance. The groups themselves, the ones that have been successful have been very successful and the work that we're doing here has been very, very important. (IRA male)

Differences between loyalist and republican activism

The coherence of the provisional republican movement's embrace of conflict transformation has augmented the presentation of former prisoners' role in the community as one of leadership and support and bolstered their claims to be an integral part of the communities they physically left when they were imprisoned. There is no equivalent hegemony within loyalism and the fragmentation and rivalry within the UDA in particular has undermined attempts to use community activism as a means of moving away from illegal action. This distinction is connected to other problematic factors that loyalist ex-prisoners have had to take into account when engaged in grassroots activities.

A perennial theme of literature about loyalism is that it is an ideology that rests on an extreme sense of insecurity (see McAuley 1998; Todd 1987). Nelson argues that:

> The very people who repeat clichés about Catholics' reluctance to work or subservience to the Church will often envy what they see as Catholics' ability to 'get on' and their greater capacity for independent social and political action. The phrases used about Irish unity suggest few can even picture a situation where they will not be annexed, repressed or submerged. (Nelson 1984: 113)

This view accords with the argument expressed in interviews with loyalist former prisoners about the ability of republicans to extract the maximum benefit from post-Agreement arrangements for their communities.

> As a military man I think I won the war, nobody will tell me any different. I know I won the war, I know we won the war. But once the war ended and our enemies transformed into political – we're losing now, we're losing it fast. And people who fought the military campaign for loyalism are slow to pass over to the political, whereas republicans were very quick to do it. All I'm trying to say is that we need to move on. We can't fight them militarily but we can let them away with it politically. (UDA male)

> Because [Catholics] have had this whole thing about the community and community development long before Protestants did they were better geared to access funding when money came in from the peace process. (UDA male)

It must be noted that some interviewees found such arguments problematic and that there were a range of nuanced opinions about the benefits accruing to loyalists and republicans across the data collected:

> I'm reluctant to say it was all the republican/nationalist community [that benefited] because that just feeds into what we are spoon fed every day … I know financially that there is money coming into loyalist communities regardless of what we hear. A lot of times you'll hear people on the ground people saying 'the Catholics get everything' but that is not my experience. (UVF male)

However, former prisoners and the groups of which they are a part have not yet offered a clear alternative to the prevailing fatalism within loyalist discourse as regards the strength and unity of republican community politics.

Loyalist former prisoners also have to contend with another long-standing problem, namely fragmentation. Another voluntary sector director has identified a pattern of 'differential development' where republicans get very frustrated with loyalists and accuse them of dragging their feet on any community initiative, when in fact loyalists are slowed down by the difficulty of co-ordinating any response across the disparate churches, political coalitions and non-state combatants on their side of the fence (Shirlow and Monaghan 2006). For former prisoners attempting to offer leadership to this fragmented coalition a further difference between republican and loyalist prisoners emerges. The republican movement is much more confident than loyalists that they will be accepted as leaders and spokespeople by their community:

> In the nationalist community, I think the ex-prisoners, they're in every single aspect of this community. They're at every level, every type of organisation that you can think of, ex-prisoners are contributing. You look around and you see ex-prisoners contributing to sport in the community, to community groups. There's a richness there, the Irish language. None of them are the sole preserve of ex-prisoners, but every facet of life in this community, in this society, I can see ex-prisoners contributing. (IRA male)

> I mean republican prisoners go back centuries. You had the hunger strikes in the 20s, you had hunger strikes in, well you know, way back, so they have a history within prisons and they were able to adapt much better than what we were. Also when they came out prison they were accepted within their community because of that whole tradition. (UVF Focus Group)

When prisoners were released under the terms of the Good Friday Agreement, *An Phoblacht* contrasted the public statements of republicans as they left the prison gates with loyalist prisoners covering their faces and hurrying away from the cameras.

> For loyalists, imprisonment was a contradiction. They were 'loyal' to the very state that imprisoned them and could never understand that they were only cannon fodder. For those loyalists who skulked away from Long Kesh, hidden from the media and the world, the question remains: why is it that the 'fight for God and Ulster' didn't bring with it the courage to face the world and explain their actions? (*An Phoblacht*, 3 August 2000)

Retrospective coverage of the prison years in *An Phoblacht* suggested that the republican movement had no such problems as regarding the position of prisoners and the values of the prison experience. The period was regularly covered as anniversaries and exhibitions were publicised. The twentieth anniversary of the Hunger Strike was marked by weekly centre-spreads on the death of each striker including a picture of each body lying in state and the subsequent funeral (e.g., 'Death of Thomas McElwee: IRA Volunteer: sincere, easy-going and full of fun'). The same issue carried 'Hunger Strike Memorial Unveiled in South Armagh, Clare Hunger Strike Exhibition' (*An Phoblacht*, 28 June 2001). The letters page in another issue included a letter from 'Grateful Ardoyne Ex-POWs' thanking everyone for their help in making their Prisoners' Day exhibition as success, including the loan of prison artifacts (14

August 2003). *An Phoblacht* also played a role as curator of these events and icons, regularly running reminiscences of former prisoners, such as Seanna Walsh's memories of the Hunger Strike in 'Mo Chara Bobby Sands' (*An Phoblacht*, 9 May 2002) and Sinead Moore ending her interview about the no-wash protest and hunger strikes in Armagh Prison with the assertion, 'I would do it all again' (*An Phoblacht*, 8 July 2004).

Publications sympathetic to loyalist paramilitaries have also indulged in nostalgia and they have highlighted the need to preserve and exhibit memorabilia of the period. 'Wanted, Wanted, Wanted' was the headline of an appeal for items made in prison and photos of the period 'hopefully to put on show' (*The Loyalist*, January 2006). However, there is palpable anxiety that republicanism has essentially copyrighted the prison experience and that Sinn Fein will monopolise the past as a means of ensuring legitimacy in the future.

Combat reported a number of anxious reactions to plans to create a museum on the site of the Maze prison. For example, 'No "Shrine" at Long Kesh' concerned a visit by members of the PUP and EPIC who could reassure readers that there would not be a republican bias to any museum and the article showed positive aspects to commemorating the prison, for example noting that the Maze 'was called by many "the University of Long Kesh" due to the number of prisoners who gained degrees and other qualifications whilst gaoled there'. However the article concluded with the concern that should Lisburn Council drop its level of commitment to the museum if the proposed stadium on the site became successful then 'republicans will swoop in like vultures to take over' (*Combat*, May 2005). Republicans had been accused by *Combat* in the past of stealing the struggle for political status whilst in prison; now there was a fear that they would claim the whole history of those years in prison for themselves and that prisoners would remain an asset only for the republican community.

This inability to establish the authenticity and authority of loyalists' years behind prison walls has led to frustration that mainstream politicians (including, or even especially, unionists) use the 'ex-prisoner' tag to undermine the standing of those engaged in community work. This is apparent from articles such as 'An Open Response – Jim McDonald Speaks Out'. McDonald, a PUP activist, argued that whilst politicians criticised UVF work in loyalist areas, they were ignoring the positive projects such as restorative justice, educational programmes and interface work: 'these are just a few of the ways in which PUP members, ex-combatants, ex-prisoners and others contribute to our communities' (*Combat*, September 2004). Similarly a riposte to a complaint from an SDLP MLA about a former UVF prisoner taking a post in the British Legion pointed out that the prisoner, Russell Watton, was the first loyalist in the H Blocks to get an Open University degree and that since his release he had been working through Flags Forum to alleviate tension during the marching season. The article stated 'The community as a whole should, with open arms, welcome not ridicule and castigate those ex-prisoners who sincerely wish to contribute positively to society' (*Combat*, Spring 2006).

Reviewing the differences between loyalism and provisional republicanism, it is apparent that former prisoners who wish to work for change in loyalist communities face a number of challenges. The communities from which they are drawn lack confidence in their own ability to improve their lives and residents in these areas are not always likely to accept people with such connections as their representatives. A lack of history of community action, coupled with fragmentation of the relational networks of civil society and severe division between the UVF and UDA and within the UDA means that loyalist former prisoners are starting from a less consolidated position than provisional republicans. Loyalist paramilitaries themselves often exhibit frustration and despondency over their position relative to those in republican areas who have been through similar experiences.

However, even with these problems, positive evidence of the impact of groups such as EPIC and Alternatives can be found. Gribben et al.'s study (2005) of Loyalist Conflict Transformation Initiatives found that members of these groups had encouraged change, such as the removal of paramilitary flags and murals. They also had a unique ability to reach the hard-to-reach and reduce marginalisation, and had promoted stability in difficult situations. For example, EPIC was directly involved in rehousing families displaced by a feud between the UDA and UVF in 2000. So although loyalist former prisoners have faced a number of difficulties that have sometimes seemed insurmountable, they have also managed to overcome these obstacles and make community activism work. In addition they have been part of cross-community activity, which is an area that former prisoners claim they are uniquely equipped to progress.

Cross-community activism

A starting point for anyone wishing to embark upon cross-community dialogue or even concerted action could be citing the shared socio-economic concerns of loyalist and republican communities. Borooah et al. (1995: 55) point out that 'there is much greater inequality within the Catholic and Protestant communities than there is between them'. Providing leadership on this at the elite level has proved difficult. Even if the institutions created by the Good Friday Agreement had managed to avoid periodic suspension and overcome their fragility, the possibility for political representatives who were combatants/and or prisoners during the conflict working together would be hindered by the mismatch of Sinn Fein's electoral dominance and the tiny mandate of the loyalist fringe parties. That said, it must be noted that PUP MLAs and former prisoners Billy Hutchinson and David Ervine were keen to support the then Education Minister Martin McGuinness in his bid to abolish the 'eleven plus' selection process for secondary education on the grounds that this was an issue that cut across sectarian divides.

McGuinness informed the assembly that 'David Ervine and Billy Hutchinson of the PUP told me that in many working class Protestant areas, a grammar school place is beyond the reach of almost all pupils. In the Shankill less than two per cent of pupils gain a grammar school place. If that is not a damning indictment, I do not know what is' (Hansard 2002). Hutchinson applauded McGuinness's commitment to abolish the eleven plus and said 'I welcome the minister's statement because it concerns future generations of working-class children and may address the most important decision to be made by the assembly' (Hansard 2002).

Education proved to be a less difficult issue for politicians associated with non-state combatants than other issues of socio-economic need, especially housing. The increasing physical segregation of working-class Northern Ireland has been intensified in areas such as North Belfast by population change. The residents of increasingly populous Catholic areas feel penned in by the inability to expand into emptying Protestant areas, but the residents there fear that these needs are a cloak for the aggressive expansionist intentions of Irish republicanism (see Jarman 2003; Shirlow 2003). Political representatives of groups affiliated to paramilitaries have often interpreted the resulting upheaval and tension at the areas where these communities meet through the language of ethnic cleansing, and former prisoners and internees have been involved in this public and hostile debate. Observing increasing tension in the Torrens area of Belfast, the then MLA, Billy Hutchinson, argued that 'Torrens is a classic case of ethnic cleansing' (Australian Broadcasting Corporation 6 September 2001), around the same time as a Sinn Fein MLA Alex Maskey said 'the increase in loyalist attacks on Catholics right across the north can only be described as a sectarian pogrom' (*An Phoblacht*, 26 September 2001).

However, it is at these flashpoints that former prisoners have established a clear and productive community leadership role. Former prisoners from all the groups interviewed have engaged in work in interface areas. They have provided emergency assistance through mobile-phone networks in times of heightened tension and committed themselves to involvement with projects that seek to ease these tensions in the long term. It is something that is seen a role that is uniquely fitted for ex-prisoners:

> It is ex-prisoner groups that are at the interfaces there. And they're speaking to other prisoner groups and other combatants. Ultimately they are the people who will solve these problems. It won't be just ordinary people who people don't have respect for. The police aren't going to solve it. It'll be the ex-prisoner groups who have been there and understand problems. I wouldn't think that the police would play any great part in anything in the six counties to be honest. (INLA male)

This low-key involvement, pragmatic co-operation and behind-the-scenes commitment to the search for accommodation reflects the prison experience, with prisoners engaging in education and debate free from accusations of selling out or treachery. It also demonstrates that former prisoners are willing to engage in co-operation with old enemies, without significantly changing their opinion of them, their intentions or their cause: a male former IRA prisoner argued that loyalists 'talk the talk when it comes to building peace and, and they pretend that they want peace' (IRA male). A UDA male (unusually) found external arguments why republicans had changed their *modus operandi*:

> I think it's just another strategy. I think for war, they can't go back, not with global terrorism because the whole attitude of America has changed. All of their support base would have changed now after 9/11. Before, they had a lot of support, but if they went back to physical war and attacked and bombed that support would be totally diminished. (UDA male)

Thus, former prisoners themselves have not left behind a sense of mistrust about the intentions of the other side, even as they prepare to work positively with their old enemies for the improvement of their communities and relations between them.

Addressing an NIO conference, the Ex-Prisoners Assistance Committee (EXPAC) Project Director, Tommy McKearney, brought up other examples of cross-community work owned by former prisoners, such as the magazine *The Other View*. However, he also highlighted the problems of projects that did not cross the same divisions:

> Unhelpful participation is where we believe that our involvement is detrimental to our overall project. The issue of 'single identity work' for example has recently arisen for us. If people have concerns about participating on an education course with old adversaries, is it wise to give them space and time to gain confidence or are we merely pandering to ancient bigotry. We don't have an answer but it is something that we must deal with. (McKearney 2004)

Former prisoners still retain their old mistrust and suspicion and there is sometimes palpable reluctance to engage with the other side. However, through involvement in interface work, from defusing tension and policing fault lines to engaging with projects designed to facilitate understanding and co-operation, former prisoners have made use of their status to cross lines for the purpose of negotiation. Having committed acts that led to years of incarceration, former prisoners can utilise this sacrifice to rebut any notion of weakness or betrayal and they can work behind the scenes while their political leaders seek to shore up their communities with public displays of intransigence. However, in terms of societal reconstruction, whilst this work has undoubtedly provided stability in troubled times, there are limited opportunities to take the work further when issues such as housing remain so controversial.

Making old soldiers fade away?

Though there is abundant evidence of the commitment of many former prisoners to community activism, this does not mean that all of those who served time during the Troubles have chosen this path and many have chosen not to join former prisoners' groups or any political organisation. Interestingly, Dwyer's (2008: 788) study has found that the release and subsequent monitoring of non-state combatants is based on the premise that 'in a post-conflict situation it is evident that risk is actually deflated if the prisoner has strong paramilitary associations' and that group leadership has been a crucial factor in maintaining stability and reducing the risk of reoffending. Her figures show that of 440 paramilitary prisoners released since 1999 only sixteen have had their licences revoked (twelve of them life prisoners). This compares favourably with a 50 per cent recidivism rate within two years for non-political prisoners (Dwyer 2008: 795).

Maintaining the separate identity and paramilitary association of this group has generally had positive results and this has been especially important given Rolston's (2007) point that reintegration programmes have been left to voluntary organisations and the combatants themselves. However, for all of the four groups studied there are some common problems.

First, although former prisoners have stressed that their legitimacy has come from the sacrifices of past actions, the uneven results of restorative justice programmes suggests that in many people's eyes, their authority stems from their current association with groups that can still deliver physical force when required. Loyalist and republican communities contain many residents who became tired and fearful of paramilitary violence, but the status of prisoners was not based merely upon 'moral authority', also owing something to fear within the community of the possibility of strong sanctions for local 'transgressors'. This also raises questions about who will take over prisoners' roles and position within their communities in future years and whether the social capital they have built up through intra-community and inter-community work will remain.

Second, there is the issue of how long prisoners will remain an important force in community politics and how they will deal with any diminution in significance.

> Well prisoners' groups, you mean EPIC and Alternatives? I think they have been probably less influential but still had a significant influence probably on the development of the PUP. I think that influence will wane, will become less as normal politics becomes more the norm, but I think that historically they were quite

significant players in the roots of the PUP as a political party. (PUP Executive male)

If 'normal' politics means that prisoners are no longer meant to contribute to political parties and community groups using the primary identity of former prisoner then this needs to be managed without discouraging the positive activities in which many of these people have been engaged.

In addition to these points, some groups have specific problems. The INLA have been considerably keenest to keep the flame alive as far as raising the profile of those still in prison. The *Starry Plough* has continued to focus on republican prisoners who were held after the releases secured under the Good Friday Agreement because they broke the conditions of their licence, belonged to an organisation that was not considered on ceasefire, or because they were held in prisons in the Republic of Ireland. There were regular demands to 'Release all political hostages now! Free Dessie O'Hare now!' (October/November 2004) and 'Restore political status now! (August/September 2005). The position of the INLA and IRSP as regards the Good Friday Agreement is that it is a 'traitors' charter' and a betrayal of republican goals (Smith 2002: 238). Their condemnation of signatories as sell-outs relates to constant references to those still in prison, either in the UK or the Republic of Ireland, because imprisonment of republicans has always been an issue that evokes suffering and symbolises effectively the ongoing struggle and objection to partition.

In 2003, the IRSP's Eddie McGarrigle urged INLA former prisoners to support the campaign by Real and Continuity IRA prisoners for segregation of republicans in Maghaberry prison, stating that: 'The IRSP fully support the right to segregation and we recognise that they are political prisoners involved in a legitimate form of protest.' Nonetheless, McGarrigle also stated that 'The IRSP are very clear about the futility of the continuation of armed actions. We urge other republicans to take the political road. It is the only way forward to progress republican objectives' (*Irish News*, 28 July 2003). Keeping the prison issue alive maintains the INLA's commitment to militancy and resistance to compromise without having to engage in an armed campaign for which they see little support or tactical advantage. This taps into the presentation of prison as an alternative battleground and prisoners as soldiers fighting on a different front that the republican movement articulated in the 1970s, as discussed earlier in this work.

The INLA and IRSP have been hemmed in by the change of events and still wish for the unity of the days of the Hunger Strike. In an article 'Political Policing – An Attack on Ex-Prisoners', the claim was made that raids on the homes and offices of Teach Na Failte members had been allowed to take place because of republican disunity and pro-agreement republicans smearing anti-agreement republicans, with Willie Gallagher quoted as saying 'the relationship I would like to see among all republicans, despite political differences, is the relationship respect and solidarity shown by IRA/INLA hunger strikers' (*Starry Plough*, January/February 2006). Without this unity the INLA remain a small group who have been sidelined by the peace process.

For former UVF prisoners the importance and worth of their work to the wider political movements to which they belong may change in future years. The UVF have had to tackle the particular problems of legitimacy that loyalists have faced and if the PUP does maintain its foothold in mainstream politics then the issue arises of the extent of public disengagement from the UVF required to develop a mandate based on social democratic politics, rather than association with an extra-legal group, whose presence many potential supporters would find off-putting. UVF former prisoners also have to struggle with the issue of being labelled as criminals not because of the actions of some of their colleagues, but because of ongoing problems within the various factions of the UDA, which reasserts the idea that loyalist paramilitaries are gangsters not community activists.

For former UDA prisoners these splits and fractiousness reflect an ongoing problem of poor leadership. From the group's inception, the UDA has not been a tight-knit group, governed by a clear hierarchical structure. Previous chapters highlighted how within prison walls the UDA were far less likely to take educational qualifications in prison and their compounds and wings were not as structured or directed as those of other groups. These weaknesses manifest themselves now with some in the UDA engaging in community work and grassroots campaigning, but with others actively hostile to such work. The fate of the UDP which began to disintegrate after failing to secure seats in the first election for the Northern Ireland Assembly is instructive. The 1998 election 'marked a turning point in UDP fortunes, with those involved directly in the UDP unable to convince the broader UDA of the merits of political involvement' (McAuley 2003: 62). The row over CTI funding, which has seen the UDA's reputation for criminality given another public airing, may have similar implications for the use of community activism as a means of transforming the UDA into an organised grouping with a positive role to play in Northern Irish civil society.

Former IRA prisoners have advantages that others who served time do not. Turning away from a military path does seem to have delivered tangible rewards and the idea that community work taps into talents developed in prison and is a new way of serving an old cause promotes confidence that has underpinned a range of republican ex-prisoner initiatives and has allowed many former prisoners to maintain a sense of coherence about the movement and their role within it:

> I have a t-shirt that says not an ounce, not a bullet and I laugh at myself when I put it on. But basically 'not an ounce, not a bullet' – what it really meant was, you know, handing over weapons to the British and that's what that mean and leaving yourself defenceless and all of that... I think there was a pragmatism involved. If

the weapons, if the ammunition was being used as a barrier to prevent us from making progress then we needed to look at that. (IRA female)

For those unable to make these adjustments, the idea that community work is an extension of a military role and therefore will aid the pursuit of the same aims and ethos has been more difficult to swallow. If these shifts cannot be accommodated, then former prisoners who cannot involve themselves in this arena can find themselves marginalised and extremely vulnerable to poverty, unemployment and 'a series of social and structural exclusions which prevent them engaging in and with civil society' (McKeever 2007: 425). This raises a further problem for all former prisoners about whether retaining the appellation of political prisoner is always a choice, or if it is a necessity to play the role and follow the direction of others in order not to slip into obscurity and poverty.

Conclusion

Just as paramilitaries were the product as well as the instigators of the conflict, they are products of the society in which they operate and so their role as community activists is shaped by the communities in which they ply this trade. Northern Irish civil society is not an entity that runs separately to the forces and actors who have taken part in violent conflict, nor is it a hearty fraternity of citizens, free from the taint of sectarianism. In considering the extent that former prisoners have managed to leave behind inter-community mistrust and attempt societal reconstruction from below this has to be taken into consideration. The relative difference in terms of legitimacy and impact between republican and loyalist former prisoners' work can be explained in part by the fact that loyalist communities have poorer social capital than republican areas and they find it harder to maintain the intra-community bonds they do have and also to build bridges to other communities and statutory agencies (Gribben et al. 2005). The divisions within Northern Irish civil society must also be taken into account when reviewing the fact that the majority of former prisoners' activism has taken place within their own areas. This is not an anomalous position, given that key civil society institutions and third sector agencies and projects also observe divisions of faith and identity.

Investigating the work of former prisoners, it is easy to find evidence of positive outcomes of their community activism. In the absence of government initiatives, former prisoners have displayed the self-reliance of the prison years and set up their own forums for education and welfare. They have utilised these talents for the wider community, for example providing advice centres and educational retreats. Political leaders have demonstrated public militancy on social and economic issues such as housing and also on cultural issues such as Orange Order parades, in order to underline their staunch defence of their constituency. At the same time, prisoners have crossed lines in order to defuse some of the violent tensions that these issues and the rhetoric around them can provoke and thus ensured that political manipulation of these emotive issues do not promote societal breakdown.

However, it must also be noted that this line crossing and openness to dialogue has not signified the end of inter-community mistrust. Former prisoners have demonstrated in interviews that they can work with the other side without dropping their innate suspicions and hostility and this means that the scope for taking these inter-community initiatives forward is restricted. It must also be noted that groups such as the UDA have been engaging in community work for decades, which suggests that community work in itself will not promote conflict transformation. Such activities provide something tangible for former combatants to do if they wish to embrace such a position and if the political process continues to restrict the room to manoeuvre for those who would wish to embrace large-scale military action then community activism can act as a clear route forwards for those who joined the paramilitaries for explicitly military ends. It remains unclear, though, as to whether maintaining the separate identity of politically motivated former prisoners will create problems in the future when this group begins to thin in number whilst the needs and issues that their work addresses remains.

Conclusion

The significant decline in state and paramilitary violence in Northern Ireland has been part guided by politically motivated prisoners who have played a vital role in conflict transformation. Former prisoners have contributed to the development of alternative modes of thinking that have challenged once-dominant militarist ideologies. The actors involved in these discursive shifts have pinpointed alternative structures and strategies within which to pursue their respective belief systems via non-violent means. Raising alternative debates has been a key feature of such actor-group relationships and such discussions have been attached to wider political shifts that are in turn translated into conflict-transformation-based activities and programmes undertaken by former political prisoners. From restorative justice groups through to former prisoner groups that undertake inter-community social economy projects, there is now a significant body of positive and meaningful non-violent former-prisoner-based intervention. This is not to deny the negative impact of previous violence, nor the pain and loss felt by victims. Nor is this to underestimate the transition of some paramilitaries into criminal gangs, but there has been an undoubted shift both in terms of practice and intent within the wider body of non-state combatants (Shirlow and McEvoy, 2008).

The role and future of the former prisoner community is set against the enduring realities of criminalisation and discrimination. The role played by that community in upholding and delivering peace has been instrumental in the relegation of violence to a mere bit player in the politics of Northern Ireland. New inter-community relationships between former prisoner groups, are beginning to unfold into programmes and projects that at one time may have seemed unlikely. However, it could be argued that the evolution of working relationships between republicans and loyalists was a rational expectation given that they were both minorities within their respective communities. The shared experiences of being incarcerated combatants, educated in a manner that would have been unlikely if it had not been for imprisonment and having shared a similar concern for their respective working-class communities may have drawn them closer together than assumed.

A central feature in the shift into conflict transformation has been trust. The release of prisoners and the state's recognition that the imprisoned were effectively political in their orientation created a sense of achievement in that criminalisation, in theoretical terms, at least, had been defeated. The leadership in gaining release and recognition showed that the trust placed in them had been fulfilled and republican and loyalist former prisoners could locate political positives in the contribution that they had made and more importantly could still make.

A precise date when this process of conflict transformation began is almost impossible to determine, given that peace-building began in the tumult of violence. The book has contended that 'top-down', leadership-on-the-outside/government-dominated accounts of how peace was formulated are too one-dimensional, offering only partial truths. Equally, accounts of the development of peace via the onset of a mutually hurting stalemate are not spurious, but they are incomplete and unsatisfactory, grounded in a military 'no complete win' scenario evident to many combatants since the 1970s. Instead, what is required is a more interpretive model highlighting the interplay of the military with the political, ideological, structural and personal.

The building of capacity via electoral politics and community activism encouraged a wider participation in republican and to a less extent loyalist activism that required engagement beyond the confines of each movement. The incapacity of militaristic republicanism to build upon the foundations of loyalty to them, given hostility from the wider nationalist community to violence, created a sense that wider electoral loyalty would grow via the erection of a non-violent, more conventional political structure. Therefore, the capacity to deliver social justice and welfare through working with state agencies and with an enlarged political mandate behind Sinn Fein meant that the justification of republican demilitarisation was linked to the pursuit, as noted, of republican ideology by non-violent means. Such a shift was important and supported by former prisoners who could present the historical sense of their incarceration as necessary, whilst part-framing and supporting the engendering of a contemporary republicanism that was increasingly relevant.

Key to this was that the development of ideas of conflict transformation had been a conscientious by-product of years of analysis within which the key emphasis was placed upon how 'struggle' encompassed more than military action. Resistance to social injustice in a post-conflict situation was understood as required and to be conducted through multi-faceted and non-violent mediums and structures. In particular, discrimination and subjugation in whatever form were to be contested through the agenda of equality-building, which ultimately was removed from the use of armed conflict to end the 'colonial' domination that 'caused' social inequity (Lundy and McGovern 2001). Republicans and to some extent loyalists were devoted to the idea that they were emerging unbroken and that the experience of prison was one of ensuring that 'attempts by our captors to criminalise us and our struggle' had failed (Mac Giolla Ghunna 1997: 2).

Republican ideological faith was to remain centred upon the achievement of a united Ireland. The new vocabularies of inclusion were accompanied by, a less antagonistic and atavistic attitude towards the British state, which was briefly and erroneously identified as a potential persuader for a united Ireland (Tonge 2005). Republicans identified a range of mediums through which to achieve political power, arguing that the goal of unification was being articulated and advanced via new tactical arrangements, even if this meant overturning many tactics which had been elevated to the status of fundamental republican principles. Nearly ten years after the Good Friday Agreement Gerry Adams, president of Sinn Féin, felt able to claim at the special *ard fheis* on policing (28 January 2007) that the role played by those who purchased *An Phoblacht* (the republican weekly newspaper) had been as important as those who had 'picked up the gun' (Adams 2007). In the same speech, Adams argued: 'Republicanism should never be about elitism or dogma or militarism. Republicanism always has to be about citizenship and people's rights and equality. We are about making republicanism relevant to people in their daily lives.' Territorial republicanism had been displaced by a softer form, in which the assertion of rights and Irish identity took primacy.

Ulster loyalism, like most pro-state paramilitarism, has been represented as having failed to determine a social space with a positive vocabulary regarding the ownership and meaning of its identity. Thus loyalists are seen as incapable of building meaningful social capital due to their promotion of a populist rhetoric and also by the infestation of such groups by criminals. Such depictions have worth, but are counter-balanced by those loyalists who in rejecting the efficacy of violence as a strategy in itself provide a powerful exercise in moral leadership. In challenging negative portrayals of them progressive loyalist leaders argue that their support and delivery of conflict transformation is generally unmentioned by external commentators. They contend that they have done much to quell elements intent upon a return to conflict and that they have also established networks that encourage dialogue with former adversaries.

There is no doubting that a progressive loyalist leadership has, through publications, political activity and community networking, articulated and promoted the principles of conflict transformation. They have also built links with statutory agencies in order to encourage social capital formation and alternative ideas and principles of inter-community linkage between Protestant and Catholic working-class communities.

Positive and negative forms of loyalism have always co-existed and the peace process is allowing 'thinking' loyalism to emerge, if slowly and unevenly (Bruce 2004). Notwithstanding the works of Bruce (2004), McAuley (2004), Gallaher (2007) and Spencer (2008) the role of 'transitional' loyalism is under-explored. Such a transition is crucial with regard to ending victimisation, encouraging citizenship and demobilising threat. Despite the immediacy of such issues it is obvious that the capacity to shift loyalism forwards has come from within, bereft of the attendant support base, international appeal and finances enjoyed by Sinn Fein.

An important lesson in the case of republicans and loyalists has been the nature and development of an organic intellectualism and the realisation that conflictual behaviour was insufficient with regard to gaining key goals and objectives. Kriesberg's (1982: 32) argument that the basis of conflictual behaviour is 'an intention to induce the other side to yield what the coercer wishes to obtain' is instructive. In the Northern Ireland case the ambiguity of success aided the claims of achievement and thus conflict transformation. Republicans believed that the British state had been forced to concede to anti-discrimination legislation, recognition of political motivation and an accept-ance that they had an obligation to persuade for Irish unification. For loyalists the failure of the IRA to 'win' and the reality that Northern Ireland remained within the United Kingdom is evidence of having 'induced' results. In either way both sets of antagonists have framed a new Northern Ireland and only the deluded would press on in what was a war that could not be won when promising alternatives were available. With that reconstruction former prisoners have moved their behaviour into a non-violent conflict. If anything and especially within loyalism, post-conflict violence aimed to remove the threat from within. In both instances the threat from within is now a more tangible fear than that from without.

In symbolic terms both loyalists and republicans depict themselves as the 'champions' of their community who actively stood against the 'tyranny' of Irish Republicanism or the British state. Violence had been a rational and legitimate response and under this worldview, in no circumstances should the label of failure stain the reputation of those who had committed violent acts. In the republican and loyalist worlds that are constituted by the boundaries of working-class territories, the cognition of such efforts and defenderism is itself a powerful medium that permitted a place in which to retire from violent action. The reality of republican and loyalist community spaces that can be influenced by former prisoners and in which power and influence is devolved via politics and community activism, is crucial in determining how peace and transition could be framed. Defeat would surely entail suffering and neither republicans nor loyalists feel such hurt.

Conflict transformation is interpreted within loyalism and republicanism as a process of contestation within and beyond loyalism. It is understood that conflict is also set within a wide social arena that encompasses suspicion, mistrust and the desire to restrain human rights development. Additional interpretations of conflict transformation within loyalism include:

- the need to transform via an interpretation of equitable social, cultural and political definitions;
- that identity construction can both facilitate and undermine the deliverance of democratic accountability;
- that conflict can only be resolved when adversaries understand the capacity for transformation and the part that they can play in resolving conflict.

The desire to prevent future occurrences of violent disunity has been divided into two general perspectives. First, a conflict transformation perspective encourages an analysis of the antecedents of conflict as a way out of disagreement. Second, seeking out better ways to represent loyalism within a process of capacity building has also emerged. Additional features include:

- a long-term process that aimed to lift loyalism and republicanism out of insularity and into a host of civic and inter-community-based relationships;
- developing better relationships with government and statutory agencies;
- promoting restorative justice schemes;
- creating alternative community narratives which link loyalism and republicanism into a post-ceasefire process;
- challenging the mythic status of violence and in so doing diverting youth attention away from paramilitaries and sectarian violence.

Loyalists and republicans have also:

- formed inter-community groups to stop interface violence;
- provided seminars to youths to promote anti-violent approaches;
- worked with republicans on shared history and prisoner issues;
- developed links with statutory agencies in order to draw resources into Protestant communities.

An important factor in the promotion of non-violence is the extent to which the military leadership offered is found to be credible among the rank and file. Credibility has been important with regard to dissuading a return to large-scale violence as it provides legitimacy to anti-violence discourse, but operates as a further example of the internalised nature of transition. As a senior UFF member concluded:

> Look you see if you went with all the goodwill in the world and said 'Lads the reasons for not going back to war are this and that'. They would listen but not heed

you. If I walk in and say 'look I whacked so and so', the same fellas would listen. We might say the same things but you don't have the stripes like I do. (Cited in Shirlow and Mongahan, 2006)

A fundamental problem for those involved in such interventionist work is the threats that are endured. As noted by a UVF member:

> You challenge the drugs dealers in your own ranks and they could just shoot you dead. These are the people who don't give a shit about the peace process. You see if we have a settled society then they will have to go. So it is in their interest to destabilise loyalism. (Shirlow and Monaghan 2006)

UVF-linked persons have been at the forefront of the internal discussions with republicans which led to the production of working papers concerning respective constituencies' attitudes towards truth recovery processes (Eolas 2003; EPIC 2005). Outside their own immediate base, loyalist and republican former prisoners have played significant roles in other truth-focused initiatives. Loyalists have campaigned on a vast range of issues on behalf of themselves and Protestant communities. These include:

- improved social services;
- facilities and rights;
- the establishment of local job-seeking and social capital schemes;
- welfare, education, counselling, advisory and advocacy roles;
- the creation of advice centres, family projects, counselling services, children's activities and social activities;
- campaigning for the rights of former prisoners and their families.

Moving on

The role of republicans and loyalists has been to build up communities and within it persons who were prepared to use violence for political and defend-erist means. Given that the *raison d'etre* of such approaches has now virtually gone it is important that any future role is centred upon demobilising the nature of ethno-sectarian enmity between communities. As noted in the Middle East context by Tzfadia and Yiftachel:

> To enhance its power, each community mobilizes its members through the construction of difference, as a convenient platform for reinforcing ethnic and racial solidarity. This does not take place in isolation but by groups in constant relation (often contestation) with other groups and interest ... Competition for spatial, cultural and political resources includes control over territory, relation to place, and the right to cultural expression. (Tzfadia and Yiftachel 2004: 43)

Evidently, there is among former prisoners recognition of the need to remove the contestation between working-class and, in particular, interfaced and highly segregated communities. Thus the role of former prisoners is to present a politics that understands the nature and quality of 'alienation' from a range of perspectives, but in such a manner that it does not lead to sectarian conflict from a new generation. It is also imperative for them to develop structures and capacities capable of mobilising community resources, but in a manner that does not lead a sense of fatalism and decline that may be manipulated into another period of conflict.

Loyalists have challenged the more malign unionist voices that suggested in the wake of the Good Friday Agreement that the Protestant community is in structural decline and is being 'swept aside' by perfidious Albion as it aims for Catholic 'aggrandisement'. In December 2008, Dawn Purvis, leader of the PUP, was the only unionist to vote in favour of the Northern Ireland Bill of Rights. Although fearful of 'expansionist' nationalism and republicanism, loyalist former prisoners have co-operated on a pragmatic basis in lowering localised territorial, sectarian and cultural tensions during the Orange 'marching season' and have supported, on social-class lines, republican efforts to abolish the eleven plus transfer test in schools. The common view of loyalist former prisoners is that having 'won' the war in terms of the constitutional question, there is a requirement to at least seek to develop class commonalities beyond the sectarian divide.

The residualisation of certain Protestant communities and the enduring poverty in working-class Catholic communities produces a need for decisions to be made over the allocation of insufficient state resources. Of all of the actors involved in developing social and community capital and challenging social exclusion, it might be hoped that former prisoners, unlike others, see resources as scant as opposed to something to be fought over and, despite the communal backdrop, that they might see beyond 'my community', a statement that has a distinctively conflictual edge in Northern Ireland. Furthermore, former prisoners have an important role to play in highlighting the reality that single-identity work underpins the legitimacy of imagined needs, feeds internal paranoia and denies inter-community opportunity.

Former prisoner groups now also possess a vocabulary that understands the need to question not merely 'are my needs being served', but instead are 'needs being resolved'? If anything, former prisoners' groups have evolved as the radical space in Northern Irish politics. As shown within this book there is an understanding that a previous discourse served to protect communities inspired by fear of insecurity and promoted a shift from defence to assault. That language no longer offers any sense of protection and has no need of such. Distancing themselves from that language has meant that former prisoners have obtained a language of political and social change, trust and community needs that are no longer reducible to simplistic ideological frameworks. As shown in Shirlow and McEvoy (2008) former IRA prisoners were usually twice as likely as non-imprisoned family members to believe that British soldiers and RUC officers were victims of conflict.

A central role for former prisoners is to endure that ethno-sectarian segregation between communities is not bolstered by the promotion of oppositional political discourses. In challenging their own communities former prisoners can make it less feasible for ethno-sectarians to engender mythic reiterations of alienation that are then funded in such a manner that removes funding from real social problems. The location of problems via either a green or orange discourse is a sustained instinct within the community sector that former prisoners are perhaps best placed to challenge. What is lacking is a serious engagement with issues in Northern Ireland that are not merely defined by stakeholders promoting their ethno-sectarian credentials. Former prisoners are beginning to stretch debates beyond the ethno-sectarian self-interest and into a realm in which the elimination of antagonism requires a constructive mobilisation of interests that are based upon democratic accountability and not an extended idea that good neighbours are best served by high walls so that they cannot offend each other. The politics of the communities blighted by apartheid – however benign in modern times – and social exclusion requires a radical edge, but not one that is single-identity based.

In their version of conflict transformation, formers prisoners' understanding of power is now understood through an analysis of multiple dimensions and not along a previous and unsophisticated medium of imagined good and bad. At the centre of this shift is the need to rethink the type of skills set required in conflict transformation which displaces sectarianism or singular identities with strategies to define common routes out of social exclusion. Understanding and evaluating the connections that explain the nature and effect of difference requires a distinctive set of methodological lenses in which participatory research, open-space approaches and more penetrative data-gathering methods would need to be prioritised by former prisoners. Although ideological continuity and negative perceptions of the other side remain, it is worth recording that former prisoners understand conflict transformation as:

- taking into account the needs of numerous different people, even those from within the other ethno-sectarian group;
- promoting a rights-based approach that incorporates a duty to promote equality of opportunity and of citizenship as rights based, as opposed to merely ethnically designed;
- engages residents in a participatory manner and in intra- and inter-community settings as equals rather than as those who opinions and beliefs are invalid.

Ultimately, the quality of conflict transformation work undertaken by former prisoners will depend, in part, on the quality of discussion, the legitimacy of such persons within their respective community and explanation and intent of partnership building. There is a responsibility and an opportunity for a range of interests to be managed and proactively driven by former prisoners that will focus on conflict transformation building projects that concentrate on exclusion and the impact of a separated past upon the future. They 'haven't gone away you know', but their role and contribution spans decades of negotiation and evaluation, often producing progressive thinking.

Bibliography

Acheson, N. and Milofsky, C. 'Peace building and participation in Northern Ireland: local social movements and the policy process since the "Good Friday" Agreement', *Ethnopolitics*, 7.1, 63–80, 2008.

Adams, G. *Free Ireland: Towards a Lasting Peace*, Dingle: Brandon, 1995.

Adams, G. *Before the Dawn*, London: Heinemann, 1996.

Adams, G. 'Presidential address', Sinn Fein *ard fheis*, Dublin, 18 April 1998.

Adams, G. *The New Ireland: A Vision for the Future*, Dingle: Brandon, 2005.

Adams, G. Presidential speech to Sinn Fein special ard fheis on policing, Dublin, January 2007.

Alden, C. 'Making old soldiers fade away: lessons from the reintegration of demobilized soldiers in Mozambique', *Security Dialogue* 33.3, 341–56, 2002.

Alexander, J. *The Civil Sphere*, Oxford: Oxford University Press, 2006.

Alexander, Y., Swetnam, M. and Levine, H. *ETA: Profile of a Terrorist Group*, New York: Transnational, 2001.

Alison, M. 'Women as agents of political violence: gendering security', *Security Dialogue* 35.4, 447–63, 2004.

Allport, G. *The Nature of Prejudice*, Reading MA: Addison Wesley, 1954.

Alonso, R. *The IRA and Armed Struggle*, London: Routledge, 2006.

Anderson, B. *Imagined Communities: Reflections on the Origin and Spread of Nationalism*, London: Verso, 1991.

Anderson, C. *The Billy Boy: The Life and Death of LVF Leader Billy Wright*, Edinburgh: Mainstream, 2002.

Anheier, H. and Kendall, J. 'Interpersonal trust and voluntary associations: examining three approaches', *British Journal of Sociology* 53, 343–62, 2002.

An Glor Gafa (*The Captive Voice*) Autumn 1989; Summer 1991; Spring 1993; Summer 1999.

An Phoblacht 22 December 1975; 16 April 1976; 21 December 1982; 12 September 1985; 12 September 1985; 11 January 1990; 2 May 1991; 23 September 1993; 16 December 1999; 3 August 2000; 28 June 2001; 14 August 2003; 9 May 2002; 8 July 2004; 24 February 2005.

Arena, M. P. and Arrigo, B. A. *The Terrorist Identity: Explaining the Terrorist Threat*, New York: New York University Press, 2006.

Arthur, P. and Jeffery, K. *Northern Ireland since 1968*, Oxford: Blackwell, 1988.

Aughey, A. *The Politics of Northern Ireland: Beyond the Belfast Agreement*, London: Routledge, 2005.

Auvinen, J. and Kivimaki, T. 'Conflict transformation in South Africa', *Politikon* 28.1, 65–79, 2001.

Bacon, D. 'Revitalising civil society in Northern Ireland: social capital formation in three faith-based organisations', paper presented at Researching the Voluntary Sector Conference, London: NCVO Headquarters, 2001.

Bates-Gaston, J. 'Terrorism and imprisonment in Northern Ireland: a psychological perspective', in A. Silke (ed.) *Terrorists, Victims and Society*, Chichester: Wiley, 2003.

BBC, *Loyalists* (television series), 1998.

BBC News, 'Mowlam persuades loyalists to back talks'. 9 January 1998.

BBC News, 'NI prisoners savour freedom', 28 July 2000.

BBC News, 'Restorative justice in spotlight', 29 February 2005.

BBC News, '"Threats" aimed at justice scheme', 7 November 2008.

BBC Radio 4, *Great Lives: David Ervine*, 9 September 2008.

Bean, K. *The New Politics of Sinn Fein*, Liverpool: Liverpool University Press, 2007.

Bean, K. and Hayes, M. (eds) *Republican Voices*, Monaghan: Seesyu, 2001.

Beem, C. *The Necessity of Politics: Reclaiming American Public Life*, Chicago: University of Chicago Press, 1999.

Bell, C. and O'Rourke, C. 'The people's peace? Peace agreements, civil society, and participatory democracy', *International Political Science Review* 28.3, 293–324, 2007.

Bell, G. *The Protestants of Ulster*, London: Pluto, 1976.

Beresford, D. *Ten Men Dead*, London: Harper Collins, 1987.

Beresford, D. and Maas, P. *Ten Men Dead*, New York: Atlantic Monthly Press, 1997.

Berman, E. and Labonte, M. 'Sierra Leone', in W. Durch (ed.) *Twenty First Century Peace Operations*, Washington: United States Institute of Peace, 2006.

Bew, P. and Gillespie, G. *Northern Ireland: A Chronology of the Troubles*, Dublin: Gill and MacMillan, 1999.

Bew, P. and Patterson, H. *The British State and the Ulster Crisis: From Wilson to Thatcher*, London: Verso, 1985.

Bew, P., Gibbon, P. and Patterson H. *Northern Ireland 1921–2001 Political Forces and Social Classes*, London: Serif 2002.

Bideleux, R. and Jeffries, I. *The Balkans: A Post-Communist History*, London: Routledge, 2007.

Billig, M. *Banal Nationalism*, London: Sage, 1995.

Birrell, D. and Williamson, A. 'The voluntary-community sector and political development in Northern Ireland since 1972', *Voluntas*, 12.3, 205–20, 2001.

Bishop, P. and Mallie, E. *The Provisional IRA*, London: Heinemann, 1987.

Bloomer, S. 'Bridging the militarist-politico divide: the Progressive Unionist Party and the politics of conflict transformation', in A. Edwards and S. Bloomer (eds) *Transforming the Peace Process in Northern Ireland: From Terrorism to Democratic Politics*, Dublin: Irish Academic Press, 2008.

Borooah, V., Heaton, N., McKee, P., and Collins, G. 'Catholic-Protestant income differences in Northern Ireland', *Review of Income and Wealth* 41.1 41–56, 1995.

Borland J. King, R. and McDemott, K. 'The Irish in prison: a tighter nick for the micks?', *British Journal of Sociology* 46.3, 371–94, 1995.

Bose, S. *Bosnia after Dayton*, London: Hurst, 2002.

Boulton, D. *The UVF 1966–1973: An Anatomy of Loyalist Rebellion*, Dublin: Torc, 1973.

Bowyer-Bell, J. *The IRA: 1968–2000: Analysis of a Secret Army*, London: Frank Cass, 2000.

Boyce, D. G. 'The suffering people and the threatened community: two traditions of political violence in Ireland', in A. O'Day (ed.) *Terrorism's Laboratory: The Case of Northern Ireland*, Aldershot: Dartmouth, 1995.

Boyce, J. 'Investing in peace: aid and conditionality after civil wars', Adelphi Paper 351, International Institute for Strategic Studies, 2002.

Boyle, K. and Haddon, T. *Ireland: A Positive Proposal*, Harmondsworth: Penguin, 1985.

Breen, S. 'Who in Sinn Fein was IRA?', *Village*, 26 February 2005.

Bregman, A. *A History of Israel*, Basingstoke: Palgrave Macmillan, 2003.

Brehm, J. and Rahn, W. 'Individual-level evidence for the causes and consequences of social capital', *American Journal of Political Science*, 41.3, 999–1024, 1997.

Brewer, J. D. *Ethnography*, Buckingham: Open University Press, 2000.

Brown, K. 'Our father organisation. The cult of the Somme and the unionist "golden age" in modern Ulster Loyalist commemoration', *The Round Table. The Commonwealth Journal of International Affairs* 96, 707–23, 2007.

Bruce, S. *The Red Hand: Protestant Paramilitaries in Northern Ireland*, Oxford: Oxford University Press, 1992.

Bruce, S. *The Edge of the Union: The Ulster Loyalist Political Vision*, Oxford: Oxford University Press, 1994.

Bruce, S. 'Unionism amongst the paramilitaries' from R. Hanna (ed.) *The Union: Essays on Ireland and the British Connection*, Newtownards: Colourpoint 2001.

Bruce, S. 'Turf war and peace: loyalist paramilitaries since 1994', *Terrorism and Political Violence*, 16.3, 501–21, 2004.

Burt, R. 'The network structure of social capital', *Research in Organisational Behaviour* 22, 345–423, 2000.

Burton, F. and Carlen, P. *Official Discourse: On Discourse Analysis, Government Publications, Ideology and the State*, London; Routledge and Kegan Paul, 1979.

Butler, A. *Contemporary South Africa*, Basingstoke: Palgrave Macmillan, 2004.

Cadwallader, A. 'Goodbye to the Maze', *Ireland on Sunday*, 30 July 2000.

Cairns, E. 'Social identity and intergroup conflict in Northern Ireland' in J. Harbinson (ed.) *Growing Up in Northern Ireland*, Belfast: Stranmillis College Press, 1989.

Cairns, E., Lewis, A. and Mumcu, O. 'Memories of recent ethnic conflict and their relationship to social identity', *Peace and Conflict: Journal of Peace Psychology* 4.1, 13–22, 1998.

Cairns, E., Niens U. and Hewstone, M. 'Contact and conflict in Northern Ireland' in O. Hargie, and D. Dickson (eds) *Researching the Troubles: Social Science Perspectives on the Northern Ireland Conflict*, Edinburgh: Mainstream, 2003.

Cairns, E., Van Til, E. and Williamson, A. 'Social capital, collectivism-individualism and community background in Northern Ireland', *Report to The Office of the First Minister and the Deputy First Minister, Centre for Voluntary Action Studies*, Coleraine: University of Ulster, 2003.

Calhoun, C. 'Social theory and the politics of identity' in C. Calhoun (ed.) *Social Theory and the Politics of Identity*, Oxford: Blackwell, 1994.

Cash, J. 'The dilemmas of political transformation in Northern Ireland', *Pacifica Review* 10.3, 227–34, 1998.

Cassidy, K. J. 'Organic intellectuals and the committed community: Irish republicanism and Sinn Féin in the North', *Irish Political Studies* 20.3, 341–56, 2005.

Cassidy, K. J. 'Organic intellectuals and the new loyalism: re-inventing Protestant working-class politics in Northern Ireland', *Irish Political Studies* 23.3, 411–30, 2008.

Cebulla, A. and Smyth, J. 'Disadvantage and new prosperity in restructured Belfast' *Economy and Society* 26.4, 560–78, 1997.

Clarke, L. and Johnston, K. *Martin McGuinness: From Guns to Government*, Edinburgh: Mainstream, 2001.

Cochrane, F. *Ending Wars*, Cambridge: Polity, 2008.

Cochrane, F. and Dunn, S. *People Power? The Role of the Voluntary and Community Sector in the Northern Ireland Conflict*, Cork: Cork University Press, 2002.

Coiste na n-Iarchimí, 'Call for prisoners in Maghaberry for political status and segregation', Press release, 18 September, 2002.

Coleman, J. C. 'Social capital in the creation of human capital', *American Journal of Sociology* 94, 95–120, 1988.

Coleman, J. S. *Foundations of Social Theory*, Cambridge, MA: Harvard University Press, 1998.

Colletta, N, Kostner, N., Wiederhofer, I., Sitarri, T. and Woldu, T., *Case Studies in War-to-Peace Transition. The Reintegration of Ex-Combatants in Ethiopia, Namibia and Uganda*, Washington DC: World Bank Discussion Paper 331, 1996.

Collins, E. *Killing Rage*, London: Granta, 1998.

Combat, August 1975; December 1977; March 1979; October 1991; September 1993; March 1994; July 1999; May 2005; September 2004; Spring 2006.

'Comm' from Maze prison regarding the end of the hunger strike protests against the withdrawal of Special Category status 1981 (held by the Northern Irish Political Collection at the Linen Hall Library, Belfast).

Community Convention and Development Company *Protestant, Unionist, Loyalist Communities; Leading a Positive Transformation – Conference Report*, Belfast: CCDC, 2006.

Community Foundation for Northern Ireland *Taking Calculated Risks for Peace II*, Belfast: CFNI, 2003.

Connolly, P. and Maginn, P. *Sectarianism, Children and Community Relations in Northern Ireland*, Coleraine: Centre for the Study of Conflict, University of Ulster, 1999.

Coogan, T. P. *The Troubles*, London: Random House, 1995.

Cook-Huffman, C. 'The role of identity in conflict', in D. J. D. Sandole, S. Byrne, I. Sandole-Staroste and J. Senehi (eds) *Handbook of Conflict Analysis and Resolution*, London: Routledge, 2008.

Corcoran, M. *Out of Order: The Political Imprisonment of Women in Northern Ireland, 1972–1998*, Cullompton: Willan, 2006.

Coulter, C. *Contemporary Northern Irish Society: An Introduction*. London: Pluto, 1999.

Cousens, E. and Harland, D. 'Post-Dayton Bosnia and Herzegovina', in W. Durch (ed.) *Twenty-First Century Peace Operations*, Washington: United States Institute for Peace, 2006.

Cox, M. 'Northern Ireland: the war that came in from the cold', *Irish Studies in International Affairs* 9, 3–84, 1998.

Cox, M. 'Rethinking the international and Northern Ireland: a defence', in M. Cox, A. Guelke and F. Stephen (eds) *A Farewell to Arms? Beyond the Good Friday Agreement*, Manchester: Manchester University Press, 2006.

Crawford, C. *Defenders or Criminals? Loyalist Prisoners and Criminalisation*, Belfast: Blackstaff, 1999.

Crawford, C. *Inside the UDA*, London: Pluto, 2003.

Crawford, R. G. *Loyal to King Billy: A Portrait of the Ulster Protestants*, Dublin: Gill and Macmillan, 1987.

Crawford, A., and Newburn, T. *Youth Offending and Restorative Justice: Implementing Reform in Youth Justice*, Cullompton: Willan, 2003.

Crenshaw, M. 'The psychology of terrorism: an agenda for the 21st century', *Political Psychology* 21.2, 405–20, 2000.

Crothers, J. *Reintegration: The Problems and the Issues*, Ex-Prisoner's Interpretative Centre, Research Document no. 2, Belfast: EPIC, 1998.

Cusack, J. and McDonald, H. *UVF*, Dublin: Poolbeg, 2000.

Dajani, O. 'Surviving opportunities: Palestinian negotiating patterns in peace talks with Israel', in T. Wittes (ed.) *How Israelis and Palestinians Negotiate*, Washington: United States Institute of Peace, 2005.

Darby, J. and Mac Ginty, R. *Contemporary Peacemaking*, Basingstoke: Palgrave Macmillan, 2003.

Darby, J. and Rae, J. 'Peace processes from 1988 to 1998: changing patterns', *Ethnic Studies Report* 17.1, 45–64, 1999.

Dawe, G. *The Rest is History*, Newry: Abbey Press, 1998.

De Paor, L. *Divided Ulster*, Harmondsworth: Penguin, 1970.

Democratic Unionist Party *Assembly Election Manifesto*, Belfast: DUP, 1998.

Dixon, P. 'Paths to peace in Northern Ireland (II). The peace process 1973–1974 and 1994–1996' *Democratisation* 4.3, 1–25, 1997.

Dixon, P. 'Rethinking the international and Northern Ireland; a critique', in M. Cox, A. Guelke and F. Stephen (eds) *A Farewell to Arms? Beyond the Good Friday Agreement*, Manchester: Manchester University Press, 2006.

Dixon, P. *Northern Ireland: the Politics of War and Peace*, Basingstoke: Palgrave Macmillan, 2008.

Dooley, B. *Choosing the Green? Second Generation Irish and the Cause of Ireland*, Belfast: Beyond the Pale, 2004.

Dowdney, L. *Neither War not Peace. International Comparisons of Children and Youth in Organised Armed Violence*, available at www.coav.org.br, 2005.

Dowty, A. *Israel/Palestine*, Cambridge: Polity, 2008.

Drake, C. J. M. 'The role of ideology in terrorists' target selection', *Terrorism and Political Violence* 10.2, 53–85, 1998.

Dwyer, C. 'Risk, politics and the 'scientification' of political judgement: prisoner release and conflict transformation in Northern Ireland', *British Journal of Criminology*, 47, 779–97, 2008.

Elliott, S. and Flackes, W. D. 'Ulster Defence Association' in S. Elliott and W. D. Flackes (eds) *Northern Ireland: A Political Directory 1968–1999*, Belfast: Blackstaff, 1999.

Edwards, A. 'The new UVF', *Fortnight* 462, May 2007.

English, R. *Armed Struggle: A History of the IRA*, Basingstoke: Macmillan, 2003.

English, R. *Irish Freedom: the History of Nationalism in Ireland*, Basingstoke: Macmillan, 2006.

Entman, R. M. 'Framing: towards clarification of a fractured paradigm', *Journal of Communication* 43.4, 51–8, 1993.

Eolas Project *Consultation Paper on Truth and Justice*, Relatives for Justice, Belfast, 2003.

EPIC 'Statement on community development', 1999, www.epic.org.uk

EPIC *Truth Recovery: A Contribution from Loyalism*, Belfast: EPIC, 2005.

Ervine, D. 'Redefining loyalism – a political perspective', in *Redefining Loyalism*, Dublin: Institute for British-Irish Studies, Working Paper 4, 1–7, 2001.

Farrell, M. *The Orange State*, London: Pluto, 1976.

Farrell, M. *Northern Ireland: The Orange State*, London: Pluto, 1996.

Feeney, B. *Sinn Fein: A Hundred Turbulent Years*, Dublin: O'Brien, 2002.

Ferguson, N., Burgess, M. and Hollywood, I. 'Crossing the rubicon: deciding to become a paramilitary in Northern Ireland', *IJCV* 2.1, 130–7, 2008.

Féron, E. 'Paths to reconversion taken by Northern Irish paramilitaries', *International Social Science Journal* 58, 447–56, 2006.

Fetterman, D. *Ethnography*, London: Sage, 1998.

Fitzduff, M. *Beyond Violence: Conflict Resolution Process in Northern Ireland*, New York: United Nations University Press, 2002.

Fitzduff, M. and Gormley, C. 'Northern Ireland: changing perceptions of the "other"', *Development* 43.3, 62–5, 2000.

Foster, P. and Woolf, M. 'Royal release for IRA bomber', *Daily Telegraph*, 27 July 2000.

Fraser, T. *The Arab–Israeli Conflict*, Basingstoke: Palgrave Macmillan, 2008.

Frisch, H. 'Motivation or capabilities? Israeli counterterrorism against Palestinian suicide bombings and violence', *Journal of Strategic Studies* 29.5, 643–69, 2006.

Gallaher, C. *After the Peace: Loyalist Paramilitaries in Post-Accord Northern Ireland*, Ithaca: Cornell University Press, 2007.

Gamba, V. 'Managing violence: disarmament and demobilization' in J. Darby and R. Mac Ginty (eds) *Contemporary Peacemaking. Conflict Violence and Peace Processes*, Basingstoke: Palgrave 2003.

Garland, R. *Gusty Spence*, Belfast: Blackstaff, 2001.

Geertz, C. 'Thick description: towards an interpretative theory of culture', in C. Geertz, *The Interpretation of Cultures: Selected Essays*, New York: Basic, 1973.

Gemayel, A. *Rebuilding Lebanon*, Maryland: University Press of America, 1992.

Gillespie, R. 'Peace moves in the Basque Country', *Journal of Southern Europe and the Balkans* 1:2, 119–36, 1999.

Gilmour, R. *Dead Ground: Infiltrating the IRA*, London: Warner, 1999.

Gormally, B. 'Conversion from war to peace: re-integration of ex-prisoners in Northern Ireland', Paper 18, Bonn: BICC, 2000.

Gormally, B. and McEvoy, K. *Release and Reintegration of Politically Motivated Prisoners in Northern Ireland: A Comparative Study of South Africa, Israel/Palestine, Italy, Spain, the Republic of Ireland and Northern Ireland*, Belfast: NIACRO, 1995.

Gormally, B., McEvoy K. and Wall, D. 'Criminal justice in a divided society', *Crime and Justice* 17, 55–135, 1993.

Gormley-Heenan, C. *Political Leadership and the Northern Ireland Peace Process*, Basingstoke: Palgrave Macmillan, 2007.

Green, M. *The Prisoner Experience – A Loyalist Perspective*, Belfast: EPIC Research Document 1, 21–32, 1998.

Gribben, V., Kelly, R., and Mitchell, C. *Loyalist Conflict Transformation Initiatives*, Belfast: Office of the First Minister and Deputy First Minister, 2005.

Guelke, A. 'Paramilitaries, republicans and loyalists', in S. Dunn (ed.) *Facets of the Conflict in Northern Ireland*, Basingstoke: Palgrave MacMillan, 1995.

Guelke, A. 'Political comparisons: from Johannesburg to Jerusalem', in M. Cox, A. Guelke and F. Stephen (eds) *A Farewell to Arms? Beyond the Good Friday Agreement*, Manchester: Manchester University Press, 2006.

Guelke, A. 'The Northern Ireland peace process and the war against terrorism: conflicting conceptions?, *Government and Opposition* 42:3, 272–91, 2007.

Guelke, A. 'The lure of the miracle? The South African connection and the Northern Ireland peace process', in C. Farrington (ed.) *Global Change, Civil Society and the Northern Ireland Peace Process: Implementing the Political Settlement*, Basingstoke: Palgrave Macmillan, 2008.

Hall, M. *Seeds of Hope: An Exploration by the 'Seeds of Hope' Ex-Prisoners Think Tank*, Newtownabbey: Island, 2000.

Hall, M. *Reuniting the Shankill: A Report on the Greater Shankill Community Exhibition and Convention*, Newtownabbey: Island, 2002.

Hall, M. *Loyalism in Transition 1: A New Reality?*, Belfast: Island, 2006.

Hall, M. *Loyalism in Transition 2: Learning from Others in Conflict*, Belfast: Island, 2007.

Hall, P. 'Social capital in Britain', *British Journal of Political Science* 29, 417–61, 1999.

Hall, S. 'The work of representation', in S. Hall (ed.) *Representation: Cultural Representations and Signifying Practices*, London: Sage, 1997.

Hamber, B. and Kelly, G. 'The challenge of reconciliation in post-conflict societies', in I. O'Flynn and D. Russell (eds) *Power Sharing: New Challenges for Divided Societies*, London: Pluto, 2005.

Hansard, 'Proceedings of the Northern Ireland Assembly', 23 April 2002, 8 October 2002.

Hareven, T. K. 'The life course and aging in historical perspective', in T. K. Hareven and K. J. Adams (eds) *Aging and Life Course Transitions. An Interdisciplinary Perspective*, New York: Guilford Press, 1982.

Harik, J. *Hezbollah: The Changing Face of Terrorism*, London: I. B. Tauris, 2005.

Harper, R. 'Social capital: a review of the literature', London: Social Analysis and Reporting Division, Office for National Statistics, 2001.

Harris, L. 'Duck or rabbit? The value systems of loyalist paramilitaries', in M. Busteed, F. Neal and J. Tonge (eds) *Irish Protestant Identities*, Manchester: Manchester University Press, 2008.

Hayes, B. and McAllister I. 'Public support for political violence and paramilitarism in Northern Ireland and the Republic of Ireland', *Terrorism and Political Violence* 14.4, 1–19, 2001.

Hayes, B. and McAllister, I. 'Who backs the bombers?', *Fortnight* 425, 11–12, 2004.

Hennessey, T. *A History of Northern Ireland 1920–1996*, Basingstoke: Palgrave MacMillan, 1997.

Hewstone, M. and Brown, R. 'Contact is not enough: an intergroup perspective on the contact hypothesis' in M. Hewstone (ed.) *Contact and Conflict in Intergroup Encounters*, Oxford: Blackwell, 1986.

Hibernia, October 1979.

HM Government, *The Agreement*, Belfast: NIO, 1998.

Holland, J. and McDonald, H. *INLA: Deadly Divisions*, Dublin: Torc, 1994

Hopkins, S. 'History with a divided and complicated heart? The uses of political memoir, biography and autobiography in Contemporary Northern Ireland', *The Global Review of Ethnopolitics* 1:2, 74–81, 2001.

Howard, D., Norval, A. J. and Stavrakakis, Y. *Discourse Theory and Political Analysis: Identities, Hegemonies and Social Change*, Manchester: Manchester University Press, 2000.

Howe, S. 'Out of Shankill', *New Statesman*, 4 February 2002.

Howe, S. 'Mad dogs and Ulstermen: the crisis of loyalism part one', *Open Democracy*, available at www.opendemocracy.net, 2005.

Hroub, K. *Hamas*, London: Pluto, 2005.

Hughes, J. and Donnelly, C. 'Ten years of social attitudes to community relations in Northern Ireland', in A. M. Gray, K. Lloyd, P. Devine, G. Robinson and D. Keenan (eds) *Social Attitudes in Northern Ireland: The Eighth Report*, London: Pluto, 1999.

Humphreys, M. and Weinstein, J. 'Disentangling the determinants of successful demobilization and reintegration', paper presented at the American Political Science Association Annual Conference, 2005.

Independent (Patten) Commission on Policing *A New Beginning: Policing in Northern Ireland*, Belfast: HMSO, 1999.

Inglehart, R. *The Silent Revolution*, Princeton NJ: Princeton University Press, 1977.

Inglehart, R. *Modernization and Postmodernization: Cultural, Economic, and Political Change in 43 Societies*, Princeton NJ: Princeton University Press, 1997.

Inglehart, R. *Culture Shift in Advanced Industrial Society*, Princeton NJ: Princeton University Press, 1980.

Inglehart, R. 'Observations on cultural change and postmodernism', in J. R. Gibbins (ed.), *Contemporary Political Culture*, London: Sage, 1989

Inglehart, R. and Rabier, J. R. 'Political realignment in advanced industrial society: from class-based politics to quality-of-life politics', *Government and Opposition* 21, 456–79, 1986.

Inter-Action Belfast *The Role of Ex-Combatants on Interfaces*, Belfast: IAB, no date.

Irish News, 17 November 1997; 28 July 2003.

Irwin, T. 'Prison education in Northern Ireland: learning from our paramilitary past', *The Howard Journal*, 42.5, 471–84, 2003.

Jamieson, R. and Grounds, A. *No Sense of an Ending: The Effects of Long-term Imprisonment Amongst Republican Prisoners and their Families*, Monaghan: Seesyu, 2002.

Jarman, N. 'Managing disorder: responses to interface violence in North Belfast', in O. Hargie and D. Dickson (eds) *Researching the Troubles: Social Science Perspectives on the Northern Ireland Conflict*, Edinburgh: Mainstream Publishing, 2003.

Jarman, N. 'From war to peace? changing patterns of violence in Northern Ireland, 1990–2003', *Terrorism and Political Violence* 16.3, 420–38, 2004.

Johnstone, G. *Restorative Justice: Ideas, Values, Debates*, Cullumpton: Willan, 2002.

Jordan, T. *Activism! Direct Action, Hacktivism and the Future of Society*, London: Reaktion, 2002.

Keane, J. *Civil Society – Old Images, New Visions*, Cambridge: Polity, 1998.

Keen, D. 'War and peace. What's the difference?', in A. Adebajo and C. Sriram (eds) *Managing Armed Conflict in the 21st Century*, London: Frank Cass, 2001.

Kennedy-Pipe, C. *The Origins of the Present Troubles in Northern Ireland*, Harlow: Longman, 1997.

Kerr, M. *Imposing Power-Sharing: Conflict and Coexistence in Northern Ireland and Lebanon*, Dublin: Irish Academic Press, 2005.

Kingma, K. 'Demobilisation of combatants after civil wars in Africa and their reintegration into civilian life', *Policy Sciences* 30, 151–65, 1997.

Klandermans, B. *The Social Psychology of Protest*, Oxford: Blackwell, 1997.

Knight, M. and Özerdem, A. 'Guns, camps and cash: disarmament, demobilization and reinsertion of former combatants in transitions from war to peace', *Journal of Peace Research* 41.4, 499–516, 2004.

Kohlmann, E. *Al-Qaida's Jihad in Europe*, Oxford: Berg, 2004.

Krause, K. and Jutersonke, O. 'Peace, security and development in post-conflict environments', *Security Dialogue* 36.4, 447–62, 2005.

Kriesberg, L. *Social Conflicts*, New Jersey: Prentice Hall, 1982.

Kymlicka, W. and Norman, W. 'Return of the citizen: a survey of recent work on citizenship theory', *Ethics*, 104.2, 352–81, 1994.

Laclau, E. and Mouffe, C. *Hegemony and Socialist Strategy: Toward a Radical Democratic Politics*, London: Verso, 1985.

Langhammer, M. '"Cutting with the grain". Policy and the Protestant community: what is to be done?', Paper to the Secretary of State for Northern Ireland and the Northern Ireland Office Team, Belfast: published by the author, 2003.

Lederach, J. P. *Preparing for Peace: Conflict Transformation Across Cultures*, New York: Syracuse University Press, 1995.

Lederach, J. P. *Building Peace: Sustainable Reconciliation in Divided Societies*, New York: US Institute of Peace, 1997.

Lederach, J. P. *The Little Book of Conflict Transformation*, Intercourse, PA: Good Books, 2003

Lesch, D. *The Arab–Israeli Conflict: A History*, Oxford: Oxford University Press, 2008.

Lister, D. and Jordan, H. *Mad Dog: The Rise and Fall of Johnny Adair and 'C Company'*, Edinburgh: Mainstream Publishing, 2003.

Little, M., Jordens, C. F. C. and Sayers, E. J. 'Discourse communities and the discourse of experience', *Health: An Interdisciplinary Journal for the Social Study of Health, Illness and Medicine* 7.1, 73–86, 2003.

Lorwin, V.F. 'Segmented pluralism', *Comparative Politics* 3.2, 141–75, 1971.

Loyalist, April/May 2004; September 2004; January 2006.

Loyalist Prisoners Welfare Association *The Need for Penal Reform in Ulster*, Belfast: LPWA, 1979.

Lundy, P. and McGovern, M. 'The politics of memory in post-conflict Ireland', *Peace Review* 13.1, 27–33, 2001.

Lynch, S. 'Lessons of a peace process', *Journal of Prisoners on Prison* 7.1, 14–18, 1986.

MacGinty, R. 'Northern Ireland: a peace process thwarted by accidental spoiling', in E. Newman (ed.) *Challenges to Peace-building: Managing Spoilers during Conflict Resolution*, Tokyo: United Nations University Press, 2006.

Mac Giolla Ghunna, M. 'Our captive voice will be heard', *Journal of Prisoners on Prisoners* 7.1, 1–4, 1997.

MacStiofain, S. *Revolutionary in Ireland*, Farnborough: Saxon House, 1974.

Magone, J. *Contemporary Spanish Politics*, London: Routledge, 2004.

Maillot. A. *New Sinn Fein. Irish Republicanism in the Twenty-First Century*, London: Routledge, 2004.

Mallie, E. and McKittrick, D. *The Fight for Peace*, London: Reed International 1996.

Mandelbaum, D. G. 'The study of life history' in R. G. Burgess, *Field Research: A Sourcebook and Field Manual*, Hemel Hempstead: Allen and Unwin, 1982.

Manning, C. 'Local level challenges to post conflict peacebuilding', *International Peacekeeping*, 10:3, 25–43, 2003.

Marguiles, P. *ETA: Spain's Basque Terrorists*, New York: Rosen, 2004.

Marshall, T. H. *Citizenship and Social Class*, Cambridge University Press, 1950.

Marxism Today, December 1981.

Mason, R. *Paying the Price*, London: Robert Hale, 1999.

Maxwell, G. and Morris, A. 'Deciding about justice for young people in New Zealand: the involvement of families, victims and culture', in J. Hudson and B. Galaway (eds) *Child Welfare in Canada: Research and Policy Implications*, Toronto: Thompson Educational Publishing, 1995.

McAllister, I. 'The Armalite and the ballot box: Sinn Fein's electoral strategy in Northern Ireland', *Electoral Studies* 23, 123–42, 2004.

McAuley, J. W. 'Cuchullain and an RPG-7: the ideology and politics of the Ulster Defence Association', in E. Hughes (ed.) *Culture and Politics in Northern Ireland*, Milton Keynes: Open University Press, 1991.

McAuley, J. W., *The Politics of Identity: A Loyalist Community in Belfast*, Aldershot: Avebury Press, 1994.

McAuley, J. W. '"Not a game of Cowboys and Indians" – The Ulster Defence Association in the 1990s', in A. O'Day (ed.) *Terrorism's Laboratory: The Case of Northern Ireland*, Aldershot: Dartmouth, 1995.

McAuley, J. W. 'A process of surrender? Loyalist perceptions of a settlement', in J. Anderson and J. Goodman (eds) *Dis/Agreeing Ireland: Contexts, Obstacles, Hopes*, London: Pluto, 1998a.

McAuley J. W. 'Ulster loyalism and the politics of peace', in J. Goodman and J.

Anderson (eds.), *Agreeing Ireland: Political Agendas for Peace in Ireland's National Conflict*, London: Pluto, 1998b.

McAuley, J. W. 'The emergence of new loyalism', in J. Coakley (ed.) *Changing Shades of Orange and Green*, Dublin: University College Dublin Press, 2002.

McAuley, J. W. 'Unionism's last stand? Contemporary unionist politics and identity in Northern Ireland', *Global Review of Ethnopolitics* 3.1, 60–74, 2003.

McAuley, J. W. '"Just fighting to survive": loyalist paramilitary politics and the Progressive Unionist Party', *Terrorism and Political Violence*, 16.3, 522–43, 2004.

McAuley, J. W. 'Whither new loyalism – changing politics after the Belfast Agreement', *Irish Political Studies*, 20.3, 323–40, 2005.

McAuley, J. W. and Tonge, J. '"For God and for the Crown": contemporary political and social attitudes among Orange Order members in Northern Ireland', *Political Psychology* 28.1, 33–54, 2007.

McAuley, J. W., McGlynn, C. and Tonge, J. 'Conflict resolution in asymmetric and symmetric situations: Northern Ireland as a case study', *Dynamics of Asymmetric Conflict* 1.1 88–102, 2008.

McBride, I. (ed.) *History and Memory in Modern Ireland*, Cambridge: Cambridge University Press, 2001.

McCann, E. *War and an Irish Town*, London: Pluto, 1972.

McCann, E. *War and an Irish Town*, London: Pluto, 1993.

McCarron, J. J. *Civil society in Northern Ireland: a new beginning?*, Belfast: Northern Ireland Council for Voluntary Action, 2006.

McCready, S. *Empowering People: Community Development and Conflict 1969–1999*, Belfast: Stationery Office, 2001.

McEvoy, K. 'Prisoner release and conflict resolution: international lessons for Northern Ireland', *International Criminal Justice Review* 8, 33–61, 1998.

McEvoy, K. 'Law, struggle and political transformation in Northern Ireland', *Journal of Law and Society* 27.4, 542–71, 2000.

McEvoy, K. *Paramilitary Imprisonment in Northern Ireland: Resistance, Management and Release*, Oxford: Oxford University Press, 2001.

McEvoy, K. and Mika, H. 'Punishment, politics and praxis: restorative justice and non-violent alternatives to paramilitary punishment in Northern Ireland', *Police and Society* 11.3, 59–82, 2001a.

McEvoy, K. and Mika, H. 'Restorative justice in conflict: paramilitarism, community, and the construction of legitimacy in Northern Ireland', *Contemporary Justice Review* 4.3–4, 291–319, 2001b.

McEvoy, K. and Mika, A. 'Restorative justice and the critique of informalism in Northern Ireland', *British Journal of Criminology* 42, 534–62, 2002.

McEvoy, K. Shirlow, P. and McElrath, K. 'Resistance, transition and exclusion: politically motivated ex-prisoners and conflict transformation in Northern Ireland', *Terrorism and Political Violence* 16.3 646–70, 2004.

McGarry, J. and O'Leary, B. *Explaining Northern Ireland*, Oxford: Blackwell, 1995.

McGartland, M. *Fifty Dead Men Walking*, London: Blake, 1998.

McGladdery, G. *The Provisional IRA in England: the Bombing Campaign 1973–1997*, Dublin: Irish Academic Press, 2006.

McGlynn, C. *How New is New Loyalism?* (Unpublished PhD Thesis) University of Salford, 2004.

McGovern, M. and Shirlow, P. 'Sectarianism, regulation and the Northern Ireland conflict', *Reclus: Journal de L'Espace Geographique* 37, 13–32, 1996.

McIntyre, A. 'Modern Irish republicanism: the product of British state strategies', *Irish Political Studies* 10, 97–121, 1995.

McIntyre, A. 'Modern Irish republicanism and the Belfast Agreement': chickens coming home to roost or turkeys celebrating Christmas?', in R. Wilford (ed.) *Aspects of the Belfast Agreement*, Oxford: Oxford University Press, 2001.

McIntyre, A. *Good Friday: The Death of Irish Republicanism*, Belfast: Ausubo, 2008.

McKearney, T. Presentation at Northern Ireland Office Conference on Peace and Reconciliation, www.expac.ie, 2004.

McKeever, G. 'Citizenship and social exclusion: the reintegration of political ex-prisoners', *British Journal of Criminology* 47, 423–38, 2007.

McKeown, L. *Out of Time: Irish Republican Prisoners Long Kesh 1972–2000*, Belfast: Beyond the Pale, 1999.

McKittrick, D. 'Amongst the paramilitaries', *Irish Times*, 20 March 1975.

McKittrick, D. 'Guns get into the Maze because it's an extraordinary kind of jail', *Independent*, 29 December 1997.

McMichael, G. *Ulster Voice: In Search of Common Ground in Northern Ireland*, Boulder: Roberts Rinehart, 1999.

McShane, L. *Politically Motivated Ex-Prisoners Self-Help Projects: Interim Report*, Belfast: Northern Ireland Voluntary Trust, 1998.

Miles, R., *Racism*, London: Routledge, 1989.

Miller, D. *Queen's Rebels: Ulster Loyalism in Historical Perspective*, Dublin: Gill and MacMillan, 1978.

Milton-Edwards, B. *Contemporary Politics in the Middle East*, Cambridge: Polity, 2006.

Mitchell, C. 'The limits of legitimacy: former loyalist combatants and peace-building in Nortern Ireland', *Irish Political Studies* 23.1, 1–19, 2008.

Moen, D. 'Irish political prisoners and post hunger-strike resistance to criminalisation', *British Criminology Conference 1999: Selected Proceedings* Volume 3, 2000.

Moloney, E. *A Secret History of the IRA*, London: Penguin, 2002.

Monaghan, R. 'Community based justice in Northern Ireland and South Africa', *International Criminal Justice Review* 18, 83–105, 2008.

Moran, J. 'Paramilitaries, "Ordinary Decent Criminals" and the development of organised crime following the Belfast Agreement', *International Journal of the Sociology of Law* 32.3, 263–78, 2004.

Morrison, D. *Then the Walls Came Down: A Prison Journal*, Cork: Mercier, 1999.

Morrow, D. 'Breaking antagonism? Political leadership in divided societies', in I. O'Flynn, I and D. Russell (eds) *Power Sharing: New Challenges for Divided Societies*, London: Pluto, 2005.

Muggah, R. 'No magic bullet: a critical perspective on disarmament, demobilization and reintegration (DDR) and weapons reduction in post-conflict contexts', *The Round Table* 94, 239–52, 2005.

Mulholland, M. 'Irish republican politics and violence before the peace process, 1968–1994', *European Review of History-Revue europeenne d'Historie* 14.3, 397–421, 2007.

Munck, R. 'Irish republicanism: containment or new departure?', in A. O'Day (ed.) *Terrorism's Laboratory: The Case of Northern Ireland*, Aldershot: Avebury, 1992.

Murphy, P. 'Contrasting symbols in a tale of two cultures', *Irish Times*, 31 August 2003.

Murray, G. and Tonge, J. *Sinn Fein and the SDLP: from Alienation to Participation*, London: Hurst, 2005.

Nelson, S. *Ulster's Uncertain Defenders*, Belfast: Appletree, 1984.

Neumann, P. R. 'The imperfect peace: explaining paramilitary violence in Northern Ireland', *Low Intensity Conflict and Law Enforcement* 11.1, 116–38, 2002.

New Ulster Political Research Group, *Beyond the Religious Divide*, Belfast: NUPRG, 1979.

New Ulster Political Research Group, *Common Sense*, Belfast: NUPRG, 1987.

Niens, U., Cairns, E. and Hewstone, M. 'Contact and conflict in Northern Ireland' in O. Hargie and D. Dickson (eds) *Researching the Troubles: Social Science Perspectives on the Northern Ireland Conflict*, Edinburgh: Mainstream Publishing, 2003.

Northern Ireland Life and Times Survey 2000, www.ark.ac.uk/nilt.

O'Brien, B. *The Long War: The IRA and Sinn Fein*, Dublin: O'Brien Press, 1999.

O'Brien, C. 'Integrated community development/conflict resolution strategies as peace-building potential in South Africa and Northern Ireland', *Community Development Journal* 42:1, 114–130, 2007.

O'Broin, E. *Matxinada: Basque Nationalism and Radical Basque Youth Movements*, Belfast: Irish Basque Committee, 2008.

O'Clery, C. *The Greening of the White House*, Dublin: Gill and Macmillan, 1997.

O'Dochartaigh, N. *From Civil Rights to Armalites: Derry and the Birth of the Irish Troubles*, Cork University Press, 1997.

O' Doherty, S. *The Volunteer: A Former IRA Man's True Story*, London: Fount, 1993.

O'Duffy, B. 'Containment or regulation? The British approach to ethnic conflict in Northern Ireland', in J. McGarry and B. O'Leary (eds) *The Politics of Ethnic Conflict Regulation*, London: Routledge, 1993.

O' Hearn, D. *Nothing but an Unfinished Song: Bobby Sands, The Irish Hunger Striker Who Ignited a Generation*, New York: Nation, 2006.

O'Kane, E. *Britain, Ireland and Northern Ireland since 1980: The Totality of Relationships*, London: Routledge, 2007.

O'Malley, P. and McCormack, J. 'Northern Ireland and South Africa: conflicts without end, guns beyond use', *Fortnight* (supplement), 386, 2004.

O'Neill, P. 'Chairperson's Report', in *Tar Isteach Annual Report 2007*, Belfast: Tar Isteach, 2007.

O'Rawe, R. *Blanketmen: An Untold Story of the H-Block Hunger Strike*, Dublin: New Island, 2005.

Office of the First Minister and Deputy First Minister *Recruiting People with Conflict Related Conviction-an Employers' Guide*, www.ofmdfmni.gov.uk/conflict-transfor-mation-news, 2007.

Omelicheva, M. 'Combating terrorism in Central Asia: explaining differences in states' response to terror', *Terrorism and Political Violence* 19.3, 369–93, 2007.

Özerdem, A. 'Disarmament, demobilization and reintegration of former combatants in Afghanistan: lessons learned from a cross-cultural perspective', *Third World Quarterly* 23.5, 961–75, 2002.

Patterson, H. *The Politics of Illusion: A Political History of the IRA*, London: Serif, 1997.

Pearce, J. 'From civil war to "civil society": has the end of the cold war brought peace to Central America?', *International Affairs* 74:3, 587–615, 1998.

Peatling, G. *The Failure of the Northern Ireland Peace Process*, Dublin: Irish Academic Press, 2004.

Pierson, C. *The Modern State*, London: Routledge, 1996.

Porter, N. *Rethinking Unionism*, Belfast: Blackstaff, 1996.

Portes, A. 'Social capital: its origins and applications in modern sociology', *Annual Review of Sociology* 24, 1–24, 1998.

Potter, J. and Wetherell, M. *Mapping the Language of Racism: Discourse and the Legitimation of Exploitation*, Hemel Hempstead: Harvester Wheatsheaf, 1992.

Powell, J. *Great Hatred, Little Room: Making Peace in Northern Ireland*, London: Bodley Head, 2008.

Pretty, J. and Ward, H. 'Social capital and the environment', *World Development* 29.2, 209–27, 2001.

Progressive Unionist Party, *Agreeing to Differ for Progress*, Belfast: PUP, 1985a.

Progressive Unionist Party, *Sharing Responsibilities*, Belfast: PUP, 1985b.

Progressive Unionist Party 'The case for corroboration: presented at Westminster', April 1985, Belfast: PUP, 1985c.

Progressive Unionist Party *Draft Policy Document*, unpublished, 1986a.

Progressive Unionist Party *War or Peace? Conflict or Conference: Policy Document of the Progressive Unionist Party*, Belfast: PUP, 1986b.

Progressive Unionist Party *Breaking the Mould*, Belfast: PUP, 1998.

Putnam, R. D. 'The prosperous community: social capital and public life', *American Prospect*, 13, 35–42, 1993.

Putnam, R. D. 'Bowling alone: America's declining social capital', *Journal of Democracy* 6.1 65–78, 1995.

Putnam, R. D. *Bowling Alone: The Collapse and Revival of American Community*, New York: Simon and Schuster, 2000.

Ramet, S. *Thinking about Yugoslavia*, Cambridge: Cambridge University Press, 2005.

Ramsbotham, D. *Report of an Inspection by Her Majesty's Chief Inspector of Prisons of HMP Maze*, Belfast: Northern Ireland Office, 1998.

Ramsbotham, O, Woodhouse, T. and Miall, H., *Contemporary Conflict Resolution*, Cambridge: Polity, 2005.

Reich, H. '"Local ownership" in conflict transformation projects: partnership, participation or patronage? Berghof Occasional Paper, Berghof Research Centre for Conflict Management 27, 1–36, 2001.

Republican News, 26 April 1975; May 1977.

Research Institute for the Study of Conflict and Terrorism *Reappraising Republican Violence*, London: RISCT, 1991.

Research Institute for the Study of Conflict and Terrorism *Reappraising Loyalist Violence*, London: RISCT, 1992.

Ritchie, M. *Conflict Transformation Initiative – Statement*, dsdni.gov.uk/conflict-transformation-initiative.htm, 2007.

Robinson, P. Speech to Democratic Unionist Party annual conference, 28 November 1998.

Robson, T. 'The community sector and conflict resolution in Northern Ireland', paper presented at The Role of Civil Society in Conflict Resolution Conference, Maynooth: National University of Ireland, 2001.

Rocks, P. 'Attitudes to participation of adult prisoners in HMP Maze (Compounds) and HMP Belfast', *International Journal of Lifelong Education* 4.1, 69–82, 1985.

Roessler, P. and Prendergast, J, 'Democratic Republic of the Congo', in W. Durch (ed.) *Twenty First Century Peace Operations*, Washington: United States Institute of Peace, 2006.

Rooker, Lord Written answer, House of Lords, 17 May 2006.

Rolston, B. 'Alienation of political awareness; the battle for the hearts and minds of Northern Nationalists', in P. Teague (ed.) *Beyond the Rhetoric: Politics, the Economy and Social Policy in Northern Ireland*, London: Lawrence and Wishart, 1989.

Rolston, B. 'Dealing with the past: pro-state paramilitaries, truth and transition in Northern Ireland', *Human Rights Quarterly* 28:3, 652–75, 2006.

Rolston, B. 'Demobilisation, reintegration and ex-combatants: the Irish case in international perspective', *Social and Legal Studies* 16:2, 259–80, 2007.

Rose, D. 'PUP moving forward: the role of former prisoners in conflict transformation', www.pup-ni.org.uk/party/article_read.aspx?a=2, 2008.

Rowan, B. *Behind the Lines: The Story of the IRA and Loyalist Ceasefires*, Blackstaff: Belfast, 1995.

Rowan, B. *How the Peace was Won*, Dublin: Gill and Macmillan, 2008.

Rupesinghe, K. *Conflict Transformation*, London: St. Martin's Press, 1995.

Russell, D. and Shehadi, N. 'Power sharing and national reconciliation: the case of Lebanon', in I. O'Flynn and D. Russell (eds) *Power Sharing: New Challenges for Divided Societies*, London: Pluto, 2005.

Ryan, B. 'Northern Ireland's district policing partnerships and the participatory ideals', *Irish Political Studies* 23.3, 341–61, 2008.

Ryan, C. *Inside the Maze: The Untold Story of the Northern Ireland Prison Service*, London: Methuen, 2000.

Ryan, M. *War and Peace in Ireland: Britain and the IRA in the New World Order*, London: Pluto, 1994.

Ryan, M. 'From the centre to the margins; the slow death of Irish republicanism', in C. Gilligan and J. Tonge (eds) *Peace or War? Understanding the Peace Process in Northern Ireland*, Aldershot: Avebury, 2007.

Saad-Ghorayeb, E. *Hizbu'llah: Politics and Religion*, London: Pluto, 2002.

Sanchez-Cuenca, I. 'The dynamics of nationalist terrorism: ETA and the IRA', *Terrorism and Political Violence* 19:3, 289–306, 2007.

Saoirse, 6 May 1983.

Saraceno, C. 'The time structure of biographies', *Enquête*, Biographie et cycle de vie, www.enquete.revues.org, 1989.

Schulze, K. E. and Smith, M. L. R. 'Decommissioning and paramilitary strategy in Northern Ireland: a problem compared', *The Journal of Strategic Studies* 23.4, 77–106, 2000.

Schutz, A. *The Phenomenology of the Social World*, Evanston IL: Northwestern University Press, 1967.

Segvic, I. 'The framing of politics: a content analysis of three Croatian newspapers', *Gazette: The International Journal for Communication Studies* 67.5, 469–88, 2005.

Shafer, J. '"A baby who does not cry will not be suckled." AMODEG and the reintegration of demobilized soldiers', *Journal of Southern African Studies* 4.1, 207–22, 1998.

Shanahan, M. and MacMillan, R. *Biography and the Sociological Imagination*, New York: W. W. Norton, 2007.

Shankill Bulletin 'Six on hunger strike', 4 July 1986.

Shirlow, P. 'The state they are still in. Republican ex-prisoners and their families: an Independent Evaluation', www.cain.ulst.ac.uk/issues/prison/shirlow01.htm, 2001.

Shirlow, P. 'Who fears to speak: fear, mobility and etho-sectarianism', *Global Review of Ethno-Politics* 3.1, 76–91, 2003.

Shirlow, P., Graham, B., McEvoy, K., O hAdhmaill, F. and Purvis, D. 'Politically motivated former prisoner groups: community activism and conflict transformation', Belfast: Research Report submitted to the Northern Ireland Community Relations Council, 2005.

Shirlow, P. and McEvoy, K. *Beyond the Wire: Former Prisoners and Conflict Transformation in Northern Ireland*, London: Pluto, 2008.

Shirlow, P. and McGovern, M. 'Language, discourse and dialogue. Sinn Fein and the Irish peace process', *Political Geography* 17.2, 171–86, 1998.

Shirlow, P. and Monaghan, R. *Ulster Loyalism: Forward to the Past?*, Swindon: ESRC, 2006.

Shirlow, P. and Murtagh, B. *Belfast: Segregation, Violence and the City*, London: Pluto, 2006.

Sinnerton, H. *David Ervine: Uncharted Waters*, Dingle: Brandon, 2002.

Sinn Fein, *Towards a Lasting Peace in Ireland*, Dublin: Sinn Fein, 1992.

Sinn Fein, *A New Opportunity for Peace* (Election Manifesto), Belfast: Sinn Fein, 1997.

Sinn Fein, *92nd Ard Fheis: Motions*, Dublin: Sinn Fein, 1998,

Sinn Fein, *93rd Ard Fheis: Motions*, Dublin: Sinn Fein, 1999.

Sinn Fein, *94th Ard Fheis: Motions*, Dublin: Sinn Fein, 2000.

Sisk, T. 'Power-sharing after civil wars: matching problems to solutions', in J. Darby and R. MacGinty (eds) *Contemporary Peacemaking: Conflict Violence and Peace Processes*, Basingstoke: Palgrave, 2003.

Smith, D. *Palestine and the Arab–Israeli Conflict*, Basingstoke: Palgrave Macmillan, 2007.

Smith, J. *Making the Peace in Ireland*, Harlow: Pearson Education Limited, 2002.

Smith, M. *Fighting for Ireland: The Military Strategy of the Irish Republican Movement*, London: Routledge, 1995.

Spear, J. 'Disarmament and demobilization', in S. Stedman, D. Rothchild and E. Cousens (eds) *Ending Civil Wars: The Implementation of Peace Agreements*, New York: International Peace Academy, 2002.

Spence, A. 'Oration delivered by the Commanding Officer, Ulster Volunteer Force in Long Kesh', Cage 21, 12 July 1977.

Spencer, G. *The State of Loyalism in Northern Ireland*, Basingstoke: Palgrave Macmillan, 2008.

Starry Plough, June 1988; February 1990; August/September 2003; October/November 2004; August/September 2005; January/February 2006.

Stedman, S. 'Spoiler problems in peace processes', *International Security* 22.2, 5–53, 1997.

Stedman, S. 'Peace processes and the challenges of violence', in J. Darby and R. MacGinty (eds) *Contemporary Peacemaking: Conflict Violence and Peace Processes*, Basingstoke: Palgrave, 2003.

Stevenson, J. *'We Wrecked the Place': Contemplating an End to the Northern Irish Troubles*, London: The Free Press, 1996.

Stone, M. *None Shall Divide Us*, London: John Blake, 2004.

Strauss, A. L. *Mirrors and Masks: The Search for Identity*, Glencoe, IL: Free Press, 1959.

Sunday Times, 16 March 1975.

Sweeney, G. 'Irish hunger strikers and the cult of self-sacrifice', *Journal of Contemporary History* 28.3, 421–37, 1993.

Taylor, P. *Provos: The IRA and Sinn Fein*, London: Bloomsbury, 1997.

Taylor, P. *Loyalists*, London: Bloomsbury, 2000.

Taylor, P. *Brits: The War against the IRA*, London: Bloomsbury, 2002.

Taylor, R. 'Northern Ireland: consociation or social transformation?', in J. McGarry (ed.) *Northern Ireland and the Divided World*, Oxford: Oxford University Press, 2001.

Tarrow, S. *Power in Movement: Social Movements, Collective Action and Politics*, Cambridge: Cambridge University Press, 1994.

Teague, P. 'Catholics and Protestants in the Northern Ireland labour market: why does one group perform better than the other?', *Economy and Society* 26.4, 560–78, 1997.

Tilly, C. *The Politics of Collective Action*, Cambridge: Cambridge University Press, 2003.

Todd, J. 'Two traditions in unionist culture', *Irish Political Studies* 2, 1–26, 1987.

Tonge, J. '"They haven't gone away y'know": Irish republican dissidents and "armed struggle" in Northern Ireland', *Terrorism and Political Violence* 16.3, 671–93, 2004.

Tonge, J. *The New Northern Irish Politics?* Basingstoke: Palgrave, 2005.

Tonge, J. *Northern Ireland*, Cambridge: Polity Press, 2006.

Tonge, J. and McAuley, J. W. 'The contemporary Orange Order in Northern Ireland', in M. Busteed, F. Neal and J. Tonge (eds) *Irish Protestant Identities*, Manchester: Manchester University Press, 2008.

Tzfadia, E. and Yiftachel, O. 'Between local and national mobilization in Israel's peripheral towns', *Political Geography*, 647–76, 2004.

Ulster, July 1978; July 1979; Vol. 2 No. 10 1980; October 1986; September 1987.

Ulster Miltant, 30 September 1972.

von Tangen Page, M. 'The early release of politically motivated violent offenders in the context of the republican and loyalist ceasefires in Northern Ireland', University of Bradford, Peace Studies Briefing Paper 45, 1–24, 1995.

Von Tangen Page, M. 'A "most difficult and unpalatable part": the release of politically motivated violent offenders', in M. Cox, A. Guelke and F. Stephen (eds) *A Farewell to Arms: Beyond the Good Friday Agreement*, Manchester: Manchester University Press, 2006.

Walker, B. *Dancing to History's Tune: History, Myth and Politics in Ireland*, Belfast: Queen's University of Belfast, 1996.

Walker, B., *Past and Present: History, Identity and Politics in Ireland*, Belfast: Queen's University of Belfast, 2000.

Walsh, P. *Irish Republicanism and Socialism: The Politics of the Republican Movement 1905 to 1994*, Belfast: Athol, 1994.

Walter, B. 'Designing transitions from civil war: demobilization, democratization and commitments to peace', *International Security* 24.1, 127–55, 1999.

Walzer, M. 'The civil society argument' from C. Mouffe (ed.) *Dimensions of Radical Democracy: Pluralism*, Citizenship Community, London: Verso, 1992.

Ward, R. *Women, Unionism and Loyalism in Northern Ireland: From 'Tea-Makers to Political Actors*, Dublin: Irish Academic Press, 2006.

Walker, R. K. *The Hunger Strikes*, Belfast: Lagan Books, 2006.

Walsh, S., 'IRA statement', *An Phoblacht*, 28 July 2005.

Whalen, L. *Contemporary Irish Republican Prison Writing: Writing and Resistance*, Basingstoke: Palgrave Macmillan, 2007.

Wheaton, B. 'Life transitions, role histories and mental health', *American Sociological Review* 55, 209–23, 1990.

White, R. *Ruairi O'Bradaigh: The Life and Politics of an Irish Revolutionary*, Indiana: Indiana University Press, 2006.

White, R. W. *Provisional Irish Republicans: An Oral and Interpretative History*, Westport, CT: Greenwood Press, 1993.

White, R. W. and Fraser, M. R. 'Personal and collective identities and long term social movement activism: republican Sinn Fein' in S. Stryker, T. J. Owens and R. W. White (eds) *Self Identity, and Social Movements*, Minnesota: University of Minnesota Press, 2000.

White, R. and Haines, F. *Crime and Criminology*, Oxford: Oxford University Press, 2004.

Whittaker, D. *The Terrorism Reader*, London: Routledge, 2007.

Wichert, S. *Northern Ireland Since 1945*, London: Longman, 1991.

Willis, C. *That Neutral Island*, London: Faber and Faber, 2007.

Winston, T. 'Alternatives to punishment beatings and shootings in a loyalist community', *Critical Criminology*, 8, 122–8, 1997.

Wolff, N. and Draine, J. 'Dynamics of social capital of prisoners and community reentry: ties that bind?', *Journal of Correctional Health Care* 10.2, 457–90, 2004.

Wolff, S. 'Conflict management in Northern Ireland', *International Journal on Multicultural Societies* 4.1 1–29, 2002.

Wood, I. *God, Guns and Ulster: A History of Loyalist Paramilitaries*, London; Caxton, 2003.

Wood, I. S. *Crimes of Loyalty: A History of the UDA*, Edinburgh: Edinburgh University Press, 2006.

Woodworth, P. *Dirty War, Clean Hands: ETA, the GAL and Spanish Democracy*, Cork University Press 2001.

Woolcock, M. 'The place of social capital in understanding social and economic outcomes', *Isuma: Canadian Journal of Policy Research* 2.1, 1–17, 2001.

Yiftachel, O. and Huxley, M. 'Debating dominance and relevance: notes on the "communicative turn" in planning theory, *International Journal of Urban and Regional Research* 24, 907–13, 2000.

Zartman, I. W. 'Conclusions: the last mile', in I. W. Zartman, *Elusive Peace: Negotiating an End to Civil Wars*, Washington DC: The Brookings Institute, 1995.

Zartman, W. 'The timing of peace initiatives: hurting stalemates and ripe moments', in J. Darby and R. Mac Ginty (eds) *Contemporary Peacemaking: Conflict, Violence and Peace Processes*, Basingstoke: Palgrave Macmillan, 2003a.

Zartman, W. 'Interview', www.beyondintractability.org/audi/William_zartman/ ?nid=2489, 2003b.

Index